AGAINST THE CURRENT

AND INTO THE LIGHT

MCGILL-QUEEN'S NATIVE AND NORTHERN SERIES

(In memory of Bruce G. Trigger)
John Borrows, Sarah Carter, and Arthur J. Ray, Editors

1 When the Whalers Were Up North
Inuit Memories from the Eastern Arctic
Dorothy Harley Eber

2 The Challenge of Arctic Shipping
Science, Environmental Assessment,
and Human Values
*Edited by David L. VanderZwaag
and Cynthia Lamson*

3 Lost Harvests
Prairie Indian Reserve Farmers
and Government Policy
Sarah Carter

4 Native Liberty, Crown Sovereignty
The Existing Aboriginal Right of Self-
Government in Canada
Bruce Clark

5 Unravelling the Franklin Mystery
Inuit Testimony
David C. Woodman

6 Otter Skins, Boston Ships,
and China Goods
The Maritime Fur Trade of the
Northwest Coast, 1785–1841
James R. Gibson

7 From Wooden Ploughs to Welfare
The Story of the Western Reserves
Helen Buckley

8 In Business for Ourselves
Northern Entrepreneurs
Wanda A. Wuttunee

9 For an Amerindian Autohistory
An Essay on the Foundations
of a Social Ethic
Georges E. Sioui

10 Strangers Among Us
David Woodman

11 When the North Was Red
Aboriginal Education in Soviet Siberia
Dennis A. Bartels and Alice L. Bartels

12 From Talking Chiefs to a Native
Corporate Elite
The Birth of Class and Nationalism
among Canadian Inuit
Marybelle Mitchell

13 Cold Comfort
My Love Affair with the Arctic
Graham W. Rowley

14 The True Spirit and Original Intent
of Treaty 7
*Treaty 7 Elders and Tribal Council with
Walter Hildebrandt, Dorothy First Rider,
and Sarah Carter*

15 This Distant and Unsurveyed Country
A Woman's Winter at Baffin Island,
1857–1858
W. Gillies Ross

16 Images of Justice
Dorothy Harley Eber

17 Capturing Women
The Manipulation of Cultural Imagery
in Canada's Prairie West
Sarah Carter

18 Social and Environmental Impacts of the
James Bay Hydroelectric Project
Edited by James F. Hornig

19 Saqiyuq
Stories from the Lives of
Three Inuit Women
*Nancy Wachowich in collaboration with
Apphia Agalakti Awa, Rhoda Kaukjak
Katsak, and Sandra Pikujak Katsak*

20 Justice in Paradise
Bruce Clark

21 Aboriginal Rights and Self-Government
The Canadian and Mexican Experience
in North American Perspective
*Edited by Curtis Cook
and Juan D. Lindau*

22 Harvest of Souls
The Jesuit Missions and Colonialism
in North America, 1632–1650
Carole Blackburn

23 Bounty and Benevolence
A History of Saskatchewan Treaties
*Arthur J. Ray, Jim Miller,
and Frank Tough*

24 The People of Denendeh
Ethnohistory of the Indians of Canada's
Northwest Territories
June Helm

25 The *Marshall* Decision
    and Native Rights
    Ken Coates

26 The Flying Tiger
    Women Shamans and Storytellers
    of the Amur
    Kira Van Deusen

27 Alone in Silence
    European Women in the Canadian
    North before 1940
    Barbara E. Kelcey

28 The Arctic Voyages of Martin Frobisher
    An Elizabethan Adventure
    Robert McGhee

29 Northern Experience and the Myths of
    Canadian Culture
    Renée Hulan

30 The White Man's Gonna Getcha
    The Colonial Challenge to the
    Crees in Quebec
    Toby Morantz

31 The Heavens Are Changing
    Nineteenth-Century Protestant Missions
    and Tsimshian Christianity
    Susan Neylan

32 Arctic Migrants/Arctic Villagers
    The Transformation of Inuit Settlement
    in the Central Arctic
    David Damas

33 Arctic Justice
    On Trial for Murder – Pond Inlet, 1923
    Shelagh D. Grant

34 The American Empire and the
    Fourth World
    Anthony J. Hall

35 Eighteenth-Century Naturalists of
    Hudson Bay
    *Stuart Houston, Tim Ball,
    and Mary Houston*

36 Uqalurait
    An Oral History of Nunavut
    *Compiled and edited by John Bennett
    and Susan Rowley*

37 Living Rhythms
    Lessons in Aboriginal Economic
    Resilience and Vision
    Wanda Wuttunee

38 The Making of an Explorer
    George Hubert Wilkins and the
    Canadian Arctic Expedition, 1913–1916
    Stuart E. Jenness

39 Chee Chee
    A Study of Aboriginal Suicide
    Alvin Evans

40 Strange Things Done
    Murder in Yukon History
    Ken S. Coates and William R. Morrison

41 Healing through Art
    Ritualized Space and Cree Identity
    Nadia Ferrara

42 Coyote and Raven Go Canoeing
    Coming Home to the Village
    Peter Cole

43 Something New in the Air
    The Story of First Peoples Television
    Broadcasting in Canada
    Lorna Roth

44 Listening to Old Woman Speak
    Natives and Alternatives in Canadian
    Literature
    Laura Smyth Groening

45 Robert and Francis Flaherty
    A Documentary Life, 1883–1922
    Robert J. Christopher

46 Talking in Context
    Language and Identity in
    Kwakwaka'wakw Society
    Anne Marie Goodfellow

47 Tecumseh's Bones
    Guy St-Denis

48 Constructing Colonial Discourse
    Captain Cook at Nootka Sound
    Noel Elizabeth Currie

49 The Hollow Tree
    Fighting Addiction with
    Traditional Healing
    Herb Nabigon

50 The Return of Caribou to Ungava
    *A.T. Bergerud, Stuart Luttich,
    and Lodewijk Camps*

51 Firekeepers of the Twenty-First Century
    First Nations Women Chiefs
    Cora J. Voyageur

52 Isuma
    Inuit Video Art
    Michael Robert Evans

53 Outside Looking In
    Viewing First Nations Peoples in
    Canadian Dramatic Television Series
    Mary Jane Miller

54 Kiviuq
    An Inuit Hero and His Siberian Cousins
    Kira Van Deusen

55 Native Peoples and Water Rights
Irrigation, Dams, and the Law in
Western Canada
Kenichi Matsui

56 The Rediscovered Self
Indigenous Identity and Cultural Justice
Ronald Niezen

57 As affecting the fate of
my absent husband
Selected Letters of Lady Franklin
Concerning the Search for the Lost
Franklin Expedition, 1848–1860
Edited by Erika Behrisch Elce

58 The Language of the Inuit
Syntax, Semantics, and Society
in the Arctic
Louis-Jacques Dorais

59 Inuit Shamanism and Christianity
Transitions and Transformations in the
Twentieth Century
Frédéric B. Laugrand
and Jarich G. Oosten

60 No Place for Fairness
Indigenous Land Rights and Policy
in the Bear Island Case and Beyond
David T. McNab

61 Aleut Identities
Tradition and Modernity in an
Indigenous Fishery
Katherine L. Reedy-Maschner

62 Earth into Property
Aboriginal History and the Making
of Global Capitalism
Anthony J. Hall

63 Collections and Objections
Aboriginal Material Culture in Southern
Ontario, 1791–1914
Michelle A. Hamilton

64 These Mysterious People
Shaping History and Archaeology in a
Northwest Coast Community,
Second Edition
Susan Roy

65 Telling It to the Judge
Taking Native History to Court
Arthur J. Ray

66 Aboriginal Music in
Contemporary Canada
Echoes and Exchanges
Edited by Anna Hoefnagels
and Beverley Diamond

67 In Twilight and in Dawn
A Biography of Diamond Jenness
Barnett Richling

68 Women's Work, Women's Art
Nineteenth-Century Northern
Athapaskan Clothing
Judy Thompson

69 Warriors of the Plains
The Arts of Plains Indian Warfare
Max Carocci

70 Reclaiming Indigenous Planning
Edited by Ryan Walker, Ted Jojola,
and David Natcher

71 Setting All the Captives Free
Capture, Adjustment, and Recollection
in Allegheny Country
Ian K. Steele

72 Before Ontario
The Archaeology of a Province
Edited by Marit K. Munson and Susan
M. Jamieson

73 Becoming Inummarik
Men's Lives in an Inuit Community
Peter Collings

74 Ancient Pathways, Ancestral Knowledge
Ethnobotany and Ecological Wisdom
of Indigenous Peoples of Northwestern
North America
Nancy J. Turner

75 Our Ice Is Vanishing/Sikuvut
Nunguliqtuq
A History of Inuit, Newcomers,
and Climate Change
Shelley Wright

76 Maps and Memes
Redrawing Culture, Place, and Identity
in Indigenous Communities
Gwilym Lucas Eades

77 Encounters
An Anthropological History of
Southeastern Labrador
John C. Kennedy

78 Keeping Promises
The Royal Proclamation of 1763,
Aboriginal Rights, and Treaties
in Canada
Edited by Terry Fenge and Jim Aldridge

79 Together We Survive
Ethnographic Intuitions, Friendships,
and Conversations
Edited by John S. Long
and Jennifer S.H. Brown

80 Canada's Residential Schools
The History, Part 1, Origins to 1939
The Final Report of the Truth and
Reconciliation Commission of Canada,
Volume 1

81 Canada's Residential Schools:
The History, Part 2, 1939 to 2000
The Final Report of the Truth and
Reconciliation Commission of Canada,
Volume 1

82 Canada's Residential Schools:
The Inuit and Northern Experience
The Final Report of the Truth and
Reconciliation Commission of Canada,
Volume 2

83 Canada's Residential Schools:
The Métis Experience
The Final Report of the Truth and
Reconciliation Commission of Canada,
Volume 3

84 Canada's Residential Schools:
Missing Children and Unmarked Burials
The Final Report of the Truth and
Reconciliation Commission of Canada,
Volume 4

85 Canada's Residential Schools:
The Legacy
The Final Report of the Truth and
Reconciliation Commission of Canada,
Volume 5

86 Canada's Residential Schools:
Reconciliation
The Final Report of the Truth and
Reconciliation Commission of Canada,
Volume 6

87 Aboriginal Rights Claims and the
Making and Remaking of History
Arthur J. Ray

88 Abenaki Daring
The Life and Writings of Noel Annance,
1792–1869
Jean Barman

89 Trickster Chases the Tale of Education
Sylvia Moore

90 Secwépemc People, Land, and Laws
Yerí7 re Stsq̓eýs-kucw
Marianne Ignace and Ronald E. Ignace

91 Travellers through Empire
Indigenous Voyages from Early Canada
Cecilia Morgan

92 Studying Arctic Fields
Cultures, Practices, and
Environmental Sciences
Richard C. Powell

93 Iroquois in the West
Jean Barman

94 Leading from Between
Indigenous Participation and Leadership
in the Public Service
*Catherine Althaus and
Ciaran O'Faircheallaigh*

95 Against the Current and Into the Light
Performing History and Land in Coast
Salish Territories and Vancouver's
Stanley Park
Selena Couture

AGAINST THE CURRENT AND INTO THE LIGHT

Performing History and Land in Coast Salish Territories and Vancouver's Stanley Park

SELENA COUTURE

McGill-Queen's University Press

Montreal & Kingston • London • Chicago

© McGill-Queen's University Press 2019

ISBN 978-0-7735-5920-2 (cloth)
ISBN 978-0-7735-5921-9 (paper)
ISBN 978-0-7735-5991-2 (ePDF)

Legal deposit third quarter 2019
Bibliothèque nationale du Québec

Printed in Canada on acid-free paper that is 100% ancient forest free (100% post-consumer recycled), processed chlorine free

This book has been published with the help of a grant from the Canadian Federation for the Humanities and Social Sciences, through the Awards to Scholarly Publications Program, using funds provided by the Social Sciences and Humanities Research Council of Canada.

Funded by the Government of Canada   Financé par le gouvernement du Canada   Canada   Canada Council for the Arts   Conseil des arts du Canada

We acknowledge the support of the Canada Council for the Arts.

Nous remercions le Conseil des arts du Canada de son soutien.

Library and Archives Canada Cataloguing in Publication

Title: Against the current and into the light : performing history and land in Coast Salish territories and Vancouver's Stanley Park / Selena Couture.

Names: Couture, Selena, author.

Series: McGill-Queen's native and northern series ; 95.

Description: Series statement: McGill-Queen's native and northern series ; 95 | Includes bibliographical references and index.

Identifiers: Canadiana (print) 20190185686 | Canadiana (ebook) 20190185813 | ISBN 9780773559202 (cloth) | ISBN 9780773559219 (paper) | ISBN 9780773559912 (ePDF)

Subjects: LCSH: Coast Salish Indians–British Columbia–Vancouver–Rites and ceremonies. | LCSH: Performing arts–British Columbia–Vancouver–History. | LCSH: Stanley Park (Vancouver, B.C.)–Social life and customs. | LCSH: Stanley Park (Vancouver, B.C.)–History.

Classification: LCC E99.S21 C68 2019 | DDC 971.1/330049794–dc23

This book was designed and typeset by Peggy & Co. Design Inc. in 10.5/14 Minion 3.

To my many supportive families

My Couture family: my parents, brothers, and sister as well as their spouses and children, scattered between the East and West Coasts of Canada and down to Texas. Being the youngest of seven taught me to listen from a young age, a skill that has served me well in this work.

My West Coast island family, always so kind, generous, and interested in whatever I'm doing. In particular, I gratefully acknowledge the love and support of Adele and Riley Hern, who have been role models for me.

My East Van folks: members of the 15-hundo block, Verity Rolfe, Amanda Fritzlan, Marcus Youssef, Am Johal, Geoff Mann, Michelle Bonner, Patti Fraser, Mark and Goo, Ashley and Cole, Shane, Finn, Tommy, Sammy, Keith, Skye, Annah, Justin, Mark Douglas, and all the youth who took part in the East Van–Fort Good Hope exchanges.

And Matt, Sadie, and Daisy, with whom I've been paddling this boat for almost thirty years; you continue to teach me so much about strength, curiosity, joy, and unending love.

Contents

Figures   xiii

On the hən̓q̓əmin̓əm̓ Orthography   xv

Acknowledgments   xix

Introduction   3

1   Land, Language, Place Names, and Performance   16
INTERVENTION: Walking alongside Quelemia Sparrow's
Ashes on the Water   42

2   Reiterations of Rededications: Surrogated Whiteness   52
INTERVENTION: Michel Tremblay's *For the Pleasure of
Seeing Her Again*   92

3   Vancouver's 1946 Diamond Jubilee: Indigenous Archival
Interventions   101
INTERVENTION: Iterations of Marie Clements's
The Road Forward   134

4   Indigenous Performative Interventions at Klahowya Village   142
INTERVENTION: Tanya Tagaq and Robert Flaherty's
Nanook of the North   160

Conclusion   167

Appendix: Self-Guided Walking Tour of spapəy̓əq/Brockton Point
and χʷay̓χʷəy̓/Lumberman's Arch   179

Notes   195

References   215

Index   233

Figures

1.1 Map of Vancouver area with hən̓q̓əmin̓əm̓ place names relevant to this research. Prepared by Craig Rust of the Musqueam Treaty, Lands, and Resources Department.   4

2.1 David Oppenheimer reading original illuminated address presented to Lord Stanley in 1889. City of Vancouver Archives, AM54-S4, REDED N9.   72

2.2 E.V. Young dressed as Lord Stanley addressing crowd at the "Rededication of Stanley Park." City of Vancouver Archives, AM54-S4, REDED N11.   73

2.3 Carriage driver Frank Plante delivering E.V. Young and David Oppenheimer to Lumberman's Arch. City of Vancouver Archives, AM54-S4, REDED N10.   74

2.4 August Jack Khahtsahlano and others at the "Rededication of Stanley Park." City of Vancouver Archives, AM54-S4, REDED N12.   75

2.5 Prospect Point, Stanley Park, Vancouver. Photo by Neeland Bros. City of Vancouver Archives, AM54-S4, LGN 474.   81

2.6 James Skitt Matthews imitating the Lord Stanley statue pose. *Vancouver Sun*, 17 May 1960.   84

2.7 "All Aboard for Beaver Lake" and "The Guests: Pioneers of Vancouver." In James Skitt Matthews's *Stanley Park, Vancouver: The Rededication 19th May 1964* (1964, 18–19).   88

3.1 Brockton Point during *The Jubilee Show*, July 1946. City of Vancouver Archives, AM54-S4-2, CVA 371-2025.   104

3.2 "Potlatch Ballet" opening sequence of *The Jubilee Show*, July 1946. City of Vancouver Archives, AM54-S4-2, CVA 371-1305.   105

3.3 Front cover of *The Jubilee Show*'s souvenir program.   106

3.4 Back cover of *The Jubilee Show*'s souvenir program.   107

3.5 Front cover of *The Indian Village and Show*'s program. City of Vancouver Archives, AM1519, PAM 1946-5.   108

3.6 Back cover of *The Indian Village and Show*'s program. City of Vancouver Archives, AM 1519, PAM 1946-5. 109

3.7 "Native Brotherhood of British Columbia." In *The Indian Village and Show*'s program. City of Vancouver Archives, AM1519, PAM 1946-5. 114

3.8 August Jack Khahtsahlano's welcome. In *The Indian Village and Show*'s program. City of Vancouver Archives, AM1519, PAM 1946-5. 115

3.9 James Skitt Matthews's note on the inside cover of *The Indian Village and Show*'s program. "Correspondence, Programmes, and Other Materials, 1946," City of Vancouver Archives, Vancouver Citizens' Diamond Jubilee Committee Fonds, ADD. MSS. 226, 514-E-6, FILE 5. 117

3.10 Description of the stage in *The Indian Village and Show*'s program. City of Vancouver Archives, AM1519, PAM 1946-5. 122

3.11 Chief William Scow and party confer an honorary chieftainship on Governor General Harold Alexander, 13 July 1946. City of Vancouver Archives, AM1184-S1, CVA 1184-3247. 123

3.12 Governor General Harold Alexander being made an honorary chief, 13 July 1946. City of Vancouver Archives, AM1184-S1, CVA 1184-3248. 126

4.1 Teepee in farmyard at Klahowya Village, July 2012. Photo by Selena Couture. 148

4.2 Headdress at Klahowya Village, July 2012. Photo by Selena Couture. 155

4.3 Safety fencing and burnt trees after arson on 21 June 2012 at the Miniature Train Station, Klahowya Village, August 2012. Photo by Selena Couture. 157

C.1 The strategic directions for reconciliation adopted by the Vancouver Park Board, 6 January 2016. 171

C.2 Pulling Together Canoe Journey landing at χʷaẏχʷəẏ, 15 July 2017. Photo by Pablo Palma. Courtesy of Aeriosa. 173

C.3 Map of the Thunderbird Sharing Ceremony events. Prepared by Colin Zacharias of Aeriosa using the standard map published by the Vancouver Park Board. 175

C.4 Members of Aeriosa in the trees while members of Spakwus Slulem and Git Hayetsk on the ground sing and dance, 15 July 2017. Photo by Pablo Palma. Courtesy of Aeriosa. 176

On the hən̓q̓əmin̓əm̓ Orthography

This book uses an orthography developed for hən̓q̓əmin̓əm̓, the language spoken by peoples surrounding the delta of the Fraser River in British Columbia. Since a focus on the knowledge embedded within Indigenous languages and a concern with the imminent danger of their loss is central to the theoretical pursuits of the book, I include here a guide to familiarize the reader.

The following guide instructs readers in how to write and pronounce hən̓q̓əmin̓əm̓ sounds. It is used with permission of the Musqueam Language and Culture Program and with acknowledgment of the curricular materials collaboratively developed through the Musqueam Indian Band and the University of British Columbia's joint Musqueam Language Program.

Pronunciation Guide
to the hən̓q̓əmin̓əm̓ Orthography

hən̓q̓əmin̓əm̓ has thirty-six consonants, twenty-two of which are not found in English and some of which appear in only a handful of languages around the world. Since the majority of hən̓q̓əmin̓əm̓ sounds are different from those of English, the English alphabet (orthography) is not a straightforward system for writing hən̓q̓əmin̓əm̓ words. So instead, Musqueam uses the North American Phonetic Alphabet, where each sound is represented by a single distinct symbol creating consistency of interpretation and predictability of pronunciation. Although they may appear foreign at first, these symbols are used worldwide to represent the Native languages of North America and Europe.

Note that upper case letters are not used in the hən̓q̓əmin̓əm̓ orthography, even at the beginning of a sentence.

Vowels

Sometimes vowels are followed by a colon, which means the vowel is lengthened.

i = the *i* in p<u>i</u>zza
e = the *e* in b<u>e</u>t
a = the *a* in f<u>a</u>ther
u = the *u* in fl<u>u</u>te
ə = the *u* in b<u>u</u>t

Consonants

Some sounds are pronounced the same in both hənq̓əmiṅəṁ and English: h, k, l, m, n, p, s, t, w, and y.

Other Consonants

c = *ts* sound in c<u>ats</u>
č = *ch* sound in <u>ch</u>eese
ł = formed by placing the tongue as though you are about to pronounce an *l* sound and then simply blowing a steady stream of air past the <u>sides</u> of the tongue (this is called a lateral fricative)
ƛ̓ = starts like a *t* and then releases into the *ł* sound
q = similar to *k* but with the tongue pulled farther back to stop the air flow at the uvula
š = *sh* sound in <u>sh</u>irt
θ = *th* sound in think (symbol from the Greek alphabet called theta)
t^θ = starts like a *t* and then releases into the *θ* sound
x = sounds like the *h* in <u>h</u>uge
χ = uvular fricative, a sort of raspy sound made at the back of the mouth
ʔ = interruption heard in the middle of "uh-oh"

WHAT DOES THE LITTLE COMMA ABOVE OR BESIDE THE LETTER MEAN?
Some hən̓q̓əmin̓əm̓ consonants, such as c̓, k̓, ƛ̓, p̓, q̓, and t̓, are categorized
as glottalized or ejective stops. They are distinguished from their nonglot-
talized counterparts by an audible popping sound upon their release.

The letters l, m, n, w, and y represent the group of consonants known as
resonants, characterized as such because of the reverberating or "resonant"
quality of their sound. Their glottalized counterparts – l̓, m̓, n̓, w̓, and y̓
– are, like glottalized stops, represented with an apostrophe. Glottalized
resonants are pronounced with a creaky sound, called laryngealization.

WHAT DOES THE LITTLE ^w NEXT TO A LETTER MEAN?
The little ^w next to a letter means that particular sound is made with the
lips rounded. So the hən̓q̓əmin̓əm̓ word "k^we:l" sounds very similar to the
English word "quell."

Acknowledgments

I express my gratitude to the hən̓q̓əmiṅəṁ-speaking xʷməθkʷəẏəm and səlílwətaʔɬ peoples and to the S̲kwx̲wú7mesh-sníchim-speaking S̲kwx̲wú7mesh peoples who hold these lands on which this research has been produced. In the words of the hən̓q̓əmiṅəṁ language, wə naṅ ʔəwʔəẏ tə nə šxʷqʷeləwən k̓ʷəns ʔi tecəl – I am very happy to be here.

This book is the result of many years of work during which a circle of supportive mentors, friends, and family members surrounded me. It is very difficult to articulate how much their kindness allowed me to both pursue and complete this project, but I will make an attempt. I begin by acknowledging my doctoral supervisor, Jerry Wasserman, who first sent me to the archives so many years ago and has encouraged my development as a scholar by allowing me to find my way while also nudging me in new directions when necessary. His careful eye and thoughtful suggestions have been instrumental in the articulation of my ideas. I also acknowledge my committee members: Daniel Heath Justice, whose open door, enthusiasm, and readiness to share his wisdom have pushed my development as a researcher engaged with intercultural relations; and Coll Thrush, who guided me through a reconsideration of how histories have been written and consistently expressed a confidence in my abilities that has buoyed me throughout these past few years.

I also recognize theatre studies faculty Kirsty Johnston and Siyuan Liu of the Department of Theatre and Film at the University of British Columbia (UBC), both for ideas generated through course work and for much invaluable guidance over the years as my research progressed. I also greatly appreciate the friendly support provided by other faculty and staff in the department.

I have been preceded by generations of Indigenous and non-Indigenous scholars and activists who have contended with the inheritances of colonialism. My work is possible only because of theirs. I have benefited from the generosity of these scholars throughout this process. I extend particular thanks to Michelle Laflamme, Dory Nason, Susan Roy, Sherrill Grace, Toph Marshall, Reid Gilbert, Alexander Dick, Helen Gilbert, Dani Phillipson, Peter Kulchyski, Katie Zien, Penny Farfan, Dylan Robinson, Keren Zaiontz, Heather Davis-Fisch, Rebecca Schneider, Peter Dickinson, Stephen Johnson, Mique'l Dangeli, and Amy Pereault.

I have been part of a cohort of passionate theatre scholars who share with me the never-ending desire to talk and think about theatre and performance. Thank you to Martha Herrera-Lasso, Seth Soulstein, Julia Henderson, Alex Ferguson, Kelsey Blair, Lindsay Lachance, and Eury Chang.

I thank my fellow hənq̓əmiṅəm̓-language students: Aidan Pine, Helene Irving, Jordana Manchester, Faith Sparrow-Crawford, Jessica Carson, Erica Baker, and Chloe Erlendson. I am also grateful to my patient and generous instructors: Larry Grant, Patricia Shaw, Marny Point, and Jill Campbell. As detailed in the following work, the experiences that I have shared with them and the learning that has resulted from our interactions continue to influence me every day.

This book was completed with financial support from the Social Sciences and Humanities Research Council of Canada; the Killam Trust; a UBC four-year fellowship; the Elsie and Audrey Jang Scholarship in Cultural Diversity and Harmony; a UBC Faculty of Arts Graduate Award; the Dorothy Somerset Memorial Scholarship in Theatre; the Errol Durbach Graduate Scholarship in Theatre; and the University of Alberta President's Fund for the Creative and Performing Arts. I also found support for this work when I took a faculty position in the Department of Drama at the University of Alberta in Amiskwacîwâskahikan/Edmonton, which is in Treaty 6 territory on Métis homelands. I thank my colleagues across the university for their support and interest in this work.

An earlier version of chapter 4 was published as "Indigenous Interventions at Klahowya Village, χʷayχʷəy Vancouver/Unceded Coast Salish Territory" in Helen Gilbert and Charlotte Gleghorn's edited collection *Recasting Commodity and Spectacle in the Indigenous Americas* (2014). It is reprinted with permission. A version of the intervention "Iterations of Marie Clements's *The Road Forward*" was published as "Theatrical Activism in Vancouver: From the Native Brotherhood and Sisterhood of BC to Marie Clements's *The Road Forward* and Back ..." in *Canadian Theatre Review* 164 (2015): 44–50. It is reprinted with permission of University of Toronto Press.

AGAINST THE CURRENT

AND INTO THE LIGHT

Introduction

In hən̓q̓əmin̓əm̓, the language spoken by most of the Indigenous peoples surrounding the delta of the Fraser River in British Columbia,[1] there are two auxiliary verbs, "niʔ" (be there) and "ʔi" (be here). Because the words locate the speaker in space according to what is being discussed, they also often locate them in time; for example, speaking of something that is not present often means speaking of the past (but not necessarily). These words can be used on their own or in conjunction with other verbs to elaborate or emphasize the existential qualities of the action (Suttles 2004, 34–6). *Against the Current and Into the Light* concerns the *there and then* as well as the *here and now* of Indigenous peoples in what is currently known as the Lower Mainland of British Columbia, using instances of the action of performance to demonstrate the fluidity of time. As with the hən̓q̓əmin̓əm̓ verbs mentioned above, this examination of time is embedded in a location – the Coast Salish village of χʷaÿχʷəy̓ near what is presently known as the Lumberman's Arch area of Stanley Park in downtown Vancouver. I have chosen this space because of the numerous Indigenous[2] performances that have taken place here over the years and currently continue. The knowledge embedded in this place name reinforces the notion that the current use of this place for performances is a continuation and adaptation of cultural practice from pre-European settlement times.

This book's examination of how performance is used to transfer knowledge also includes the performative activities of settlers that have occurred in this place. The settler history of Stanley Park is well documented in archives as well as in popular culture; however, the use of performance as a method of creating and maintaining a colonial space has not yet been considered. In keeping with much recent scholarship regarding colonialism that focuses on the mutual influence of settlers and Indigenous people, establishing that this is a significant place of performance for Coast Salish peoples brings new insights into why it has also been the site of so many settler performances. So, although this book is mainly concerned with Coast Salish cultural continuation through performance, I demonstrate

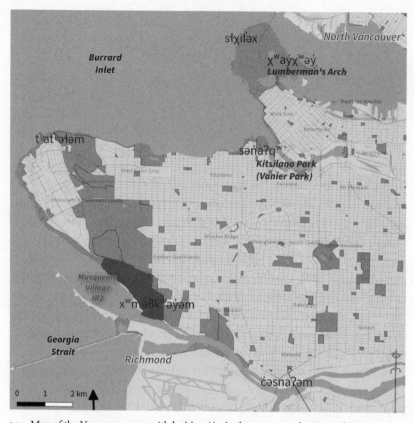

1.1   Map of the Vancouver area with hənq̓əminə̓m place names relevant to this research.

the cultural construction of whiteness through performance in this place as well.

Examining intercultural performances from the establishment of the city of Vancouver in the late nineteenth century through to the first decades of the twenty-first makes evident the importance of performance as a mode of knowledge transfer, cultural continuity, and intercultural influence that connects people to place. In so doing, this work also locates histories that have been ignored by settlers and newcomers up to now, aiming to aid in the process of Indigenous resurgence and the work of transitioning away from existing settler colonial power structures.

Since European settlement, Vancouver has been a site of contention between settlers and the Musqueam, Tsleil-Waututh, and Squamish, as well as other peoples of this place. Indigenous groups have consistently used cultural performance to establish their persistence and political legitimacy in the face of settler efforts to dispossess them of land and to control a romantic narrative of Indigenous peoples through cultural homogenization (Roy 2002, 62–4; Hawker 2003, 101–25).

Beginning with an exploration of the significance of land as an organizing cultural concept for Indigenous peoples generally as well as locally and then enhancing this with hənq̓əmin̓əm̓-language research, I explore performance as an enunciation of land through language and place naming. In this context, critically engaging the colonial origins of much of Vancouver's written history through an analysis of the city archives allows for a new consideration of historical assumptions and opens up an understanding of performance as it was used both by settlers aiming to connect with land throughout the twentieth century and by Indigenous organizations countering and intervening in these performed histories. Once this history has been established, I examine how the contemporary presence of Indigenous performers at a tourist spectacle can demonstrate the way that Indigenous performance continues to assert cultural identity and relationship to land at this site.

Many Indigenous performances at this site in the twentieth century have occurred in the context of related intercultural settler performances of whiteness. Included in my study are reenactments of the naming and dedication of Stanley Park produced by the city archivist as well as an examination of *The Jubilee Show* of 1946, which celebrated the sixtieth anniversary of Vancouver with a historical pageant. These performances also include instances of what Philip J. Deloria (1998) has termed "playing Indian," exemplified by the opening "potlatch ballet" scene of *The Jubilee Show*, and instances of what Jean Barman (2007) has called "the erasure of indigenous Indigeneity" (4) in the Lower Mainland, shown by efforts to import a Kwakwaka'wakw village in the early 1900s, which resulted in an iconic totem pole display still popular with tourists (Phillips 2000, 28; Hawker 2003, 44).

Understanding this history in its full complexity requires one to trace histories not found in print-based colonial archives (Bratton 2003). It means not only exploring the ways that Indigenous people resisted colonial invasion and maintained cultural continuity despite centuries of violence but also looking at ways of transmitting Indigenous history that do not depend on the colonial archive. These efforts necessitate a definition of performance that can account both for purposeful theatrical presentations and for performance that seeks to assert identity by publicly challenging cultural norms. Diana Taylor's (2003) emphasis on the fruitful complexity in defining performance is helpful here. She suggests that we embrace the difficulty of defining performance in order to remember "that we do not understand each other – and [to] recognize that each effort in that direction needs to work against notions of easy access, decipherability, and translatability" (15). Although I am opening up the definition of performance to expand it beyond those events held in a theatre, I am also aware of the tensions involved in imposing a definition. Bringing works on theatre and Indigenous historiography as well as performance studies into conversation emphasizes the importance of performance as a method of Indigenous history, while also bringing insights from non-Western epistemologies to the study of theatre and performance.

This place-based study is situated mainly in a section of Stanley Park, a large urban park in the city of Vancouver that is also the site of a village used by Musqueam, Tsleil-Waututh, and Squamish people, known in hәṅq̓әmiṅәm̓ as x̌ʷay̓x̌ʷәy̓ and in Sḵwx̱wú7mesh as X̱wáyx̱way.³ In 1870 this was documented as the site of a very large ceremony (known as a "potlatch" in Chinook Jargon), and it hosted other ceremonies until at least 1885, one year after the federal potlatch ban came into effect (Barman 2005, 67–9; Kheraj 2013, 24).⁴ The village was acknowledged by colonial authorities to be one of the oldest in the Lower Mainland because of its extensive midden (Roy 2010, 45–6); further archeological research has found some artifacts to be 3,200 years old (Kheraj 2013, 25). The peninsula was designated a naval reserve in the 1860s, although proper British legal procedures were not followed by the colonial government. This oversight became an issue later when the people living in the park were taken to court (Barman 2005, 24–9; Kheraj 2013, 37). Shortly after the incorporation of Vancouver in 1886, the first City Council immediately made plans to use the peninsula as a public park, and it was officially opened in 1888.

The park is approximately 1,000 acres in area and is easily accessible from the downtown core of the city. Brockton Point is the most protected part of the land formation on the south side of the first narrows of the inlet, over which the Lions Gate Bridge spans. Once the Stanley Park causeway was built, enclosing the tidal flats, which became known as Lost Lagoon, this point of the park became very accessible from the downtown core. Many of Vancouver's iconic tourist attractions have been situated here over the years, including the Vancouver Aquarium, the totem poles, Malkin Bowl (home to Theatre Under the Stars during the summer), the Rose Garden, the Shakespeare Garden, the Stanley Park Pavilion, Lumberman's Arch, the Lighthouse, and the 9 O'Clock Gun.

Although the main site of this study is the area surrounding χʷay̓χʷəy̓, inquiries have also led me to activities at other village sites within Vancouver: c̓əsnaʔəm[5] (through museum exhibits), the Musqueam Reserve, and sən̓aʔqʷ (now known as Vanier Park). Chronologically, this research spans the era of European settlement from the 1880s to the first two decades of the twenty-first century and also reaches back, through knowledge embedded in the hən̓q̓əmin̓əm̓ language, to times previous to European contact. It is also worth noting that Vancouver and British Columbia generally are fertile sites for this research. They are the spaces where oral history and performance have become essential to substantiating Aboriginal title, as seen in *Delgamuukw v. British Columbia* (1997)[6] and as reflected in the performative activities of the Four Host First Nations at the 2010 Winter Olympics.

Against the Current and Into the Light is an inquiry into how, when, and why Indigenous performance is employed to create and transfer historical knowledge, connect to land, and assert identity. It does so in the context of intercultural and related settler performances with the aim of understanding the constructed nature of white settler identity in Vancouver and the use of performance to make and maintain colonial space. The book also engages with a range of interrelated disciplines and methodologies, primarily performance studies, theatre history, archival research, fieldwork, and Indigenous research methodologies, while seeking to understand the knowledge embedded in the endangered languages traditionally spoken by the Indigenous peoples in whose unceded, ancestral territory the city of Vancouver is situated. It also works to develop decolonizing research methodologies for use by non-Indigenous researchers that are in conversation with established Indigenous methods as a way of taking up the responsibilities of a settler inheritance.

Against the Current and Into the Light offers a number of contributions. First, by inquiring into the City of Vancouver Archives and its founder, James Skitt Matthews, who served as archivist for forty years, this book replaces histories that have been silenced within settler archives. As Matthews also used reenactments to constitute civic history, performance studies methodologies can bring attention to these strategic events and deconstruct these inherited histories. Each of the other case studies also engages in theorizing the role of performance in the making of space/history. Second, the book develops the conceptual terms "grounded practices" and "eddies of influence" as ways of placing and examining Indigenous-settler cultural negotiations that exist, in Senecan film scholar Michelle Raheja's (2010) phrasing, "between resistance and compliance" (193). The demonstration of these concepts models a methodological adjustment for much settler scholarship on Indigenous performance. Third, by examining place names that are progressive verbs, this work expands on scholarship about the importance of Indigenous place names to consider performance as the expression of a "reciprocal *relationship*" with land (Coulthard 2014, 60, italics original). I also reflect on the process of learning an Indigenous language as a method to further understand Indigenous performance practices and ways of knowing as well as to demonstrate a space-based method of "self-decolonization" for a non-Indigenous person. This precise investigation of a plot of land and the specific geo-historical relationships that exist there and grow from it also aims to model a practice that can be applied more broadly in terms of site, time, and scholarly discipline. Finally, the use of a seriously endangered Indigenous language through-out the text intends to contribute to the project of hǝṅ̓q̓ǝmiṅǝm̓-language revitalization. Although I acknowledge that this requires extra effort on the part of my reader, my commitment to the use of the language responds to the time-sensitive nature and severity of the language's endangerment as well as to the reciprocal research relationship that I have developed with the Musqueam Language and Culture Program.

Although *Against the Current and Into the Light* is focused on a par-ticular site and the development of one western Canadian city, I write this book in the hopes that it will have a broader reach than is suggested by this focus. Recent activities led by Indigenous peoples in Canada, particularly the ongoing Idle No More movement, which has demonstrated leadership concerning issues of environmental protection and global warming, have garnered international attention. The building resurgence of Indigenous peoples continues to grow transnationally as demonstrated by the recent international tribal support for the Standing Rock Sioux's protest against the Dakota Access Pipeline.[7] British Columbia is the site of significant legal decisions involving Indigenous rights, land, title, and performance as well as a place of internationally influential Indigenous leadership; therefore, a study emerging from this place will be of interest to others engaged with decolonization and the protection of Indigenous peoples and lands.

Much of the scholarship I engage with employs the term "decolonizing," which has multiple meanings that depend on the times and places it has been deployed. In this book, I use "decolonization" to describe specifically located work that not only aims to reconnect with Indigenous laws and epistemologies of this land but also aspires to recognize and dismantle the particular existing settler colonial structures of this nation-state. I am informed by Eve Tuck (Unangax̂) and K. Wayne Yang's "Decolonization Is Not a Metaphor" (2012), in which they explain that land is the most valuable commodity in the settler colonial state and that disruption of Indigenous relationships with land as well as the disappearance of Indigenous peoples are necessary for the maintenance of settler colonial structures (5–6). Tuck and Yang further assert that "decolonization in the settler colonial context must involve the repatriation of land simultaneous to the recognition of how land and relations to land have always already been differently understood and enacted" (7). My understanding of decolonization therefore includes attention to the specific histories of Indigenous peoples enacting relations to this land, with the goal of supporting the rematriation/repatriation of Indigenous lands.

I am also informed by Māori scholar Linda Tuhiwai Smith's influential *Decolonizing Methodologies* (2012). Although she focuses on the fields of education and health, she poses some of the most relevant questions to cross-cultural research when she asks who has designed its questions and framed its scope and how its results will be disseminated respectfully (175). My research questions took form over many years, initially under the influence of graduate coursework in the University of British Columbia's First Nations and Indigenous Studies Program as well as with support from faculty and students in its First Nations Languages Program (FNLG). My second chapter, which addresses conceptions of land contained within hənq̓əmin̓əm̓ grammar, words, and place names, has been approved by the Musqueam Language and Culture Program as well as by the former FNLG chair, Patricia Shaw, and it has been reviewed by a representative of the Tsleil-Waututh Nation's Treaty, Lands and Resources Department. This effort to obtain approval and review involved a multiyear process of relationship building and continual learning. I collaborated with members of Full Circle First Nations Performance, at times conveying information to them in order to aid in their development of a site-specific performance at χʷayχʷəy̓. While working in collaboration, I have learned that I need to discuss my research in process in order to be able to incorporate responses. One of the most compelling sections of Smith's work is her questioning of who benefits from the research and how it will be disseminated: "Sharing is the responsibility of research ... [S]haring is about demystifying knowledge and information and speaking in plain terms to the community" (162). In response to this idea, I aim to disseminate my research conclusions in multiple formats, such as the book you hold in your hands, as well as in-person walking tours of the site and a recorded audio walking guide.

In doing this work, I am also aware of critiques of settlers whose work attempts to engage with Indigenous peoples and ideas, specifically Stó:lō scholar and ethnomusicologist Dylan Robinson's explanation in "Welcoming Sovereignty" (2016) of the upriver Halq̓eméylem word for non-Indigenous people who arrived in their lands during the Fraser River Gold Rush: "xwelítem" (starving ones) (6).[8] This word is still used for white people generally but can also be a pointed concept that asks non-Indigenous people seeking intercultural contact and understanding to reflect on the source of their hunger and to fill it elsewhere before making further demands on Indigenous resources. In making this observation, Robinson also demonstrates that the spirit of welcome and sharing of sovereign spaces can be achieved only if there are also times and spaces of exclusion or "un-welcome," which he deems useful as a method "to re-situate the assumption from being a welcome guest to the actuality of assuming welcome as an 'uninvited guest'" (17). This action of exclusion can then "define a space outside of Indigenous knowledge extractivism" (20). To this critique of easy assumptions of decolonizing, political scientists Corey Snelgrove, Rita Kaur Dhamoon, and Jeff Corntassel (Cherokee) in their collaborative article "Unsettling Settler Colonialism" (2014) add a discussion of how the scholarly institutionalizing of settler colonial studies attempts to move to innocence without decentring whiteness. They explain the necessity of relationality in responsible intercultural work as well as the importance of examining the conditions that enable settler colonialism in a way that does not reify it and present it as inevitable but instead pays attention to contingencies. They conclude that the most powerful decolonial actions are a mix of "temporary solidarities" of the kind demonstrated by the Idle No More movement and "spatial solidarities," which involve the "regeneration of Indigenous languages, ceremonial life, living histories, and nationhood" as a way to localize struggles (24). Although they do not engage with concepts of theatre or performance, and at times use "performativity" as a way to describe insincerity, I find their approach to be a useful way into thinking about theatre and performance solidarities, which are necessarily engaged with space and time. Michi Saagiig Nishnaabeg poet, performer, and scholar Leanne Betasamosake Simpson in a talk on "Decolonizing Solidarity" (2017) concurred that the decentring of whiteness is a key consideration of allyship with co-resisters of capitalism, white supremacy, and heteropatriarchy. She also insisted that conceptions of solidarity must be expanded to include land, lakes, and rivers as well as plant and animal nations. From these explanations, I have synthesized a methodology that works to understand the hungers that have resulted from my specific settler inheritance while not assuming a welcome despite my long-time inhabitation of Coast Salish lands and waters. In this work, I focus on the contingencies of settler capitalist resource-extraction projects in these lands and waters, while also doing my best to centre local Indigenous thought as expressed through the hən̓q̓əmin̓əm̓ language. Through this focus, I have begun to recognize what I call a settler privilege of oblivion that allows non-Indigenous people to continue to occupy and extract from Indigenous lands while refusing to acknowledge that, as noted by Anishinaabe-Ashkenazi theatre scholar and artist Jill Carter (2015), we live off the crimes of our ancestors and remain bystanders while injustices are continued against Indigenous peoples (423–4). Understanding with more fullness the early interactions of settlers and Indigenous people is a step out of the forgetfulness that supports a continuation of settler thinking, one that can lead to a more equitable and decolonized future for all.

Although this book is deeply concerned with historical activities, its chapters are organized thematically. They move from engaging with knowledge contained in the hən̓q̓əmin̓əm̓ language and expressed through performative practices to examining performative interventions in archival knowledge. Although I cycle back and forth in time while looking at events and performances from different perspectives, the chapters move gradually from the pre-1880s to the present. I also aim to avoid the still common colonial view of Indigenous peoples as being of the past and seek to rectify the absence of Indigenous women from the archival record. To support these goals, I include short sections between each chapter in which I respond to contemporary theatrical works written and/or performed by Indigenous women in Vancouver. I have named these short pieces "interventions" in relation to ideas put forward in Leanne Betasamosake Simpson's *As We Have Always Done: Indigenous Freedom through Radical Resistance* (2017). She uses the word throughout her book to describe actions taken by Indigenous people. Her book's index entry for "intervention" says, "see embodied resurgent practice" (295), which is part of the title of her eleventh chapter, "Embodied Resurgent Practice and Coded Disruption," in which she explains that she learned about "Nishnaabeg aesthetics of reenactment and presencing from watching the performances of Nishnaabeg performance artist Rebecca Belmore and Nishnaabeg artist Robert Houle. I've learned that my voice, my body, and my physical presence are interventions in a settler colonial reality, in a similar way to the work of Audra Simpson, but in this case not intellectual, or not just intellectual, but as a physical presence" (203). Simpson then goes on to say, about Belmore's presence in a space, that she "is intervention. She is theory. She is both presence and the doorway, and in her performances she often gives birth to the flight paths out of settler colonial reality and then literally takes those flight paths in front of the audience as witness" (203). Although I have learned from Simpson's engagement with these performing artists, I am also aware that she is discussing them from within a Nishnaabeg world-view, so I do not adopt her terminology of "embodied resurgence" and "presencing" but instead focus on her naming of the actions as interventions into settler colonial realities. Each of the performances with which I engage was a demonstration of Indigenous women intervening in settler colonial narratives, whether by reconsidering the building of the city of Vancouver, documenting the origins of a significant Québécois theatre artist's theatrical storytelling skills, challenging the dehistoricizing of a continuum of Indigenous resistance, or questioning the exotic framing of Inuit people in filmmaking of the early twentieth century. In each of these works, the performers pushed back against the historical narratives in order to make space for Indigenous bodies, actions, knowledge, and relations to be transmitted. Whereas two of the performances took place on and were about the history of this land, the other two were performed there but concerned distant Indigenous peoples and lands. I include discussions of these performances here because one of the core insights of this work is that the content of the theatrical text and the performing embodied actor are equally important: we must understand how performance generates meanings beyond ostensible textual or plot content.

Chapter 1, "Land, Language, Place Names, and Performance," begins by examining the significance of Indigenous relationships to land and their practice-based expressions. The expressions I examine include museum exhibits that encourage careful listening, the decolonizing experience of studying and performing in hən̓q̓əmin̓əm̓, the grammar and etymological constructions of words and place names in the language, as well as the strategic and tactical use of place naming by Indigenous peoples. In this chapter, I argue that performance, both theatrical and the everyday reiterations of gesture and speech, is a necessary conceptual structure through which to expand understandings of Indigenous relationships to land. To aid in this analysis, I coin two terms that I use throughout: "grounded practices" and "eddies of influence." Immediately following this chapter, I include a reflection on my experience of Musqueam actor and playwright Quelemia Sparrow's podplay *Ashes on the Water* (2011) to assert that this format is uniquely suited to intervene in settler cultural assumptions about land and history. The play gives its audience the intense experience of listening to a dramatization of the Great Fire of 1886, which destroyed the new city of Vancouver, and the Indigenous women's decision to rescue settlers, while the audience walks through the space in which it happened. Sparrow's work theatrically illustrates concepts of a grounded practice of performance as well as the eddies of influence in the history of this city.

Chapter 2, "Reiterations of Rededications: Surrogated Whiteness," continues my inquiry into the knowledge contained in place names; however, in this chapter it is the name "Stanley Park" that is under scrutiny. I examine this name through an analysis of the influence of city archivist James Skitt Matthews on the archival record in Vancouver, as well as his work on reenactments of Lord Stanley's "dedication" of the park through publications, stagings, and monument. Using Sara Ahmed's (2007) theory of the phenomenological construction of whiteness and white spaces, I argue that Matthews's interventions and manipulations have recruited settlers and newcomers to invest in a particular British imperial identity that, through disaffiliation, retroactively claims the creation of a multicultural space despite historical evidence to the contrary. The intervention following this chapter continues to seek an understanding of the construction of whiteness by engaging with Western Canada Theatre's production of Michel Tremblay's *For the Pleasure of Seeing Her Again* (1998), staged during the Talking Stick Festival in Vancouver in February 2014. My interest in responding to the play here is connected to director Glynis Leyshon's decision, based on evidence in Tremblay's text, to cast Indigenous actors and change the final imagery to connect with Cree life in Saskatchewan. I assert that this decision, while emphasizing the Cree heritage of Tremblay's mother and opening a line of inquiry into many of his works that were inspired by his mother, also illuminates the gendered nature of the colonial process. This production was both a vehicle for a virtuosic performance by Cree-Saulteaux actor Margo Kane as Nana and one where the representational mode of performance of Nana as a Cree woman connected with what Bonita Lawrence (Mi'kmaw) (2004) has called a "metanarrative about encounters with genocide" (xvii).

Chapter 3, "Vancouver's 1946 Diamond Jubilee: Indigenous Archival Interventions," undertakes an inquiry into the nature of the archive by examining the archival records of two performance events during Vancouver's

Diamond Jubilee in 1946, *The Jubilee Show* and *The Indian Village and Show*, the former of which presented the settler vision of Vancouver's history and future as crafted by the citizens' committee. The absences in the archive, which at first seem to be part of the colonial disavowal of Indigenous people, may instead be Indigenous assertions of power through cultural restriction. I argue that the narrative of Indigenous displacement and settler emplacement performed nightly in *The Jubilee Show* at spapəẏəq/Brockton Point was countered by *The Indian Village and Show* performed twice daily during the same period across False Creek at a space alternately known as səńaʔqʷ, Sen'ákw, Snauq, or Kitsilano Park. Thus the citizens' committee failed to create a dominant large-scale narrative of the city's history in *The Jubilee Show*. The fact that the committee revised the colonial script and commissioned the Native Brotherhood of British Columbia (NBBC) to present *The Indian Village and Show* suggests that there was already some doubt that such a historical narrative could exist. This chapter is followed by an intervention that analyzes the phenomenological performance modes balanced in Métis-Dene playwright and director Marie Clements's production of *The Road Forward* during the 2013 PuSh Festival in Vancouver. I assert that this production, which makes extensive use of the archives of the NBBC and developed out of a commission by the 2010 Winter Olympics for the Aboriginal Pavilion, is a continuation of the use of performance as intervention during a mega-event.

Chapter 4, "Indigenous Performative Interventions at Klahowya Village," offers an analysis of the Indigenous performative presence at Klahowya Village from 2010–14 and argues that the performing artists at this culturally significant site in Vancouver – metres from χʷaẏχʷəẏ – asserted a grounded practice. Expanding on Seneca literary and film scholar Michelle Raheja's (2010) analysis of "visual sovereignty" in Indigenous filmmaking to consider the performative aspects of a live event, I show the significance of the embodied experience of both performers and audience members at Klahowya Village, which was layered over the archival architecture of this tourist space. Focusing on multiple modes of performance observed over repeated site visits in the summer of 2012, I examine, with reference to Taylor (2003), the "scenario" (28) of the touristic encounter that was layered into the village, taking into account the historical context of Indigenous performance in this region and the physical location of the site. Following Taylor's emphasis on the fact that the repertoire and the archive are not sequential or binary (22) in order to analyze the site design of the tourist village as an eddy of influence, I demonstrate how Klahowya Village presented an enterprise that asserted a connection to land while enabling some intra-nation Indigenous transfer of knowledge, although it was also structurally limited as a site of Indigenous critique of settler society due to its status as a touristic spectacle. The final interchapter intervention is a response to Inuit throat singer Tanya Tagaq's performance at the 2014 PuSh Festival, where she sang to Robert Flaherty's *Nanook of the North* (1922), a film that Raheja (2010) has discussed in the context of its knowledge transfer and Indigenous filmmaking methodologies. Similar in ways to Clements's *The Road Forward*, Tagaq's performance also engaged with archival footage through song. I argue additionally that it demonstrated performance as historiography since Tagaq's throat singing can be considered a form of research that accessed knowledge of land and people held within the film.

The book concludes with a reflection on the performative activities at the site throughout the twentieth century while also reviewing more recent actions that have taken place since the publication of the Truth and Reconciliation Commission of Canada's *Calls to Action* (2015). New policy recently adopted by the Vancouver Park Board is examined in order to consider what the next years will bring as local Indigenous people assert their relationship to the land while also teaching newcomers how to be respectful visitors.

Included in an appendix is a self-guided walking tour for the site surrounding χʷay̓χʷəy̓. As a part of my reciprocal research practice, I have been engaged in conversations along this walking route with many people who are interested in decolonizing the land that is currently known as Stanley Park.

Returning to the hən̓q̓əmin̓əm̓ language, in consideration of the work done by Indigenous performers discussed throughout the book, I am struck by the concepts that constitute the word "hiw̓aʔqʷ" (head person, chief). Contained within this word, which is formulated as a progressive act – creating a sense of continuous, repeated, and long-lasting action – are the concepts of both moving into the light of the fire at the centre of a communal house as well as having the strength not just to withstand, but also to move against, a current (Shaw and Campbell 2013b, 334; Shaw 2015). *Against the Current and Into the Light* is ultimately an examination of the work of Indigenous performers – both in the past and in the present – who have acted as leaders in this way, documenting how their work has contributed to cultural continuation and the maintenance of Indigenous spaces.

Land, Language, Place Names, and Performance

Land has always been a defining element of Aboriginal culture. Land contains languages, the stories, and the histories of a people. It provides water, air, shelter, and food. Land participates in the ceremonies and the songs. And land is home.

Thomas King, The Inconvenient Indian (2012), 218

Cherokee writer and scholar Thomas King (2012) concludes his account of Native people in North America by engaging with the significance of land in a chapter subtitled "What Do Indians Want?" (215–33). King explains that this is the wrong question to ask, partly because "Indians" do not exist but are an imaginary category. Instead, he asserts that the more import-ant question is "what do Whites want?" and he answers this with one word: "Land" (216). This conflict, which he explains as the commodifi-cation of land by settlers operating within a capitalist economy opposing Indigenous cultural connections to land, must be grasped: "Land. If you understand nothing else about the history of Indians in North America, you need to understand that the question that really matters is the question of land" (218). And so, guided by King's words, I begin this inquiry into history and performance by examining manifestations of the significance of land in Indigenous cultures, as explained philosophically through political and cultural theory as well as in practice through knowledge contained within the hən̓q̓əmin̓əm̓ language. I argue that performance, both theatrical and the everyday reiterations of gesture and speech, is a useful conceptual struc-ture through which to expand understandings of Indigenous relationships to land. I begin by engaging with Yellowknives Dene political theorist Glen Sean Coulthard's *Red Skin, White Masks: Rejecting the Colonial Politics of Recognition* (2014), connecting his concept of "grounded normativity" (62) with French Jesuit philosopher Michel de Certeau's influential engagement with urban spatial practices in *The Practice of Everyday Life* (1984). I then synthesize these ideas with concepts from theatre and performance studies and propose the use of two terms that express a localized connection between land and performance: "grounded practices" and "eddies of influence." I elucidate these terms both through an examination of spatial knowledge contained within hən̓q̓əmin̓əm̓-language grammar and etymology that demonstrates land-based thinking and through accounts of the use of place names as a performative expression of past, present, and future relationships to land.

Grounded Practices

Coulthard begins *Red Skin, White Masks* (2014) by asserting the colonial-capitalist nature of contemporary Canadian politics of recognition, and then in his second chapter, "For the Land," he goes on to explain that "Indigenous struggles against capitalist-imperialism are best understood as struggles oriented around the question of *land* – struggles not only *for* land but also deeply *informed* by what the land as a mode of reciprocal *relationship* (which is itself informed by place-based practices and associated forms of knowledge) ought to teach us about living our lives in relation to one another and our surroundings in a respectful, nondominating and nonexploitative way" (60, italics original). He regards this understanding as an ethical framework that he calls *grounded normativity*. Coulthard explains that place "is a way of knowing, of experiencing and relating to the world and with others; and sometimes these relational practices and forms of knowledge guide forms of resistance against other rationalizations of the world that threaten to erase or destroy our senses of place" (61). He supports this understanding with an explanation in terms of his community's Weledeh dialect of Dogrib where "dè" (land) is translated to encompass land, people, animals, rocks, trees, lakes and rivers, and more. This usage demonstrates that people are as much a part of land as other elements – which are also considered to hold agency – creating reciprocal ethical obligations among all things (61). Although he takes his example from his own community, Coulthard asserts that the significance of land for Indigenous peoples is widespread.[1] I examine this claim in terms of local West Coast peoples whose land has been developed into the urban Lower Mainland area of Metro Vancouver. Coulthard invokes the concept of "place-based practices" in his definition of *grounded normativity*, but he does not connect this with de Certeau's influential discussion of spatial practices in *The Practice of Everyday Life*. Because de Certeau's work is often evoked in considerations of urban experience as well as site-specific performance, it is useful for this study of Indigenous connection to place through performative practice within an urban setting to relate his concepts to Coulthard's ontological framing of land within Indigenous thought.

De Certeau (1984) introduces his investigation by explaining his focus on how *users* – as opposed to *makers* – of representation or culture operationally manipulate and thereby invent everyday life by "*poaching* in countless ways on the property of others" (xi–xii, italics original). He terms this a hidden "*poiēsis*," which he exemplifies through a description of Indigenous peoples' actions in response to Spanish colonizers, observing that "their use of the dominant social order deflected its power, which they lacked the means to challenge; they escaped without leaving it" (xii–xiii). He then moves on to discussing methods of invention, first defining "strategy" as "the calculus of force-relationships, which becomes possible when a subject of will and power ... can be isolated from an 'environment.' A strategy assumes a place that can be circumscribed as *proper* (*propre*) and thus serve as the basis for generating relations with an exterior distinct from it" (xix, italics original). I would like to focus on his use of relations – he calls them "force-relationships" – and on his idea that *strategies* are used for generating relations with an exterior distinct from the subject of will and power and from the circumscribed *propre* place.[2]

Although de Certeau assumes that Indigenous peoples are *users*, not *makers*, his description of strategic actions does not necessarily exclude Indigenous relations to land as described by Coulthard (2014), which include practices of resistance against forces "that threaten to erase or destroy our senses of place" (61). De Certeau (1984) then contrasts "strategy" with "tactic," defined as "a calculus that cannot count on a 'proper' (a spatial or institutional localization), nor thus on a borderline distinguishing the other as a visible totality ... [A] tactic belongs to the other" (xix). This understanding of tactic can be applied to how Indigenous people have responded to invaders or settlers who do not recognize their relationship with land. He then asserts that the political and rational use of strategies is the victory of space over time, whereas "a tactic depends on time" and is therefore "always on the watch for opportunities that must be seized 'on the wing'" (xix). He concludes that the form of the tactic is not discourse but "the act and manner in which the opportunity is 'seized'" and that it is "an art of the weak" (xix, 37). He therefore links strategies with spatial control and tactics with the inability to depend on a localization. He develops these concepts further in a later chapter, describing the place from which one can look down upon and see the totality of a city as a strategic vantage point and the movement of walking through the city as tactical yet blind (91–110). Theatre and performance theorists have taken up de Certeau's concern with action, movement, and power but have developed a reading that assumes that strategy and tactics are not necessarily as oppositional as he lays out.

Diana Taylor cites these concepts in *The Archive and the Repertoire* (2003), but when discussing the nonbinary nature of the relationship between archive and repertoire, she says, "Performance belongs to the strong as well as the weak; it underwrites de Certeau's 'strategies' as well as 'tactics'" (22). Later, when discussing the importance of physical location in the analysis of a "scenario" of repertoire, whereby the "action defines the place," she comments that de Certeau's suggestion that "space is a prac-ticed place" means that "there is no such thing as place, for no place is free of history and social practice" (29). She is responding to de Certeau's assertion that, in relation to place, which he defines as an "instantaneous configuration of positions," thus implying "an indication of stability," space is "like the word when it is spoken ... caught in the ambiguity of an actualization, transformed into a term dependent upon many different conventions, situated as the act of a present ... and modified by the trans-formation caused by successive contexts" (117). Taylor's assertion supports a decolonizing understanding of land. She dismisses the concept that there can exist a place that is a stable configuration of elements in relation to one another and that is not created through its use and the ensemble of movements within it. In her formulation, a performance is a strategy as well as a tactic, and all of de Certeau's *places* are continually constructed through spatial practices, never stabilized, and therefore, in terms of his definition, do not exist.

In *Performing Conquest: Five Centuries of Theater, History, and Identity in Tlaxcala, Mexico* (2009), Latinx theatre scholar, dramaturge, and dir-ector Patricia Ybarra also engages with de Certeau's concepts of strategies and tactics. However, she does so less "to delineate tactics of resistance than to further explore how Mexican artists, historians, and local elites employ actions that are more like strategies than tactics" (201). She describes the strategic Tlaxcaltecans as neither "powerless nor powerful" but as "mak[ing] do somewhere in the middle," saying that they have made a place for themselves (201). Ybarra's assertion that they "'have a place'" (202) – which she puts in quotation marks – may be a reference to Taylor's dismissal of the idea that places exist, yet instead of arguing against this dismissal, Ybarra says that the Tlaxcaltecans, through their use of strategy to create place, may be exposing the "'operational logics' of historiography itself" (202). Ybarra's and Taylor's refusals to separate the users of strategies and tactics align well with Coulthard's concept of *grounded normativity*, while also declining to separate space and time.

Although the terms "space" and "place" are not easily transferrable between de Certeau and Coulthard, the concepts behind them can be discussed productively. De Certeau took pains to make a distinction between the concepts, identifying space with an enactment of relations and as therefore lacking the stability of place; yet within Coulthard's (2014) definition of *grounded normativity*, these concepts can be combined through what he calls the "reciprocal *relationship* (which is itself informed by place-based practices and associated forms of knowledge)" (60, italics original). Just as discussed by Taylor and Ybarra, de Certeau's separation of space and place is not valid in the context of Indigenous thought and actions. Interestingly, however, Coulthard aligns with de Certeau in creating a dichotomy of space and time. As mentioned above, de Certeau considers the *strategies* of those with will and power to be aligned with space and the *tactics* of the weak to be aligned with time. Quoting Lakota philosopher Vine Deloria Jr's *God Is Red* (1972), which asserts that "American Indians hold their lands – *places* – as having the highest possible meaning, and all their statements are made with this reference point in mind," Coulthard (2014) contrasts this view with Western societies, which hold time as the narrative of central importance (60, Coulthard's italics). This unacknowledged difference between the significance of space and time is what Deloria says leads to misunderstandings. A strict separation of space and time into Indigenous and Western ontologies, however, can contribute to the portrayal of Indigenous people as being outside of time or as being of the past. Although Coulthard cites Deloria, he does include in his definition of *grounded normativity* place-based practices and relationships – both of which must happen durationally or through time. This interdependent relationship of space and time is fundamental to theatre and performance scholarship, and therefore it is not surprising that Taylor (2003) has dismissed de Certeau's assertion that there could be a place that "is free of history and social practice" (29).

Nor could such a place exist in terms of theatrical dramaturgical practices that engage with embodied historiographic method and land, as demonstrated by a project that its performers, Guna-Rappahannock scholar Monique Mojica, Choctaw novelist and poet Leanne Howe, and Chickasaw literary scholar Chadwick Allen have been working on since 2011. As described in Mojica's article "In Plain Sight: Inscripted Earth and Invisible Realities" (2012), their method is to visit earth mounds in order to access deep knowledge that has been obscured by colonial violence. Mojica describes this process as her mode of "realism," in contrast to a modernist realism that depends on her erasure as an Indigenous woman (219). She explains that the earthworks they visit are "encoded visual language" that she is using to inform her research – which she considers archival, field, and studio. They are making an inquiry into "Indigenous aesthetics and performance principles in theory, process, and practice" and are using "the practical application of these investigations and principles as the structural base from which to construct a performance, design a set, or dramaturge a script" (219). After detailing their visits to multiple earthworks sites, some visible and others hidden, Mojica concludes, "This hyperreal invisibility [is] made visible by privileging ancestral knowledge: feats of astronomy, engineering, architecture, physics, and social organization that manipulate the landscape to evoke a heart-spirit response that can impact and align the human body in relationship to the earth and stars ... across all these centuries" (242). One expression of this ongoing project is *Sideshow Freaks and Circus Injuns* by Howe and Mojica, which explores the complexities of both the hypervisibility of Indigenous enfreakment and the invisibility of "deliberate concealment and erasure of the evidence that marks our sustained presence on the landscape" (Knowles 2016, 101). Their project, which privileges a reciprocal relationship to land and the knowledge that can be gained from it, is a conscious aesthetically engaged example of Coulthard's political theory, as well as Taylor's and Ybarra's wide-ranging descriptions of performative theoretical approaches.

In a synthesis of this discussion of Indigenous, cultural, and performance scholarship, I propose the term "grounded practices" to illuminate the interaction of land and performance-based practices, making use of both strategies and tactics as described by de Certeau, while also emphasizing Coulthard's idea of being deeply informed by what the land teaches through reciprocal relationship. These grounded practices, as I explain in the next section, include the enunciation of land through language that accentuates the relations of space and time.

Eddies of Influence

On a warm February day late in the afternoon, with the sunlight slanting sharply in through the large windows of the University of British Columbia's Museum of Anthropology, I stood at the entrance to an exhibit, transfixed by a projection on the floor. The sunbeams made it a little hard to discern the moving images on the institutional grey carpet, but eventually I perceived that this was a video representation of waves hitting a shore of smooth rocks in a slow rhythm. I was entering one of three sister exhibits in the series *c̓əsnaʔəm, the city before the city*, which opened in January 2015 at the Musqueam Cultural Centre, the Museum of Vancouver, and the Museum of Anthropology.[3] I stopped in the entrance space and let the images wash over me while I listened to the voice of Larry Grant speaking words of welcome in hən̓q̓əmin̓əm̓:

> ʔa:: si:y̓ém̓ tə siyey̓əʔ ct ʔiʔ tə n̓a:ɬtən ʔiməxneʔtən,
> [Our respected friends, relations, and visitors,][4]

> ʔəm̓i ce:p kʷətxʷiləm ʔi ʔə tə n̓a šxʷməθkʷəy̓əmaʔɬ təməxʷ ʔiʔ tə shən̓q̓əmin̓əm̓qən.
> [come into the land and language of the Musqueam people.]

> ʔiʔ hay ce:p q̓ə tə ɬwələp k̓ʷəθ xʷʔəm̓i *c̓əsnaʔəm, the city before the city.*
> [And thank you to all of you for coming to *c̓əsnaʔəm, the city before the city.*]

The greeting ended with Vanessa Campbell's voice saying (also in hən̓q̓əmin̓əm̓), "You will honour us to become witnesses. Commit our ancestral village of c̓əsnaʔəm to your hearts and minds. Commit also to your hearts and minds the land, traditional teachings, history, and language of the Musqueam people."

Most significant for this discussion of land and performance is the emphasis, in all three exhibits about the village of c̓əsnaʔəm, on talking, listening, and witnessing. Each featured multiple examples of oral histories, and one of the most effective, titled "sq̓əq̓ip – gathered together," was at the Museum of Anthropology in a dimly lit room set up with a kitchen table and chairs, on which a teapot, mugs, and some photos were laid out. The room also had four speakers hung in the corners with a chair underneath each one for visitors. A twenty-five-minute conversation played in a loop. Four Musqueam men and two Musqueam women spoke in English, laughing and telling stories.[5] They discussed their parents and Elders, as well as younger generations, touching on methods of teaching and learning through talking and listening. This part of the exhibit demonstrated experientially the significance of taking the time to listen. Both times that I was in the room, other people were present, and we all sat still and silent, making little eye contact, intent on the voices speaking out of the darkness above, much like children listening to adults (as hən̓q̓əmin̓əm̓-language instructor Larry Grant explained to me). Unlike the usual flow of a museum exhibit, this one expected prolonged attentive listening while sharing a space with others (in contrast to the often employed insulated listening space of headphones). Musqueam community member and exhibit co-curator Jordan Wilson explains the process of creating this section in his article "Gathered Together: Listening to Musqueam Lived Experience" (2016), where he reflects on the significance of the skilled collective narration of lived experiences as a method of continuing his community's "distinct values, worldviews, laws, history and practices (otherwise known as snəweyəł – teachings received since childhood)" (470). Wilson discusses this moment of the exhibit as one that aimed to intervene in the conventions of a museum with an aural experience of conversation listening that would have a quality of warmth and comfort (484). The recording was done in one of the group members' homes after a home-cooked meal and was originally two and a half hours long, but it was edited for public sharing in order to create an experience of what Paige Raibmon, quoted by Wilson, calls "transformational listening" that should be understood as a gift (485).

All of the exhibits were filled with the voices and images of contemporary Musqueam people and offered extensive opportunities for listening. The significance of this feature was emphasized through Musqueam co-curator Terry Point's comments in a video near the end of the Museum of Vancouver

exhibit. When asked what he hoped would come of the museum presentation, he made a request for settlers and newcomers to listen to Musqueam
people. The three exhibits, filled with voices, words, images, and language,
were clear cultural enunciations of land, identity, technology, and ways of
knowing, ready for the attention of the ears, hearts, and minds of visitors.

In his introductory essay in *The Practice of Everyday Life* (1984),
de Certeau likens his investigation to the enunciation of speech, explaining that he privileges the act of speaking because "it establishes a *present*
relative to a time and place; and it posits a *contract with the other* (the
interlocutor) in a network of places and relations" (xiii, italics original).
He cites John Searle with regard to speech act theory and later describes
walking as "pedestrian speech acts" that appropriate the topography by
spatially acting out place just as a speaker appropriates a language by acous-
tically acting out its words, noting that both walking and speaking also
imply relations with others (97–8). Whereas de Certeau uses speech as a
metaphor to illuminate the concept of walking as a "space of enunciation,"
in this section I connect language and land more explicitly. Spurred on by
the use of spoken language and listening relations in the museum exhibits
about the space of čəsnaʔəm, I examine a process of decolonization through
my experiences of learning hən̓q̓əmin̓əm̓ and performing in the language at
community gatherings in order to convey the Indigenous epistemological
conceptions of relationship to land that are embedded in the enunciation
of the language. The significance of language has been emphasized by multiple Indigenous scholars, activists, and community members who look to
their languages for Indigenous epistemologies. This focus is demonstrated
throughout Michi Saagiig Nishnaabeg poet, performer, and scholar Leanne
Betasamosake Simpson's *Dancing on Our Turtle's Back* (2011), in which
she asserts that "Indigenous languages carry rich meanings, theory and
philosophies within their structures. Our languages house our teachings
and bring the practice of those teachings to life in our daily existence" (49).
She further explains, "Breaking down words into the 'little words' they are
composed of often reveals a deeper conceptual – yet widely held – meaning.
This part of the language and language learning holds a wealth of knowledge and inspiration ... [T]his 'learning through the language' provides
those who are not fluent with a window through which to experience the
complexities and depth of our culture" (49). In Peircean semiotics, this
way of understanding is termed "the interpretant," which depends on a

community participating in a shared code system. This section details the work of a community to restore its interpretant system to wider use within the community as well as a way for settlers and newcomers to better understand the space and people with whom they live.

As a necessary part of an effort to better know the Indigenous peoples and their ways of knowing the lands on which I have been living and working, at the core of my method is the study of an Indigenous language. Although undertaken as a student, this learning has involved far more than preparatory training. I have benefited in myriad ways from the opportunity of being permitted to study the hǝńq̓ǝmińǝm̓ language with Musqueam teachers Larry Grant, Marny Point, and Jill Campbell as well as with Patricia Shaw of the University of British Columbia's First Nations and Endangered Languages Program (FNEL). I recognize and respect the intellectual property rights associated with the knowledge I have acquired through the Musqueam Indian Band and the FNEL as well as its culturally sensitive nature; and I therefore respectfully acknowledge the many hands that have prepared, organized, and presented the information. The course work and materials were arranged with the guidance and teachings of the late Adeline Point, Ed Sparrow, Edna Grant, Dominic Point, and Arnold Guerin Sr. We were taught the orthography developed in 1999 by the Musqueam Indian Band and the FNEL as well as its correspondence to Arnold Guerin Sr's system developed in the 1970s based on symbols available on a typewriter. The orthography used in the courses I took is based on the North American Phonetic Alphabet, and there is a single unique symbol for each distinct sound (Shaw and Campbell 2012, 118).

In learning the language, I made extensive use of digitized sound files paired with writing. Shaw (2015) emphasizes that every word, phrase, sentence, and role in a narrative or dialogue is paired with digitized sound files to provide students with a diversity of native speaker voices as role models. These sound files allowed me to listen carefully (and repeatedly) until I had an audio memory of words and sentences that was supported by the writing system but not completely dependent on visualizing the written words. In the absence of an immersion environment, the sound files approximated the opportunity of learning through imitation by introducing sounds, words, and concepts alongside the linguistic terms to describe them. By learning the language in this way, I also gained the basic research skills to be able to access the knowledge contained within Coast Salish ethnographer and linguistic anthropologist Wayne Suttles's the *Musqueam Reference Grammar* (2004).

The hən̓q̓əmin̓əm̓ language is referred to by Suttles (2004) as the "downriver" dialect of the Salishan language classified as Halq̓eméylem. It is spoken by multiple groups in the area surrounding the delta of what is known as the Fraser River, extending from Musqueam, Tsleil-Waututh, Katzie, Kwantlen, Langley, Marpole, Burrard, Jericho, and Coquitlam to Tsawwassen (Shaw and Campbell 2012, 1–3; Tsleil-Waututh Nation n.d.). These groups are based in the metro Vancouver areas known as North Vancouver, Tsawwassen, Vancouver, Richmond, Surrey, Langley, New Westminster, Coquitlam, and Pitt Meadows and were part of a complex network of communities that is not accurately represented through the colonial reserve system. The language is currently described as part of the hən̓q̓əmin̓əm̓-Hul̓q̓umin̓um-Halq̓eméylem language continuum.[6] Suttles (2004) explains that his reference grammar primarily reflects the speech of Christine Charles (1894–1968) and James Point (1881–1979) along with some additional materials from Andrew Charles (1893–1961), Della Kew (1929–1982), and Arnold Guerin (1910–1987) (xxi). Suttles also describes the language as providing a link between the "upriver" and "island" dialects of Halq̓eméylem and explains that, based on their experiences of living in multiple communities, the Musqueam people with whom he worked demonstrated "no great differences in speech within" the downriver dialect (xxv, xxix). Thus, although my research is deeply embedded in the relationships that have developed between the University of British Columbia – situated on unceded Musqueam territory – and the Musqueam people, the knowledge contained within the language may be considered to reflect the interpretant system of a range of Indigenous groups throughout the Lower Mainland.

My experience over the two years that I studied the language profoundly shifted my understanding of where I am living and of some of the people on whose land I am a visitor. This has been part of the process that Stephanie Irlbacher-Fox (2014, 146) regards as the overcoming of settler privilege through efforts of self-decolonization and that Matthew Wildcat and colleagues (2014) describe as settler reckoning with colonial past and present to undertake a decolonizing journey. Learning the language was difficult, and I often felt at sea given how unfamiliar everything was and how inept I seemed – similar to the way that Irlbacher-Fox (2014) describes the experience of land-based education for settlers who are "forced to under-stand themselves in relation to the limits of their knowledge contrasted with the superior capabilities possessed by Indigenous Elders and land-based knowledge holders" (155). She describes this as a process of transition "from a position of dominance to one of dependence [that] constitutes an important moment of 'unsettling': reaching a place of potentially trans-formative discomfort" (155). I recognized that my discomfort was likely productive, and by continuing to engage, I began to build understanding and relationships that are part of my unfinished, continual, and "messy process of relational in-the-world becoming" that is self-decolonizing (156).

As well as this personal learning, the courses included an expecta-tion of performance, which also triggered discomfort and feelings of dependence.[7] At the end of each term, language students performed at a community potluck where we enunciated the language we had learned for community members.[8] This use of performance as a public summative evaluation of learning was intimidating, and as a performer, I felt that the stakes were very high. It was also generative in that we were expected to write our own skits and create characters while responding to our present experiences. Our performance involved using the language we had learned about the hunting and preparation of ducks in order to per-form a skit about elves preparing Santa's duck dinner, including singing a hənq̓əminəm̓ version of the French song "Alouette," called "nə maʔəqʷ, nə ɬəkʷəm̓ maʔəqʷ," as we plucked the head, wings, and backside of stuffed ducks. Another event featured a rap written by Aidan Pine, a student in the University of British Columbia's First Nations Languages Program, called "ʔi ct ceʔ xʷcəməstəl̓ qəlet" ("We Will Meet Again"), sung to an instrumental of A Tribe Called Quest's song "Can I Kick It?" (1990). These performances challenged me to put into practice my language learning in order to communicate with community members. The urge for creative expression made me realize how little I knew and motivated me to learn more.

Evenings were structured around the sharing of a meal, with food pro-vided by the FNEL, Musqueam administration, and the language learners. Students then took turns presenting their poetry, songs, and skits. Elder Larry Grant hosted by introducing and responding to student perform-ances. The vulnerability that is involved in performing connects to the sense of dependence mentioned by Irlbacher-Fox (2014) above, which also creates an opening through which it becomes possible to offer care and nurturing. During the performances, students and Musqueam community members often described their emotional journeys using words like "tension," "humility," "gratitude," "regret," "longing," "pride," and "courage." At the December 2014 performance, Grant shared his experience of first speaking publicly in hən̓q̓əmin̓əm̓, describing how, when he speaks, he hears the voices of his grandparents again. He explained how emotional this experience was for him and how for the first five years, whenever he spoke publicly, he wept. Gina Grant also took the opportunity to state how proud she was of all the Musqueam community members who were learning their language and explained that it was not in her to learn because of her experiences at residential school (Gaertner 2014a). During these evenings, the dynamics of tension and dependence created through the action of performing and spectating (or witnessing) were used to begin to bridge the separation between settlers/newcomers and Musqueam people as well as between generations, helping to establish a place from which to engage in the process of decolonizing. As de Certeau (1984) would posit, these acts of speaking established a *present time* and *place*, creating a network with others that comprised those with whom I performed, those who responded to us, and the language teachers whose work allowed us to stand up and speak aloud in hən̓q̓əmin̓əm̓ to Musqueam community members in their cultural centre at the mouth of the river.

The courses took place on Musqueam Indian Reserve 2, first in the Elders' Centre and later in the community centre. Although I have lived in Vancouver since 1991, this was the first time I had been on the reserve. As a settler/newcomer, I had never felt invited and was unsure whether I would be trespassing if I entered the area. This confusion is part of the legacy of the unceded nature of these lands and the present-day tension that underlies settler assumptions. The FNEL coursework and materials were very explicitly concerned with knowledge of land. The first chapter of the textbook for the first course is subtitled "Introduction to the Musqueam People, Their Territory, and Their Language" and includes five maps of the area and over thirty place names. The first homework assignment included an exercise in which we plotted the great Musqueam warrior qiyəplenəxʷ's multiday journey through the waters of the area. Before we learned how to introduce ourselves, we learned the names of the places surrounding us. Eventually, I began to understand some of the knowledge about this land contained within the words of the language. I will now focus on spatial conceptions, examining the imbrications of land, including water, with expressions of language in order to show how speaking in hәṅ̓qәmiṅәṁ can also be a way of philosophically moving through land and water.

In the *Musqueam Reference Grammar* (2004), Suttles summarizes concepts of space required by hәṅ̓qәmiṅәṁ grammar. He explains elements of the language that require the identification of a location relative to the speaker: use of the auxiliary verbs "ʔi" and "niʔ" to add "here, now" or "there, then" to a verb; how movement is expressed in terms of away from or toward the speaker; and the fact that every noun is described by an article or demonstrative that also locates it either as present and visible, nearby but invisible, or remote and/or hypothetical (487). These three elements of the grammar embed every speaker's expression (using auxiliary verbs, movement, and/or nouns) in its relative location. Suttles then explains the significance of the expression of movement in relation to land or water: "[D]irection of movement and location on land or water are commonly indicated with words that refer to the shore and the flow of water ... [T]hese words are the counterparts of cardinal directions in English" (488). Furthermore, directions within a house are derived from the same roots used to express directions in relation to water. For example, "xʷiwәl" means both to move upstream and to move toward the centre of the house, or toward the fire (488). These are just a few examples of how location and relation to water are grounded in the practice of speaking hәṅ̓qәmiṅәṁ.[9] I move on now to a few words that elucidate connection to land, leadership, and care.

The word for moving upstream or toward the fire, "xʷiwәl," is related to the word "hiẁaʔqʷ" (head person, chief), which is constructed from the progressive reduplication – which creates a sense of continuous, iterative, and durative action – of "hiẁ-," comprised of the root "hiw-" (take/bring someone toward the centre of the house, or toward the fire) with both a glottalized "w" to indicate continuous reduplication and a lexical suffix[10] meaning "head" (Shaw and Campbell 2013b, 334; Shaw 2015). The way that this word for leader conveys the motion and connection to land, water, and home – as going upstream against the current or moving toward the fire – within leadership is quite powerful. It carries images of both coming into the light to address and be seen by community members as well as having the strength not just to withstand, but also to move against, a current.

Another philosophical connection of people, particularly women, to land is through the construction of words using lexical suffixes and prefixes. In "The Origin of the Name 'Musqueam,'" James Point tells the story of a dangerous two-headed sʔiłqəy̓ monster that lived in a small lake but came out one day, killing all the plants as it moved over the ground on its way to the river. Its path became the creek and wherever its droppings fell, a new plant, the məθkʷəy̓ grass, grew.[11] It was considered sacred, and the "xʷəlməxʷ tən̓a təməxʷ" (people of this land) named the area xʷməθkʷəy̓əm (Suttles 2004, 539–46). In the phrase "people of this land," Suttles hypothesizes that the word "təməxʷ" (land, earth) is made up of the lexical suffix "-məxʷ" (land, people) added to the consonant "t," thus connecting land, people, and earth (288). The word "xʷəlməxʷ" is given as "people" or "Indian" (82). Suttles also suggests that the lexical suffix "-əlməxʷ" (breast milk) is related to the lexical suffix mentioned above for "land, people" (286). Following Suttles's hypothesis, it seems that, using the connective suffix "-əl" (movement), the lexical suffix for "land" is expanded to mean "breast milk," metaphorically connecting this essential life-giving nourishment to land. Suttles also gives multiple meanings for the prefix "xʷ-," each of which can generate a vivid sense of land. This prefix can indicate an oblique relater, which connects something with something else, a verbalizing prefix for "move toward," or a lexical prefix for "inward," "inhering," "possessing," or "vulva" (557). Together, these possible meanings create a constellation of ideas that could be encompassed in the word for "people of this place" – connection, moving, possessing, vulva, breast milk, and land – perhaps demonstrating a notion of land and people that is constructed in terms of the life-giving potential of women's bodies.

I employ these examples of locative strategies and word constructions to show how leadership, land, water, people, and women underlie the expressive practice of speaking in hən̓q̓əmin̓əm̓. I also propose to use a cluster of hən̓q̓əmin̓əm̓ words to inspire a metaphor with which to consider the interrelation of space and time with, as will be discussed throughout the rest of this book, cultures. I am concerned here with the movement that happens where water meets an obstruction in an eddy, a formation where currents interact with an obstacle, either an element of the land or an object in the water. There are multiple hən̓q̓əmin̓əm̓ words for interacting with an eddy, signifying the cultural saliency of this water formation, including "qem̓" (to get in the eddy), "qeqəm̓" (in the back eddy), and "qam̓əθət" (to get into the back eddy) (Shaw et al. 2010, 6).[12] For those travelling through water as well as gathering resources, knowing the areas where eddies form is essential for both harnessing their power and staying safe. I propose a use of this significant water formation as a metaphorical conception of the interaction between space and time given that the movement of the water is shaped by the land, yet over time the water shapes the land as well. This reciprocal relationship helps avoid dichotomies. The metaphor also supports much discussion in theatre and performance studies concerning interaction and relation, such as Diana Taylor's (2003) assertion of the interdependent connection of the archive and the repertoire and her denial of the surrogation of Indigenous cultural practices, which she asserts multiply through simultaneous action within colonially commanded behaviours. The "temporal drag" and temporal reach that create "inter(in)animation," concepts discussed by Rebecca Schneider in *Performing Remains: Art and War in Times of Theatrical Reenactment* (2011, 14, 7), can also be represented by the motion within an eddy.[13] This metaphor, which I term "eddy of influence," is also a corrective, and perhaps a localization, of Joseph Roach's (1996, 28) concept of the "vortices of behavior."

For Roach, *vortices of behavior* are spaces of gravitational pull that bring audiences together and produce performers from their midst. Throughout *Cities of the Dead: Circum-Atlantic Performance* (1996), he identifies numerous vortices, all of which are areas of exchange of emotions or ideas where behaviours demonstrate culture through performance that is both a mixing and a creating of new norms. Roach never interrogates the force of attraction pulling behaviours together, nor does he examine how the new norms are created. By using the words "vortex" and "gravitational pull" to describe the phenomena he is working with, Roach masks the human agency involved in the creation of this type of performance place and also focuses on new behaviours without considering the continuation of old actions interacting with the new. To trace a local genealogy of performance that engages with Indigenous perspectives, it is essential to articulate the powers that channel performative behaviours to these designated spaces. The eddy of influence includes motion as well as a seemingly static obstacle – either natural or constructed by humans – around which the water is flowing, an obstacle that stays, creating swirling eddies in front and in back. An eddy may be powerful, acting on objects caught within it, or it may create a resting place from a strong current. An eddy also has a clear cause: the enduring object around which the river's current or ocean's tide must make its way. The eddy that forms around and/or within an object will eventually influence the shape of that object, and as the object changes, it will change the formation of the current. All of these things must happen through time and space. I propose that this metaphor more accurately represents the continuing and dynamic presence both of the Musqueam people and of the knowledge contained within their language and place names for what is now known as Vancouver.

This discussion also brings me back to the projection on the carpet in the foyer of the c̓əsnaʔəm exhibit at the Museum of Anthropology accompanied by the hən̓q̓əmin̓əm̓ words of welcome. Hours later, as I left the area, the sun had set and I could see the definition of the rocks very clearly as the water rhythmically washed over them. It was a visual representation of innumerable small eddies and an appropriate way to frame an exhibit that explains the Musqueam people's endurance through time as well as their engagement in contemporary culture and their influence on the city of Vancouver. One means of endurance has been through place names, both those adopted by settlers/newcomers and those that have been officially overwritten, although the knowledge they contain about the land and their performative reiterations cannot be completely emptied out. This is the topic of the final section of this chapter.

Simultaneity of Place Names and Tactics

I began the first section of this chapter with a discussion of Coulthard's (2014) concept of *grounded normativity*, which understands land as a mode of reciprocal relations and obligations. In this section, I examine how part of that relation is enacted through the naming of places. Naming articulates a relationship to the land; it is necessary as a way to guide travel to a specific destination or to pass on knowledge of resources available in that area. The relationship can also be one that holds stories about something significant that happened or about something that continuously, iteratively occurs there. Therefore, paying attention to place naming can be a way to learn what land, as Coulthard suggests, "ought to teach us about living our lives in relation to one another and our surroundings" (60). Keeping in mind what I have termed "grounded practices," which illuminate the interaction of land and performance-based strategies and tactics, an examination of the knowledge held and performed through place name articulation by Indigenous people resisting colonization will also speak to the affective swirling[14] about in the eddies of influence since European invasion and settlement. I begin with a short discussion of the significance of place names from anthropological scholarship. I then examine the etymological construction of three place names in the area of this research project. I conclude with a discussion of how three examples of interventions in settler cultural activities through place name enunciation and wayfinding demonstrate place names as a performative way of capturing relationship to land through times past, present, and future.

Keith Basso's *Wisdom Sits in Places: Landscape and Language among the Western Apache* (1996) is a foundational work that has inspired a reconsideration of the significance of place and naming that resonates particularly well with the notions of time, place, and embodiment as they are discussed in theatre and performance studies. Basso asserts that place names for the Western Apache not only represent their history as being comprised of ancestors' words and viewpoints grounded in a place but also describe human activity in that place, some of which marks people as being from there and some of which passes on cultural values. He learns from Western Apache Elders about the connection between the ability to visualize place name stories and the ability to communicate in a deep, concise way as well as to react to both internal and external disturbances with wisdom. Basso's work demonstrates the importance of places and how their names are integrated into meaning making in the Western Apache system of knowledge, giving an understanding of the important role that living surrounded by named places has in the continuation of culture. His extended inquiry into "socially given systems of thought ... that mold and organize the experience itself" opens up a world, showing that "to casually ignore them ... is to suppose that matters are much smaller in fact than they really are" (144). Although not explicitly concerned with performance, Basso's work is deeply concerned with the placement of bodies in time and space, which links well with the durational spatiality discussed in theatre and performance studies theory. Insights on performativity and land in anthropologist Crisca Bierwert's *Brushed by Cedar, Living by the River: Coast Salish Figures of Power* (1999) are also helpful in considering place names that connect to reiterative actions. Bierwert closes her book with a discussion of methods by which people enact their relationships to place through cultural practice. She asserts that "memories attached to a place are not only the associations they have with dear relatives who also lived there and have died"; what is also "important here is the attachment felt when people recapitulate the performative knowledge of those others" (280–1). Bierwert is not speaking of theatrical performance but of the everyday actions of cultural practices, which can include theatricality.

An examination of knowledge enacted through three local place names concurs with the "multiplication and simultaneity" asserted by Taylor (2003, 46); it also illuminates the grounded practices embedded in the hən̓q̓əmin̓əm̓ language, which connect to knowledge that is held by the land. These hən̓q̓əmin̓əm̓ place names are verbs constructed as progressive, durative, and iterative acts that continue and are repeated throughout time, unlike perfective verbs, which imply a complete action taken to its conclusion. A beach on the west side of Vancouver, known to settlers as Spanish Banks, is called tᶿatᶿələm̓ (shivering from cold) in hən̓q̓əmin̓əm̓ (Shaw and Campbell 2012, 1; Suttles 2004, 570). The area is on a point of land unsheltered from ocean winds; as anyone who spends time there knows, it is a cold place. In Suttles's (2004) reference grammar, he cites a story about this name told by Musqueam Elder James Point, which connects it to "a rock of white granite ... [that] was an old lady who was crying here (presumably when χe:l̓s came and transformed her)" (570). Given that this name is the progressive reduplication of "shiver," it seems to be commenting on both the shore as a cold place and the transformation story embedded in the name. As the woman in the story was crying, she may also have been shivering since these two actions often go together. In this way, the name holds environmental knowledge as well as a sχʷəy̓em̓, which is a narrative involving χe:l̓s and his transformations of the world (264).

Along the seawall that rings Stanley Park is a significant rock formation; its name in hən̓q̓əmin̓əm̓ is "sɬχiləx," which is constructed of the progressive verb "be standing" and an s-prefix nominalizer or resultative (Suttles 1996, 14; Shaw 2015). A few stories tell of the rock being a man who was transformed – in each version because he refused to stop ritually bathing, which he was doing either to ensure that his child would be born properly (Johnson 1911, 11–20) or to prepare to protect his fishing rights (Bierwert 1999, 91–3). There is a beauty to this place name, which expresses the transformation story particularly well with its combination of a progressive verb (which indicates continuous action) and a nominalizer (which immobilizes the verb into a noun) or a resultative (which describes the end result of the action). Both versions of the sχʷəy̓em̓ narrative of the transformation of the man resonate with a manifestation of strength in action, of standing up for what is right. However, the current settler name, Siwash Rock, has a pejorative connotation. Bierwert explains that the original Chinook Jargon word "siwash" shifted "from an equivalence with 'Indian' to a suggestion of a relic and then to the suggestion of a derelict ... [What once] would have also suggested that there was an old story attached to [the rock] ... would have been empty of spiritual significance" (287). What we are left with is a name of a rock formation in a very public place that denigrates Indigenous people – a name that continues to be repeated by newcomers and descendants of settlers who have little knowledge of its connotations.[15]

The last progressive-verb place name I discuss, χʷay̓χʷəy̓, also brings us to the main site considered in this book: the village that was located at Lumberman's Arch in Stanley Park. The meaning is given variously as "masked dance performance ... from the tradition that an ancestor received a privilege there" (Suttles 2004, 571) and as "clearly [sχʷayχʷəy] ... [the] performance by masked dancers, without the s-prefix" (Suttles 1996, 13). In *A Stó:lo–Coast Salish Historical Atlas* (2001), Albert (Sonny) McHalsie (aka Naxaxalhts'i) translates this place name as "masks" or "little masked performance," suggesting a diminutive of the performance (153). None of these meanings is given as a progressive verb, but the reduplication of the syllable, the glottalization of the resonants, and the possible diminutive form indicate that it may be one.[16] That would give the meaning a sense of continuation: instead of "performance," it would be "performing" or, taking into account the full vowel in the first syllable, "several are performing." If the root of the word is "χʷəy," it could be related to the verb "χʷəyem" (tell a story), which Suttles (2004) describes as possibly a durative form indicating that an action is prolonged or a position is held (177).[17] If the suffix "-em" on "χʷəyem" is the intransitive,[18] it could perhaps indicate that the root of "χʷay̓χʷəy̓" is the word "story" without the intransitive added. Intransitive verbs are those that involve only one direct participant who experiences the verb (Shaw and Campbell 2013b, 252), and Suttles (2004) explains that the intransitive suffix is added to roots that are logically transitive, naming actions that have objects – as in the telling of a story to people (231). We usually conceive of telling a story as an action that involves a listener, yet if both the verb "χʷəyem" (tell a story) and its related noun "sχʷəy̓em̓" (a story from the time of χe:l's) have an intransitive ending, it may indicate the effect that these types of stories have on the teller rather than the listener. The absence of the intransitive suffix, as seems to be indicated if "χʷəy" is the root of "χʷay̓χʷəy̓," shifts the emphasis away from the state experienced by the subject of the verb.[19] In terms of theatre and performance theory, this is a fascinating possibility for the place name formation. A place name that indicates performance but has the status *not* of a transitive verb acting on the audience *or* of an intransitive verb acting only on the performer but of something in between, or perhaps both, describes the relationship between the performers and audience that is often discussed in theatre theory and performance studies. It is also in keeping with conceptions of ritual in oral cultures that is intended to achieve something and have an outcome affecting others.

Indigenous performers and scholars Monique Mojica (Guna-Rappahannock) and Floyd Favel (Cree) have discussed the tension inherent in performing without violating the ceremony/tradition/knowledge that is not meant to be shared (Favel 2005, 114–15; 2013, 118–22) as well as the need to create a bridge that can transform tradition in order to fulfil the needs of theatre (Mojica 2013, 129). So, although it is very important to note the connection of the place name to the sχʷayχʷəy dance that belongs to certain families and is performed for distinct purposes only in restricted community contexts, there is a difference between this dance and the public performances that have occurred at this site since settler invasion. This part of the knowledge held within the place name marks the site as one that is spiritually significant. It is certainly not within the scope of this book, nor is it appropriate for me as a newcomer and settler descendant, to investigate or comment on spiritual practices. So, without going into all the simultaneous meanings that are held within the name, my inquiry will note the significance of the continuity of performance and the reciprocity between performers and spectators but will focus on public activities at the site.

I now shift focus slightly in order to consider place names and wayfinding, both in terms of physical orientation and as a way to constitute destinations along a decolonizing pathway. Schneider's (2011) discussion of live reiterative acts, such as the gesture of a pointing finger, is generative when considering place names and wayfinding. She says the gesture "casts itself both backward (as a matter of repetition) and forward (it can be enacted again) in time" (37–8). I assert that the use of place names for wayfinding – especially in a touristic-recreational site – is a performative act along the lines of Schneider's reiterative gesture and Judith Butler's (1988) formulation of the construction of gender through performativity, repetition, and the normative. Wayfinding, either through the reading of maps or through the interaction between people, can both implicitly and explicitly contain the gesture of a pointing finger while also enacting the speaking of a place name.

Along the lines of Butler's (1988) configuration, if a spoken place name does not follow the "socially shared" and "historically constituted" expectation, there can be anxiety and punishment, yet there is also an opportunity to reclaim power through subversive performances that gesture to the contingency of the normative and the potential to transform it (528–31). For instance, in the summer of 2013 my partner and I hiked along a (somewhat) gruelling and isolated trail in the mountains north of Vancouver. When we met with the few other hikers, we would discuss the conditions and name our destination. In our usual social milieu, these peaks north of Vancouver are generally referred to as The Sisters, a translation of their Skwx̱wú7mesh place name. When we would mention them as our first night's destination, our easy conversation would often stall, as a look of confusion came over our interlocutors. They would then invariably say, "You mean The Lions," and we would respond with, "Yes, The Sisters." No one ever asked us why we called them that, perhaps just taking us for fools wandering in the wilderness. In this context, the reiteration of "The Lions," the authority of which is supported through signage and maps, produces a normative assumption of the singularity of a place and, I assert, the attempt to create a singular place of whiteness. Our minor subversive naming, albeit ephemeral, was also an effort to respect and effect local Indigenous cultural continuity.

The naming of these peaks is a towering example of the enactment of multiple eddies of influence. They have been called The Lions since the 1890s when Judge John Hamilton Grey suggested the name because of his view of their similarity to the "lions couchant" of heraldry (Akrigg and Akrigg 1997, 154). [20] There are, however, some significant obstructions of the colonial name. Mohawk-English writer and performer Pauline Johnson (aka Tekahionwake) comments on the origin of the settler name in her opening story of *Legends of Vancouver* (1911), in which she describes a discussion with Chief Joe Capilano (aka Su-á-pu-luck),[21] a well-respected Sk̲w̲x̲wú7mesh leader whom she met in London in 1906. She explains the settler name for the peaks by referring him to the statues of the *Landseer Lions* he saw in Trafalgar Square. In her narrative, Su-á-pu-luck/Capilano recognizes the similarity but then tells her story of "The Two Sisters," in which a chief's two daughters entering womanhood prevail upon their father to invite their enemies to their feast, creating a lasting peace. They are memorialized for this act and transformed into the two peaks by the Creator, Sagalie Tyee (2–10). A similar story is told by Squamish Elders of the "Sch'ich'yúy – The Sisters Mountains" in Johnny Abraham and colleagues' *People of the Land: Legends of the Four Host First Nations* (2009). In this version, the Squamish twin sisters are captured during a raid and willingly marry twin Stek̲'in brothers. Their good conduct convinces the Stek̲'in to sue for peace with the Squamish, and they are memorialized as the mountains after a long life (81–90).

The two publications of similar stories, almost 100 years apart, are entwined with political performances and demonstrate the tensions of *simultaneity* and *inter(in)animation* that can be present in an eddy of influence. In 1909 Johnson moved to Vancouver to retire after an internationally successful career as a recitalist and poet. Throughout 1910–11 she published stories about the region related to her by Su-á-pu-luck/Capilano, who had gone to London as a leader of the first delegation of BC Indigenous people on a mission to present grievances to King Edward IV with the intention to circumvent discriminatory Canadian government channels by dealing nation to nation with the monarch (Carlson 2010, 269–70). He was considered a "flamboyant and gregarious" leader and was often described in newspapers as inciting unrest throughout the province before the trip as well as afterward (Carlson 2005, 1). Johnson and Su-á-pu-luck/Capilano became friends when she moved to Vancouver. Her publication of these stories in *The Daily Province* newspaper's weekly Saturday magazine, which was usually quite critical of him, was certainly a political and performative act attempting to obstruct settler colonial assumptions through the enunciation of names. Portrayed as her "tillicum" (friend), Su-á-pu-luck/Capilano speaks in accented English as they roam the waters and forests of the Vancouver area and she awaits his decision to share stories with her. She generally opens the stories by locating herself and Su-á-pu-luck/Capilano and then shifts narrative perspective when he speaks. As with much of

Johnson's writing, the stories are composed for recitation with a particular attention to orality and the presence of listeners (Gerson and Strong-Boag 2002, xxx). Although her status as a celebrity attracted a flooding tide of settler attention, she and Su-á-pu-luck/Capilano used their strengths to strategically place themselves as obstacles that created an eddy so that both place names in this story could exist simultaneously.

Using the performative to exert continuous, and adaptive, connection to land continues to be a strategy. The source of the second story, "Sch'ich'yúy – The Sisters Mountains," is Abraham and colleagues' *People of the Land* (2009), published by the Four Host First Nations (FHFN)[22] just prior to the 2010 Winter Olympics in Vancouver. During the opening ceremonies of the games, members of the FHFN entered immediately after the national anthem in regalia, speaking words of welcome in their own languages while four massive welcoming statues with arms outstretched rose from the stage (olympicvancouver2010 2010). The games also featured an Aboriginal Pavilion that showcased live performances as well as the film *We Are Here*, which was projected multiple times daily on the inside of the dome, and they closed with a performance of Marie Clements's *The Road Forward* (VANOC 2010, 85, 82).[23] The FHFN's involvement was both a practical and performative effort to mark the territory with contemporary Indigenous presence, creating a small obstruction around which the Winter Olympics flowed.

Abraham and colleagues' *People of the Land* (2009) features stories from all four nations and is illustrated not by stylized drawings but by contemporary photographs of people and places. Besides this Squamish place name story of The Sisters Mountains, there are other assertions of land and connection. The first Lil'Wat contribution is a description of the Transformer's creation of the territory featuring the stories of five place names based on transformations, demonstrating how Lil'Wat history is "written upon the land" (9–19). The Musqueam section also asserts connection to the land through transformation, citing archeological evidence as well as oral history that "xʷənəθət – our first ancestors – are said to have descended from the sky, wrapped in clouds, before there was anything else here. These supernatural beings populated the land until χe:l's, the Transformer, changed them into their present form as rocks, animals, and features of the landscape that remain to this day" (45). This narrative asserts that the Musqueam people do not just belong to the land but *are* also these "places and beings," and it cites "the many hənq̓əmin̓əm̓ names for the sites and features throughout our territory" as evidence (45). This book's publication coincided with significant international attention to the region, and it is noteworthy that much of the work focuses on transformations linking peoples to place and naming. The use of photographs of contemporary Indigenous people to illustrate the legends of the land is an example of the "DNA of performance" described by Taylor (2003, 175), where "surrogation" (46) is refused.[24] The editors and the Elders who granted permission for the stories to be shared were also strategically placing themselves in the swirling current of international attention, creating an eddy of influence.

In marking a narrative of place connected to people, both of these published accounts of the mountain peaks' names take advantage of the opportunity to reach a large-scale audience – either through celebrity or a mega-event – in order to create witnesses of those who attend to the stories. However, the nonhomogeneous nature of the audience and the persistent racist views of many contemporary settlers, newcomers, and visitors make it possible that the influence exerted will be muddied. Recent Indigenous organizing, through the Idle No More events and the Indigenous Nationhood restoration movement, makes use of performative tactics and naming for very different sorts of audience relations.

During the resurgence of Indigenous actions known as Idle No More, which began in the winter of 2012–13, there were reclamations of names across the country. Leanne Betasamosake Simpson (2014) writes of the significance of the WSÁNEĆ nations' reclamation of the original name of PKOLS, also known as Mount Douglas, on Vancouver Island, and she chronicles other activities, such as the project to restore Anishinaabemowin place names to Chi Engikiiwang/Tkaranto/Toronto.[25] She describes this restoration as a saturation of Indigenous homelands with peoples, languages, and ceremonies (360–2). These projects are in concert with Taiaiake Alfred's (2014) call to "start to reoccupy Indigenous sacred, ceremonial and cultural use sites to re-establish our presence on our land and in doing so to educate Canadians about our *continuing connections* to those places and how important they are to our *continuing existence* as Indigenous peoples" (349, italics added).

This type of claiming of names without government cooperation or recognition is a way of manifesting eddies of influence that can appear and disappear, sweeping up some unawares, while being used to their own advantage by those who have knowledge because of their continuing presence. In a movement imbued with performance – full of round dances,

. drumming, and singing in public spaces – the marking of Indigenous spaces that have not been successfully surrogated by colonial powers is an important performative tactic. By using names that have circulated outside of official documents or names that respond in mutually affective ways to colonial choices, Indigenous peoples and their allies are using enunciation to constitute the much larger world that Basso (1996) proposes is generated through systems of thought created by place naming.

In this section, I have discussed the way that a performative relationship to land is held within hənɊəminəm progressive-verb place names and have also demonstrated how this grounded practice was enacted through the creation of eddies of influence by Pauline Johnson and Su-á-pu-luck/Capilano in the early 1900s and by the Four Host First Nations in 2010 and how it continues to be employed as a spatial tactic by those working for an Indigenous resurgence across Canada. The enunciations of Indigenous place names are the obstructions that affect the swirling flow of colonial cultural assumptions. Through the knowledge held within the names, and their use as tools for wayfinding, place names become a performative method of expressing the relationship with land both in times past and in the current flow of settler-Indigenous culture, a relationship that will, in the manner of an eddy, relentlessly shape the future.

Although this chapter on land, language, and the enactment of the relationship between the two through place names has reached its conclusion, this is not the end of my discussion of the significance of all these elements. The next chapter follows through with a consideration of naming, but it is concerned with the extraordinary efforts undertaken by settlers and the archivist of Vancouver to create and maintain a "proper name" (de Certeau 1984, xix) for the area surrounding χʷayχʷəy̓, known since 1888 as Stanley Park. I also continue my exploration of the grounded practices of strategies and tactics connected with performances since the beginnings of the European invasion, settlement, and founding of the city of Vancouver, including the ways that eddies of influence have manifested through a response to Quelemia Sparrow's podplay *Ashes on the Water* (2011) in the next section.

Walking alongside Quelemia Sparrow's *Ashes on the Water*

The recorded greeting in hən̓q̓əmin̓əm̓ that welcomed people to the 2015 c̓əsna?əm exhibits discussed in chapter 1 used the word "?iməxnə?tən" for visitor, or one who walks alongside; this is a useful term to describe my experience of Musqueam playwright and actor Quelemia Sparrow's *Ashes on the Water* (2011).[1] This podplay is an excellent example of a theatrical grounded practice that can engage a visitor in reciprocal learning through a spatially enacted experience of the past and present. It has a unique status within the burgeoning form of podplays[2] and, along the lines of David Gaertner's (2014b) analysis of Indigenous new media, compels audience members to confront present Indigeneity while disrupting settler assumptions of land. Although the experience does employ practices similar to other works in order to give listener-walkers new understandings of space and history, this podplay goes further because of the confluence of its content, site, and authority in the storytelling.

The advancing sophistication of mp3 audio technology and the popularity of personal media players have enabled an upsurge in use of the podplay form,[3] but there has been discussion since the introduction of the Sony Walkman in the 1980s about audiowalking and how the personal audio player creates a form of "secret theatre" that isolates the listener while also enhancing perception of spatial signification in urban settings (Hosokawa 1984; Chambers 1994; Balme 2006). Kimberley McLeod's article "Finding the New Radical: Digital Media, Oppositionality, and Political Intervention in Contemporary Canadian Theatre" (2014) positions audiowalks within Alan Filewod's call for digital media to reconstitute activist theatre (204–5). McLeod adds nuance to the use of digital media for intervention by comparing Montreal-based playwright Olivier Choinière's *Projet blanc* (2011) with Toronto-based urban activist Jonathan Goldsbie's *Route #501 Revisited* (2012), the first of which was a surreptitious one-night audiowalk during which seventy-two listeners attended Théâtre du Nouveau Monde's staging of Molière's *L'École des femmes* (1662) while listening to Choinière's criticism of the production, whereas the latter was a collaborative streetcar guided tour employing Twitter, which harkened back to the history of urban spaces while creating a distributed discourse. McLeod (2014) deems the former a reinscription of theatrical hierarchy that, in comparison to Goldsbie's event, failed to "harness the interactive potential of the digital" and instead treated its audience as listeners (213, 218). What I want to consider, however, is deployment of the podplay on unceded land as an appropriate use of the structured form to encourage new ways of perceiving site, which is a necessary step in the unsettling of space. So although McLeod is correct to comment on the untapped activist potential of collaborative new media, she is too quick to dismiss the interventionist opportunity inherent within listening.

The content of a podplay is more than the plot of the story and the sound design; the recorded audio file is the stable element that interacts with the body of the visitor moving through the continuously shifting site. As with any performance response, the experience is filtered through an embodied sensual encounter. The difference here is that the sound and voices are stable, whereas the elements of the setting – the time, weather, plants, animals, space, water, and other people – are not. The presences experienced through both the recording and the body moving in space are also distinguished by the absences of the bodies of the performers and by the impossibility of a collective audience experience. Neworld Theatre's Adrienne Wong acknowledges this dynamic of distance and presence and says that it is the tension between the two that keeps her interested in the potential of the form (Wong and Kinch 2012, 41–2). My response, which incorporates my presence in the space while the format of the podplay simultaneously distances me from others and my immediate surroundings, is based on my experience of the podplay *Ashes on the Water* with University of British Columbia professor David Gaertner's Indigenous new media class on 31 October 2014.

On a late-fall day in Vancouver, you can almost be guaranteed that it will rain, so I grab two umbrellas as I leave the house. I'm on my way to meet up with the class for the podplay, and I figure someone else may need one. We'll be outside, listening and walking as we follow the route from close to the corner of Alexander and Main Streets, across the train overpass, and into CRAB Park in the Downtown Eastside neighbourhood of Vancouver. There are a number of variables that are not within our control besides the weather. This is all happening outside, on the street, so it is uncertain what might be part of the experience. Once we've gathered beside the plaque at 157 Alexander Street that marks a church that once stood in that spot, we pair off. I'm sharing my earbud-style headphones with a woman who doesn't have a media player with her. This context affects the sound design; I can hear ambient noises from the street more easily than if I had both ears covered. It may not have been the intention of the designers, but I'm happy to have a partner in this experience, and I'm interested in remaining present with the landscape as the story unfolds. We have to organize ourselves so that the wire between us doesn't tangle, and then I press play. We're instructed to read the plaque and told that we are facing what was once Old Hastings Road and that it is the year 1886, Sunday, 13 June. The play then starts with a voice named Song saying that this is the story of her birth. The narrative shifts to a woman who steps out of the St James Anglican Church doors and describes the smoky air, the sounds of carriages and horses underlying her voice. She recounts the growth of the Canadian Pacific Railway townsite, with new buildings going up and the clearing of land. We hear her baby fussing, and she shushes it as she walks. I wonder if the baby is named Song. I'm also focused on following the directions. I'm worried about navigating while distracted, and I also notice the tension of wanting to focus on the story being told so that I won't miss anything despite the action around me.

The voice of Song directs us to walk toward Main Street, and the mother's voice describes her frustrations with her crying baby. Song then indicates the way into the past, directing us to let the cement fade to wooden sidewalks and to allow a quietness to descend. The background noises in the sound design decrease. We walk slowly, listening to this change, aware of our surroundings. There are only a few cars on the streets down here where Main Street ends and the Port of Vancouver lands begin. The railway overpass beside us mainly leads to the restricted-entry port facilities and the public space of CRAB Park. Nevertheless, we wait for the stoplight to change. Even though we could cross the empty road, being linked together and focused on the audio of the podplay, we don't take any chances. I press pause on my iPod to stop the play, but we don't talk. I look around and see low-rise brick buildings on this side of Main Street, marking this as an older part of the city. The train tracks

are on my left under the roadway, and once we cross the street, we'll be at
the base of a set of stairs with accessible ramps, set well off from the edge
of the road, to take us up over the tracks. This is an impressive amount of
pedestrian infrastructure for this area of the city.

When the light changes, we resume listening and cross the street.
Song recounts her beginning, when she came into the world through
"the ashes of destruction," and our ears are filled with the sounds of
trees falling. Wind sounds blow in from the west, and she describes the
smoke that hangs over the area. Song says she is the song of water, of
mercy, of women. The mother's voice returns, along with the sound of
her crying baby. She hears a man shouting. We are told to stop and look
back to the city from the elevation of the overpass. At this time of day,
it is unremarkable. There are few people around, mainly just the other
pairs in our group ahead and behind us as we all follow the directions.
My partner and I are unsure where we are supposed to be; it seems as
though we should be higher up on the rise in order to see back, so we
hurry to catch up with the play. Ahead of us are two others from the
group, also listening and orienting themselves. I mark their spot in my
mind, taking note of which way they go so that we can follow.

Fire. We hear the sounds of flames and the confusion of voices shouting. The mother's voice rises and describes a man running, the church in
flames. She runs, holding her baby. The sidewalk begins to burn, and she
runs on the road. We are directed to turn to the north and told that there
is a mission reserve on the North Shore. The North Shore is visible from
here, but mainly we see the port machinery and buildings and behind
that the creep of the city up the North Shore Mountains. The water is
steel-grey today, as are the clouds. The air is clear but cold and damp. I
feel very distant from a warm spring day with a fire chasing me down.

Another woman's voice is added to the polyphony. It is that of an
Indigenous woman who is attending a feast on the North Shore. This
woman's speech stresses the first syllable of each word, making it notably different from the voice of Song, which is melodic and soothing,
and from the mother's, which was marked by clipped sharp enunciations until the fire started. Now she speaks in bursts, breathless. The
Indigenous woman notices the wind, the choppy water, and the haze
of smoke over the town, and then she sees the flames across the inlet.
We are directed to walk down a staircase off the overpass. This is where
the people ahead of us were confused. This does not seem like a public

staircase. The Port of Vancouver, especially since the attacks in the United States on 11 September 2001, has security measures surrounding it. Much of the area may be public, but few thoroughfares are left. Most streets end at gates to the port, so few people use these areas. Trusting the voices on the podplay, my partner and I walk down the stairs. The mother speaks again; she is running from the fire, which is right at her ankles. A narrator describes the panic and looting, noting a drunken man passed out on the ground with desperate people fleeing past him. At the bottom of the stairs, we are directed to walk across the grass to the sidewalk. Up to this point, we haven't been sure if we are in the right place. Now the very specific descriptions match our surroundings. My partner and I share words of relief. We are in a strange space; it doesn't feel public. Under the overpass, along the side of the road, there is a dirt path through the grass that leads to the left and the port buildings, but we're told to move to the right and toward the park. Although that trajectory seems to go against the flow of the usual pedestrian traffic on these stairs, it is much more in the direction that I want to go. The mother describes the crowd and then, with horror in her voice, the sight of a man who bursts into flames.

The Indigenous woman speaks again, describing the people around her on the shore who are looking across to the fire, people from Sechelt, Sliammon, Musqueam, and elsewhere. Song interrupts, saying, "Just act, don't think." The Indigenous woman says, "It was the women who wanted to go," declaring that they must make the twenty-five-minute crossing, that they must have mercy. The narrator again intervenes – directing our thoughts to how much a fire can consume in that period of time. We walk along under the concrete structure, away from the working port and toward the public park at the shore. We wait again to cross a street. A little unsure which way we should turn at the corner, we enter the park. Song speaks again, connecting sounds with emotions of love, pain, and joy. Adding breath to these sounds, she is there as a song. She says she is from this place.

We are directed to walk into the park, past the benches, and to stand and look toward the mountains as the Indigenous woman speaks again. She talks of the decision to help, of the brief hints on the men's faces that they think it would be best to let the town burn so that they can be finished with "those people" who take everything they want, forbid the potlatch, bring disease, and treat them poorly, destroying their homes.

The women insist nevertheless on helping, and they set out to make the crossing of the choppy inlet. We walk closer to the water, away from the manicured park lawn and off the concrete footpath, until we reach the sand and stones of the beach. There is little wind today and the waves slowly lap the shore. Others from our group are here already, and I can see a few more behind us. We walk to the middle of the beach area. Looking out across the water, I hear the story and try to imagine a fire at my back and canoes crossing the inlet, but all I can see is the activity of the port, including the SeaBus crossing to my left and a floatplane descending. But I can smell the ocean. The smell brings me to a place without time, full of plants and creatures, life and decay. It's a green, rich smell but cold, too. I forget it when I'm far from the shore, and when I get close, it connects me again with the edge of this coast and all the times I've been out in these elements, sometimes trying to protect my own children from the extremes.

We hear the sounds of paddling and water. The Indigenous woman speaks with passion of the mercy driving what she calls her "fire-heart" as they move toward a rescue. We are told to keep moving toward the water. The landscape behind me fades away. I look only at the water and try to imagine people crossing toward me. The mother's voice returns, along with the baby's whimpers. Saying that she cannot breathe, she wades into the water and holds her baby up. We hear the woman in the canoe, who sees the mother up to her neck in the water. She is desperately holding something up for the rescuers. Realizing what it is, the Indigenous woman collects the baby from the mother and pulls her to safety in the canoe, covering her with a blanket. It's cold by the shore, the wind stronger here, but that's not why I shiver. The combination of the panic in the mother's voice, the urgency in the rescuer's words, and the flames roaring underneath while the baby cries triggers an affect of dread. The first-person point of view of these characters going directly into my ear shuts out my present surroundings. I'm struck by the fears and difficulties that the characters are overcoming.

Together in the canoe, the Indigenous woman and the mother look at each other. Song then speaks again: "I came into this world through the ashes of destruction. It started off with what felt like a deep yawn, a deep yawn that shot across the inlet, through the paddles that cut the water's surface and into the hearts of the people." Breathing and vocables start up and then a drum beats quietly. A number of women's voices join and a rattle starts. It is all in the time of a group paddling steadily. The Indigenous woman speaks again, explaining that the song was sung to calm the mother and lift her spirits. She invokes the "mother, mother of us all, to have mercy, mercy on all human beings." I note that these words bring to mind the Catholic invocation to Mary, "mother of us all," while also recognizing that they don't need to be interpreted this way. The song continues underneath until the voice of Song closes the play, repeating, "This, this is the story of my birth."

Adrienne Wong's voice returns, explaining the credits and funders and noting that the podplay's production was supported by the City of Vancouver's 125th anniversary funding. I remove my earbud and turn to the woman next to me. In the climax of the rescue, I hadn't thought about her or her experience. I'm feeling quite vulnerable. Hearing the voices of the characters as they underwent this crisis has brought to mind my experiences as a mother caring for young children. I've never had to run from a fire, but I do know what it is like to feel that you are the one who has to protect someone who is completely vulnerable. However, I can't stay with these thoughts and feelings for long. I'm in a public park, where a couple on a bench not far away are looking at us, a man is walking along the shore with his dog, and another man is sitting and staring at the water. We talk quietly. I ask the woman I've been walking with if she's ever been to this park before. She's not from Vancouver, and she doesn't know the park. I tell her I used to bring my daughters here to look for crabs under the rocks when they were little. I remember the wedding I attended here last summer and the dance festival my neighbours took part in. I tell her that we are close to the Women's Memorial Rock.[4] Walking past it on our way to join the rest of the group, we stop to read the inscription and look at the flowers left beside it.

There are many practical and historically based reasons for setting this play in this exact space. Our walk started at what was the edge of the town in 1886, and people would have fled to the shore. This beach is across the inlet from the mission, where it would have been possible for a gathering of people to see the fire. The resonance with the site continues, however, with its present use. CRAB Park, property of the Vancouver Port Corporation, has been leased to the City of Vancouver. Yet it is also a space over which the local low-income and urban Indigenous community has a degree of control, blocking its use by those seeking to generate capital. In the early 1980s during preparations for Expo 86, community activists rallied around the slogan "Create a Real Available Beach" (CRAB) in efforts to hold space for collective resources against threatening development. Community members started organizing in 1982, occupying the site for three months in the summer of 1983, and the park was eventually opened in 1987. Since that time, the area has repeatedly been defended against further development plans – first for a casino and cruise ship terminal in 1997 and then for a soccer stadium in 2005 (Blomley 2004, 46–73). The site is recognized as an asset in the Downtown Eastside according to mapping done by the Carnegie Community Action Project. The park is identified as a necessity that is both free and nearby, as a space where residents can volunteer as well as connect to a rich cultural and community heritage of social justice work, as a green space that connects residents to nature in a way that has spiritual importance, as a space to grieve at the Women's Memorial Rock, and as a space to continue Indigenous traditions (Pederson and Swanson 2009, 6–12). CRAB Park as a mutable space for performance (or enactment) of counter-narratives has been part of this unsettlability, as evidenced by the occupations with which the park began and by the hosting of annual festivals. As the site for Sparrow's *Ashes on the Water*, this history, including the story of the fire recounted within the podplay, is triggered for community members who know and use the site.

The area around the park also has a few place names associated with it. In the hən̓q̓əmin̓əm̓ language, it is known as q̓əmq̓əməlaɬp (big leaf maple trees) and is derived from the word "q̓əməl" (paddle) (Suttles 2004, 572), and in the Sḵwx̱wú7mesh language it is known as Lek'leki (grove of beautiful trees) (Suttles 1996, 12). These names, both based on trees, highlight the importance of the forest and also of the history of the lumber industry in the transformation of the space. The Hastings Mill originally sat just past the eastern edge of the site, literally transforming trees into lumber. The fire in the podplay consumes the trees referenced by these place names.

The vulnerability and the heroism of the women in the story find an echo in this site of a memorial for murdered and missing women. The vulnerability of mothers and daughters didn't end with the fire, nor did the heroic and merciful acts. The attitudes and policies that may have caused the fire – clearing of the town site with rapacious disregard for the environment or existing communities – continued after the town was rebuilt and still affect us today. After experiencing the podplay, we all gather by the rock, and I feel grounded in the continuum of this history and in what Adrienne Wong regards as a temporal enlargement (Wong and Kinch 2012, 40). Although I am a relative newcomer to this coast, Indigenous people also supported my ancestors in eastern Canada through the difficulties of creating lives far from home. I am here both as a result of mercies shown over many years and as a result of the withholding of mercy and the taking of more than was offered.

I've heard the women's paddle song sung before at many events, as well as the story of how it came to be. I was struck then at the generosity shown to settlers, but hearing the story and song here on the shore, where the water laps at the land and it's possible to visualize the effort it took to offer support to those in need, I am once again humbled. It's particularly poignant to stand next to a site meant to hold the memories of women whose vulnerabilities were exploited and to whom, perhaps, not enough care was offered.

I conclude now with a consideration of the impact of the authority with which this story has been shared. Quelemia Sparrow is a descendant of the people who chose to offer help and of the women with whom the song originated, as is Squamish performer Bob Baker (aka S7aplek), who leads the dance group Spakwus Slulem[5] and is listed as a cultural adviser and song creator for *Ashes on the Water* (Olson 2019). Sparrow's encounter with this historied space is reminiscent of Monique Mojica's (2012) "Indigenous artistic research methodology" (219). As discussed in chapter 1, Mojica says that this methodology "speaks to the embodiment of place," calls the land "our archive," and says that "our embodied relationship to the land defines Indigenous identities, history, science, cosmology, literature – and our performance" (219). By recounting this story and this song, Sparrow and Baker return to a moment when their ancestors permitted the continuation of settlement, offering comfort to newcomers and allowing them to walk alongside them on this land. The authority with which the story is shared is another example of how an eddy of influence can be formed. It is an obstruction in the flow of contemporary settlers/newcomers' spatial understanding, creating a moment to rest from the current while opening up potential for future reciprocity. This understanding is also in line with Tomson Highway's (2005) comment connecting performance to land, where he says that Indigenous performers "keep hoping" that non-Indigenous audiences "may just learn … something new and something terribly relevant and beautiful about that particular landscape they too have become inhabitants of" (3). The use of this podplay format, which has a stable and unchanging soundscape that permeates the shifting personal urban landscape, creates an opportunity for learning through respectful listening – a listening that is a necessary part of the decolonizing process because a great deal of colonization, as demonstrated in the next chapter, has been about selective hearing.

Reiterations of Rededications:
Surrogated Whiteness

I begin this chapter with a short biography of a man who emigrated with his family at the age of nine, travelling 20,000 kilometres by boat for six weeks to a settlement that had recently been established on tenuous grounds, existing only due to the threat of state violence. He learned agricultural skills along with his parents and two brothers – the younger of whom died from infection within a few years. His family moved repeatedly in the next six years. He left school at fifteen and was abandoned by his parents and older brother, who emigrated without him to a new country when he was seventeen. He worked for two years and then left that land himself, going to an even younger settlement that was also based on land theft and violence. As a citizen of the state illegally seizing the territory, he prospered in this new land. He did struggle; his lack of education, limited job skills, and marriage at the age of twenty to his girlfriend who was pregnant with twins meant that his early adulthood was full of anxiety and strife.

He developed a fascination with the military and joined the local militia. He also began to collect discarded relics and oral histories. When his country of origin declared war, even though he was in his late thirties, he volunteered to fight. He was put into a position of leadership, and within less than a year, he was in charge of infantrymen, enduring possibilities of sniper attacks and chemical warfare while waiting to be ordered into armed raids. During combat, he was hit in the side of the head by a bullet from a machine gun. He received first aid but had to wait five days before his head wound was cleaned. The wound turned septic and he became deaf in one ear. He was given a medical discharge on the basis of the hearing loss as well as irritable nervousness, insomnia, and anxiety.

On the night he returned home from war, his wife of almost twenty years left him, but he pursued her and at one point abducted her in an effort to save his marriage. Left alone with his youngest son, he tried to reintegrate into civilian life but found that the management position he had left to serve in the military was no longer available. He opened a business but then suffered further loss when his youngest son broke his neck and died suddenly at the age of twenty-two. From this point on, he moved from job to job. He found a supportive woman he respected, and they got married. Although he remained an active community volunteer, in his early fifties he was unemployed and had few career prospects.

I have just described in general terms the biography of James Skitt Matthews as chronicled in the first hundred pages of Daphne Sleigh's *The Man Who Saved Vancouver: Major James Skitt Matthews* (2008).[1] His story is perhaps not unusual for a British immigrant born in 1878, yet it is an important one to note in a historical endeavour that engages with the City of Vancouver's archival collection. At the moment of Matthews's possible despair – unemployed in his fifties during the Depression – he convinced Vancouver City Council to allow him to create the city archives in 1931; he then stayed on as archivist until he died at the age of ninety-two in 1970. He exerted a dominance over the collection during this time that was unusual for an archivist. He was self-taught and acted as a public historian, intervening in the city by placing monuments and organizing commemorative events. Matthews was uninterested in municipal records and instead collected memoirs, photographs, objects connected to events or significant personalities, and stories, including those of working-class people, the unemployed, and at least one Indigenous man; he also commissioned paintings of historical events (Keirstead 1986–87, 87; Sleigh 2008, 199).

As detailed in this chapter, the concept, collection, and even physical space of the City of Vancouver Archives have long been attributed to Matthews's efforts, but a more thorough examination of his work to create the archives as well as to memorialize the naming, opening, and dedication of Stanley Park in 1888–89 is of relevance to this research project. I argue that Matthews hailed and recruited settlers/newcomers to an imperial British construction of whiteness through his founding of and continuing influence on the city archives, his publications, and his production of site-specific reenacts and monuments.

This analysis continues to make use of Joseph Roach's, Diana Taylor's, and Rebecca Schneider's performance studies methodologies. Roach demonstrates the connections between racialization and performance throughout his *Cities of the Dead: Circum-Atlantic Performance* (1996), along with methods that enabled white forgetting, fostered through "complex and ingenious schemes to displace, refashion, and transfer those persistent memories into representations more amenable to those who most frequently wielded the pencil and the eraser. In that sense, circum-Atlantic performance is a monumental study in the pleasures and torments of incomplete forgetting" (7). Although this research site is far from the circum-Atlantic, the phrase "the pleasures and torments of incomplete forgetting" does resonate, particularly with the efforts of Matthews, who "wielded the pencil and the eraser" and also enacted seemingly compulsive behaviour with his collecting and interventions in the city – possibly driven by the torment of forgetting and the pleasure of selective remembering. There is much in Roach's book that resonates here, including Matthews's reenactments using "kinesthetic imagination" (27) as a way to create colonial thinking through movement as well as the spatial-temporal contingencies leading to "displaced transmissions" (59) that have resulted in a monument to Lord Stanley at the entrance of the park (27–30). The reenactments also, however, feature at least one possibility of what Taylor (2003) has termed "multiplication and simultaneity" that refuse "surrogation and absenting" (46). The archival documents and photographs generated by Matthews, along with his staging of reenactments, are also examples of Schneider's (2011) assertion of the performativity of the archive, its use in the colonial process, and the "temporal drag" (14) and temporal reach that create "inter(in)animation" (7) through these reiterative actions. However, as much as the theoretical frame of performance studies is useful in the analysis of colonial racializing processes, to engage fully with Matthews's work as part of the construction of whiteness through performance, I must also enlist theoretical work from the field of critical whiteness studies.

Whiteness

I begin with critiques of whiteness studies from cultural studies theorists Sara Ahmed and Rey Chow. In "Declarations of Whiteness: The Non-Performativity of Anti-Racism" (2004), Ahmed critiques declarations of whiteness, which she regards as nonperformative speech acts (in the Austinian sense). She cautions that one of the foundational declarations in the field – that whiteness is invisible – is true only for those who inhabit it and that this assertion assumes a white seeing and is therefore an exercise in white privilege, *not* a challenging of it. It also offers a possibility of transcending whiteness through the recognition of the self as racist and through shameful feelings, which, if moved through too quickly, allow those with white privilege to restore a positive white identity. Ahmed asks "whether learning to see the mark of privilege [automatically] involves unlearning that privilege." Rey Chow also questions the ability of those who embody white privilege to disengage themselves from it. In *The Protestant Ethnic and the Spirit of Capitalism* (2002), she discusses what she terms the "coercive mimeticism" (95) of the performance of ethnicity. She contrasts the ethnic subject (who is disciplined to properly behave in line with an essentialized identity or to refuse the identity and be deemed an inauthentic traitor) with the white subject (who, in sympathizing or identifying with nonwhite culture, never becomes less white) (107–17).

Following these critics, I agree that identifying the marking of privilege is not enough but argue that it is nevertheless necessary so that it becomes more possible to seek an understanding of how the privilege is constructed, maintained, and possibly hidden from those who hold it. Ahmed (2004) closes by saying that critiques of whiteness involve staying implicated in the critique and turning toward one's individual "role and responsibility in ... histories of racism," which remain part of the present. So although I employ theories of critical whiteness studies to recognize the construction of Vancouver, I also do so in the effort to shoulder responsibility for the present that resulted from these histories of racism. The city archives have often been uncritically employed by historians; therefore, an analysis of the archives as a performance of whiteness brings to light the present of this history. In such a public, iconic (and in many ways continuing) site of colonial whiteness as Stanley Park, the implications of its use to construct this identity may be able to deeply unsettle assumptions of city dwellers and newcomers.

Ahmed engages in a consideration of what she frames as the world of whiteness in "A Phenomenology of Whiteness" (2007, 153) and in *Queer Phenomenology: Orientations, Objects, Others* (2006, 129). Although neither is specifically about performance, her focus on the body in space is instructive. Following Pierre Bourdieu and Maurice Merleau-Ponty, she asserts that whiteness holds its place through habits (i.e., bodily and spatial forms of inheritance) and that "spaces acquire the shape of the bodies that 'inhabit' them" (2007, 156). This ongoing and unfinished inhabitation "orientates bodies in specific directions, affecting how they 'take up' space" (2007, 150). She discusses the recruitment of new white subjects through hailing, or bringing in new bodies to cohere as a group (2006, 132–3).

Matthews's archival and publishing activities as well as the reenactments and monuments that he established are all forms of hailing and recruitment to the unstable institution (or body) of Vancouver whiteness.

Ahmed (2007) cites Frantz Fanon's assertion that bodies are shaped by histories of colonialism that make the world "white" and "'ready' for certain kinds of bodies ... [with] certain objects within their reach" (152–3). She contends that white bodies go unnoticed in white spaces and have an extended reach, arguing that space consequently takes shape by "being orientated around some bodies, more than others" (157). She gives the example of the way that black bodies are noticed entering a white institutional space – and the way that white bodies' entrances are unremarkable – creating a need for nonwhite bodies to attempt to take on characteristics of whiteness in order to inhabit white space (156–8). Ahmed asserts that the ease with which white bodies inhabit and move through white spaces is interesting to connect with the discussion of movement in Indigenous studies.

One of the methods of colonization was to create private property and mark reserves as the only places for authentic Indigeneity in order to make spaces through which Indigenous people could not move. This right to move through public space is very much in line with Ahmed's (2007) assertions about comfort and discomfort: "To be not white is to be not extended by the spaces you inhabit. This is an uncomfortable feeling. Comfort is a feeling that tends not to be consciously felt" (163). Ahmed asserts that white space can be created through the privilege assumed via the right to movement and that this is particularly significant in an area that is considered to be for the recreational use and enjoyment of the public. So although Ahmed voices reservations about the nonperformative anti-racist possibilities of the mere recognition of whiteness, she has also created a formulation that is helpful in seeing how white bodies, holding their inheritances of privilege, create spaces of comfort and enjoy an ease of movement.

It is also useful to consider how Ahmed in Queer Phenomenology (2006) draws upon Jacques Derrida's assertion that archives are homes around which worlds gather, dwellings that mark the passage from private to public, and therefore contends that if "archives allow documents to dwell, then they, too, are orientation devices, which in gathering things around are not neutral but directive" (118, italics added). Ahmed discusses orienting in terms of the phenomenology of space, saying that it is the practice of finding one's way and differentiating between ways of doing so. Orienting toward something (facing it), she argues, is "determined by our location."

That which one is oriented toward is "not me," allowing one to do things with this other thing that extend the body's reach (113–15). She discusses orienting *around* something as being taken up by it, constituting ourselves at its centre, and becoming the same as that which surrounds us (115–16).

The field of critical whiteness studies has been productive, particularly in the context of the United States and Britain, and although both of these nations have been influential in the formation of Canadian (including specifically British Columbian and Vancouverite) constructions of whiteness, they are not transferable because of the historical-geographic specificities. Here, a brief overview of keywords and concepts considered with regard to representation through film, visual arts, and performance is necessary for this discussion. In *White* (1997), Richard Dyer describes whiteness as a construction that draws on imperialism, Christianity, enterprise, heterosexuality, and conceptions of race to create a common identity among European settlers. He asserts that this identity is unstable and aspirational, one that has moved from local and particular to universal, a "subject without properties" that exists through *dis*embodiedness (38–9). Mary Brewer's *Staging Whiteness* (2005) identifies systematized racism as developing in the context of capitalism and the slave trade. She suggests that disparities between capitalism and democratic ideals as well as Victorian morality created a permeable, unstable whiteness. In the context of the construction of whiteness in the United States, she explains that immigration to populate Indigenous lands linked whiteness to control of property. Margot Francis in *Creative Subversions: Whiteness, Indigeneity and the National Imaginary* (2011) focuses on the gendered nature of the Canadian colonial legacy and on the ambivalent symbol of the beaver, the Canadian Pacific Railway as an essential technology for extension of colonial rule, and the creation of wilderness parks as another method of enclosure. She also identifies the spectral hauntings of Indigeneity in each of these symbols, which she argues are essential to a Canadian identity of whiteness. In *The Resettlement of British Columbia: Essays on Colonialism and Geographical Change* (1997), Cole Harris explains the creation of the Lower Mainland's white culture by immigrants during European settlement who had to make their lives anew "without a local past" (102). A strategy for creating belonging was to focus on race as an organizing category that weakened class divisions. He also asserts that usually unremarked details became symbols of difference and that the dominance of British immigrants created an expatriate identity in British Columbia through which the racialized European colonial discourse of the late nineteenth century was superimposed on the uncertainties of an emerging immigrant society, resulting in race becoming an overriding symbol (272–3). Renisa Mawani supports Harris's assertion of British dominance. In "Genealogies of the Land: Aboriginality, Law, and Territory in Vancouver's Stanley Park" (2005), she comments on the colonial categories of Europeanness, explaining that the Portuguese fishers who married Indigenous women and lived at Brockton Point were not seen as European or Native. She attributes their status in between colonial categories partly to their life choices but also to their lower status on the racialized hierarchy of whiteness as southern Europeans (328).

Throughout this book, geo-historical specificities, performance, and space are deeply entangled. As a way to understand how this tangle has been created, I undertake an exploration of the tension around the identity of the white colonial as a "subject without property" (Dyer 1997, 39), an identity that allows a universalizing worldview that permits colonial actions, and I examine the subsequent deep need for the creation and ownership of property in the colonial project.

Insights about whiteness and ownership put forward by Quandamooka scholar Aileen Moreton-Robinson in *The White Possessive: Property, Power, and Indigenous Sovereignty* (2015) are in tension with this concept of whiteness as something generated through a subject positionality that is *without* property and that therefore aims to assume a proprietarian relationship to land wherever it goes. She builds on African American legal scholar Cheryl Harris's argument that whiteness is a form of property in law. Moreton-Robinson's work comes out of an Australian context, but, she argues, it is applicable anywhere that the British (or their descendants) colonized – including the United States, Canada, Hawaii, and New Zealand. She asserts that "[w]hite possession is the common denominator we all share, even though its specificities and manifestations vary. We are no longer the sole possessors of our ancestral lands taken by conquest, cessation or as *terra nullius* (land belonging to no one). These lands are appropriated in the name of the Crown, signifying the rule of the king and the masculine capacity to possess property and to bear arms" (xx). Moreton-Robinson discusses "possessive logics" as a "mode of rationalization ... that is underpinned by an excessive desire to invest in reproducing and reaffirming the nation-state's ownership, control and domination," which circulate meanings about ownership of the nation as common-sense knowledge (xii). She associates this situation with immigration acts passed in Australia, Canada,

New Zealand, and the United States, seeing "inextricable connections between white possessive logics, race, and the founding of nation-states," and she regards this process of nation building as "materially and discursively linked" to the "disavowal of Indigenous sovereignty" (xii).

All of this work resonates significantly with the timeframe and activities of the formation of the city of Vancouver shortly after the province of British Columbia joined the newly formed Canadian Confederation in 1871. Yet another significant contribution of Moreton-Robinson's (2015) argument fuels my study of the creation of whiteness through performance at this time and in this place. She explains that since the 1970s, critical Indigenous studies has taken as its main focus an endogenous engagement with Indigenous belief systems and cultural difference. She argues that although the work is extremely important, it has unintentionally resulted in the "reification of cultural difference. We compel 'culture' to function discursively as a category of analysis in the process of differentiation, while exogenous disciplinary knowledges that have been produced about us operationalize 'race' as the marker of out difference, even when defining Indigenous 'cultures'" (xv). She notes Métis scholar Chris Anderson's call for Indigenous scholarship to include critiques of colonial society and his insistence that it is essential to engage with the concepts of race, ethnicity, and nation (and she adds gender) because they reflect the density of Indigenous subjectivity within modernity and aim, as Anderson puts it, to "counter hegemonic representations of Indigeneity which marginalize or altogether ignore our density" (xvi). In response, I offer this work as a contribution to endogenous whiteness studies that supports this epistemological turn in Indigenous studies as one that aims to expose the logics of possession as enacted through performances on Indigenous land.

Throughout the analysis below, as I aim to elaborate how the logic of the white possessive was created in the late nineteenth century in Vancouver and continues to this day, I employ Ahmed's (2006, 113–16) terminology of orienting *toward* as part of the way that Matthews configured Indigeneity in order to construct whiteness and orienting *around* as the way that reiterative maintenance of white space of the park through performance is used to centre white identity. The reenactments, archival documents, publications, and monument are also discussed in terms of attempting to create habits that can then be passed on to descendants through inheritance and to newcomers through recruitment. I now move on to a discussion of Matthews's work in the creation of the dwelling space of the archives in the 1930s.

Archives and Conversations:
"It would be more in keeping ..."

Jean Barman (2008), who has written extensively about BC history, notes that "those of us who write about the history of Vancouver walk in Major Matthews' shadow" (xi), and her books *The Remarkable Adventures of Portuguese Joe Silvey* (2004) and *Stanley Park's Secret: The Forgotten Families of Whoi Whoi, Kanaka Ranch and Brockton Point* (2005) draw extensively on his collections. She also states that the unique nature of the City of Vancouver Archives based on Matthews's work makes "available *virtually* the entirety of the city's past" (2008, xi, italics added). I stress the word "virtually" in this statement because, although there is a range of documentation in the archives, it cannot come close to encapsulating the city's past. It is also imperative that we interrogate the nature of Matthews's shadow and how our eyes may have adjusted to the limited amount of light that it has afforded us.

As Sleigh (2008) documents, Matthews founded the City of Vancouver Archives in the spring of 1931 after a successful appeal to City Council (104–5). It was first housed in the library annex adjacent to the Carnegie Centre and then moved to the ninth floor of the new City Hall, built in 1936 in time for the fiftieth anniversary of the city's incorporation, staying there until 1959 (137). The collection was then housed in the Vancouver Public Library, where it stayed until two years after Matthews's death in 1970. He forced the construction of an archival building, the first purpose-built one in Canada, through the conditions of his will. He bequeathed his extensive personal collection of documents and artifacts not to the city but instead to the province and, further, "decreed that unless suitable accommodation for the collection was created within the space of one year, his material would be put up for sale" (197). Construction started at the end of 1971, and the present dwelling of the archives, the Major Matthews Building, opened on 29 December 1972 in Vanier Park[2] adjacent to the Vancouver Museum, built as part of the Canadian Centennial celebrations of 1967 (204–5). Matthews has been celebrated for his visionary push to create the archives for the City of Vancouver more than two decades before any other Canadian city (Barman 2008, ix). I suggest, however, that this emphasis on archives for the city was tied to the unstable nature of the European settlement on unceded land and to the discomfort of living "without a local past" (Harris

1997, 102), which drove not only Matthews but also the subsequent city councils that supported his work.

The archive's relationship to the past, present, and future as well as the ways that it intervenes and interacts with performance have been a part of the discourse in performance studies and more broadly for some time (Phelan 1993; Derrida 1996; Roach 1996; Taylor 2003; Schneider 2011). There has also been much discussion of the archive as a method of colonial governance (Thomas 1993; Stoller 2002, 2009; Mawani, 2004), so the fact that it was Matthews, a British immigrant, who controlled the city archives is not much of a revelation. Useful, however, for this examination of how performance has been employed to create and maintain land as a white space are the ways that Matthews intervened in the city archives and in public life with his manipulation of official records and publications. He was quite prolific – writing numerous books and compiling seven volumes and over 3,300 single-spaced typed pages of interviews with early settlers ("About the Early Vancouver Project" n.d.). He also published two books on Stanley Park's naming, opening, dedication, and rededication events (Matthews 1959, 1964a, 1964b), produced numerous archival documents, including two copies of a sixty-two-page album of the 1943 rededication event (one of which is held in the city archives and another of which was sent to Lord Stanley's son in England), and funded, designed, and placed a monument depicting an impression of Lord Stanley's pose and words of dedication in 1889. His focus on the moment of dedication of the land, when its status changed in the colonial imaginary from a federal military reserve to parkland, his belief that this change needed to be reiterated through reenactment, text, and sculpture, and his status as the archivist all make for a compelling case study of the colonist's archive, the instability of settler property assertions, and the construction of whiteness in Vancouver through the performance of Matthews's archival impulses. This study also responds to Adele Perry's insistence in *On the Edge of Empire: Gender, Race, and the Making of British Columbia, 1849–1871* (2001) that "the historical processes by which whiteness was constituted and empowered can and must be excavated" (197), and it takes into account her assertion that the limited whiteness that was achieved "was accomplished through human action and history rather than destiny" (201).

I now turn to an event reported in Matthews's *Conversations with Khahtsahlano, 1932–1954* (1955). Matthews made five copies of this book of over 500 pages, depositing one in Ottawa at the National Archives and one in Victoria at the British Columbia Archives, while keeping the last three in Vancouver.[3] Matthews opens the manuscript with a letter to Dominion archivist Dr William K. Lamb, explaining the dependability of Khahtsahlano given his status as a "living link" to the "Stone Age" (3–4).[4] He closes his letter to Lamb with a statement that the records "are not copyright but are my possessions. Nothing to do with City Archives" (4). This final statement is an indication of the ongoing dispute over the ownership of the collection that Matthews waged with the City of Vancouver. The conversations are dated as starting in 1932, shortly after Matthews took up his position as archivist. He began at this point to document conversations with any of the surviving settlers who had been in the area before the fire of 1886, publishing them as part of his seven-volume work on *Early Vancouver* (1931–56, vol. 1, 1932, 2). His book of conversations with Khahtsahlano is a compilation taken from this seven-volume work. In 1938 Matthews helped Khahtsahlano to officially change his name from August Jack to August Jack Khahtsahlano. Six years later, on 8 May 1944, Khahtsahlano approached Matthews, likely in his office on the ninth floor of City Hall, with a request. The following is Matthews's rendition of the conversation, given under the title "Place of Birth Chaythoos, not Snauq":

August came carrying with him his framed copy of his declaration of, I think 1938, anyway before the "Change of Names Act" came into force, in which he renounces the name of August Jack and assumes for himself and his descendants the name of August Jack Khahtsahlano, which name was formally sworn to under oath before a notary public, and lodged with the Vital Statistics branch Victoria. It states that he declares that he was born at Snauq, an Indian Village at the False Creek Indian Reserve. He now wishes to retract this, as he says, "everybody tells me I was born at Chaythoos," Stanley Park, (an Indian clearing where his father lived, also known as "Supplejack's [sic][5] Grave"; where Lord Stanley dedicated the park).

I explained to August that he had sworn to a place of birth under oath, and it would take another oath to alter that, and that copies would have to be lodged at the record office in Victoria, and that our frame would have to be undone and fixed up again, and that I was not pleased with the prospect of proving that a man who was, in fact if not in name, Chief Kitsilano, was born in Stanley Park; it would be

more in keeping if he was born in Kitsilano. Whether August caught
the point or not I do not know, but finally he said "too much bother."
He decided not to have any change made. (Matthews 1955, 146)

There are many things here to which I would like to draw attention. The
first is the oath (or speech act) on which the certificate is based, which
Matthews says would take another oath to undo. This matter of the oath
highlights the dependence of the official record on a (possibly) unstable
speech act. Matthews also discourages Khahtsahlano by saying that his
certificate would have to reframed, which strikes me as a minor concern for
someone who values historical records. Also of note is Matthews's reasoning
regarding the name of the neighbourhood and Khahtsahlano's birthplace,
which shows his willingness to manipulate in order to better narrate or
design a (tidier) history of the city. Having his birthplace in Stanley Park
would make apparent the settler work in deciding the name of Kitsilano,[6]
whereas reinserting Khahtsahlano's birth into the space of Kitsilano would
legitimate the settler use of that Indigenous name.

   Matthews's collection and creation of the city archives and their dwelling
are aptly described by Ahmed's (2006, 115–16) phenomenological orientation of *around*, which allows a holding of the centre and constitution of
oneself at and as that centre. The example of Matthews discouraging the
correction of Khahtsahlano's birthplace in the official documents is one of
the ways of structuring the dwelling place through exclusion of inconvenient details. It is also remarkable that Matthews includes this conversation
in his official record kept at three different archival institutions, perhaps
giving a clue to either his ambivalence about the project or his position
of arrogance. In the next section, I briefly depart from sources generated
by Matthews in order to afterward contrast his accounts of the 1888 and
1889 events with those of contemporary newspapers, exposing his further
intervention in the narrative of the city of Vancouver's history.

The Naming, Opening, and
"Dedication" of Stanley Park, 1888–89

The creation of Stanley Park as the first resolution by the newly formed
Vancouver City Council in 1886 has been well documented by Jean Barman
(2005), Sean Kheraj (2013), and numerous others less aware of the entangled
connections among European settlers, emparkment, property preemption,

and the transcontinental railway. This section chronicles what was recorded through newspaper accounts and documents (produced by people other than Matthews) and then suggests a chronology for Matthews's developing narrative of the events.

On 27 September 1888, Mayor David Oppenheimer and other city officials, including the newly appointed parks commissioners, went by procession to an area described as "an open space [that] has been cleared at the top of the bluff" and also as "the grassy spot where Supple Jack's grave used to be."[7] Once there, Oppenheimer spoke about the clear need for a park near the city for citizens to "spend some time amid the beauties of nature away from the busy haunts of men" and how the honour of having the park named after him was given to one of the directors of the Canadian Pacific Railway (CPR) in order that they "should feel that their efforts to promote the general welfare are appreciated." That director, Donald Smith (afterward Lord Strathcona), declined the honour and instead asked that the park be named after Lord Stanley. Oppenheimer announced the name of the park, and then they raised the Union Jack, played the national anthem, and gave three cheers for Queen Victoria. Oppenheimer then handed a copy of the bylaw creating the position of park commissioner to Alderman Alexander. Letters between Oppenheimer, Smith, and Stanley regarding the naming were read as well as letters of regret from those officials who could not attend. Officials and mayors of other municipalities spoke, and then there was a display of "day fireworks," which let out inflated forms upon exploding that resembled men, animals, and other things. People stayed to picnic, and in the evening the mayor hosted a ball.[8] I make special note that this ceremony, which was intended to change the status of the land, included the reading of the letters aloud, the presentation of a paper copy of the bylaw, and the emphasis on the narrative of the naming. Perhaps these elements were all ways to further validate the performative act of opening and naming the park through archivable text. This was the extent of the ceremony in which the name was announced and the land "opened" as a park. In the following year, the man who named the park made a visit to the city as part of his cross-country tour on the recently completed Canadian Pacific Railway.

From 26 to 31 October 1889, the *Vancouver Daily* and *Weekly News-Advertiser* as well as the *Vancouver Weekly World* chronicled Governor General Lord Stanley's visit. He was welcomed as his train proceeded through the decorated streets, the schoolchildren of the city singing a song when he arrived at the Hotel Vancouver. Mayor Oppenheimer then read from an illuminated scroll an address about hopes for Vancouver since the CPR and steamships to the Orient would aid in developing a commercial relationship with China and Japan as markets for Canadian manufacturing, drawing together the British Empire through commercial ties. He expressed hope that the "Dominion of Canada will form the central position in a great route for travel and trade between the Mother Country and the Greater Britain in the Southern seas."[9] Oppenheimer also invited Stanley to visit "that noble tract of forest which granted by your Government for the benefit of our people, you were pleased to consent should be called after your illustrious name and to view the proportions of this noble gift to the people of this city for their *use and enjoyment for all time to come*"[10] (italics added). Stanley then replied with thanks, and upon noticing a banner that read, "The welcome of a happy people without a grievance," he commented that he hoped the people would never have a grievance. He also suggested that the schoolchildren should have a holiday on Monday so that they would remember his visit.[11] Events during his six-day stay included a steamship excursion up the north arm of the inlet, a fireworks display, illuminations of the city at night, a visit with the "Mission Indians" on the North Shore, as well as a ball and a levee.

On 29 October city officials took Lord Stanley first to visit Hastings Mill and then on a drive around the park in carriages. They stopped "at the site of the cairn." According to a writer in the *Weekly World*, "owing to the inclemency of the weather the ceremony was much curtailed." There is no mention that Stanley made a speech or a dedication of any sort. The article also contains a reprint of the mayor's address, "accepted by" Stanley, about the construction of a cairn as a memorial of the visit. It was chosen, he explained, so that "citizens of all classes can participate in its erection" and would consist of flowers, plants, and "specimens of British Columbia's minerals." Oppenheimer also made the point that the "samples of the stones before you – galena ore and red hematite – are intended to represent the mineral wealth of our Province."[12] Oppenheimer laid the foundation stone of the cairn, and then "the Dominion ensign was floated to the breeze and the proceedings came to a close."[13] Erecting a monument to Stanley built out of mineral resources of the province could be considered a miniature pre-enactment of the taking of resources for the benefit of the empire and a symbol of a colonial-capitalist project *around* which settlers could constitute an identity.

The *Weekly World* also published a detailed article outlining the plans for the Stanley Cairn: it was to be a three-tiered circular construction of stones and minerals from around the province with a forty-five-foot flagstaff on top, ledges for vases, and a tablet recording the event on the front.[14] This report is similar to the one published in the *Vancouver Daily News-Advertiser* on 30 October 1889, which also states that Lord and Lady Stanley helped to lay stones for the foundation of the cairn ("Around the Park" 1889). These articles are very specific in details and plans for the cairn, yet none of the pioneer memories recorded by Matthews mention it. None of these articles are quoted by Matthews in his 1959 and 1964 books on the 1889 dedication – except to say that "it rained a little in the morning; a passing shower" (1959, 25; 1964a, 25). It seems odd that Matthews had access to the papers from 1888 and reprinted the texts from them yet did not use the papers from 1889. I will now trace a timeline of Matthews's efforts to document the process of the naming, opening, and what he termed the "dedication" of the park as taken from his archival files and publications.

In 1937 Matthews dropped in unannounced on Frank Harris, caretaker of the city's water works for fifty-five years and the father of a young man killed in the First World War who had served under Matthews. The conversation took place at Harris's cottage near the water system pipes at the end of Pipeline Road in Stanley Park. Matthews asked him if he had been present at the 1888 opening and 1889 dedication by Lord Stanley. He recorded Harris's reply with his own parenthetical comment: "He stood outside there, just where the curve is; he waved his arms a bit (Mr. Harris extended his arms as though embracing the whole park between them) and dedicated it; said a few words; that was all" (Matthews 1931–56, vol. 4, 1944, 202–3). This was the first source Matthews found that indicates Stanley gestured and said a few words. According to the records in his archive, Matthews then worked with this gesture and through "kinesthetic imagination" and "displaced transmission" (Roach 1996, 27, 59) eventually created a dedication ceremony. Also consider that the gesture, which Matthews interpreted as embracing the park, could have been one intended to embrace all of British Columbia and its resources. This would have been more consistent with Oppenheimer's address and the symbol of the cairn.

In 1940 Matthews compiled an album about Dr J.L. Telford, who served as Vancouver's mayor from 1939 to 1940. It contains a copy of a letter Telford wrote on 2 October 1939 to the 17th Earl of Derby, Lord Stanley's son. It is an emotional letter written at the outbreak of the Second World War, a few weeks before the fiftieth anniversary celebrations of the "dedication" of Stanley Park. Telford described the park as "one thousand acres of primeval forest, interspersed with patches of smooth green sward; sea girt with sandy beaches where tens of thousands gambol on a summer's day," adding that he wished he could magically transport Lord and Lady Derby to "stand upon the same old Indian clearing above the rushing waters of our First Narrows on which your noble father, the Governor-General, stood, and, throwing his arms into the air as though embracing the whole expanse of towering forest before him, besought the Almighty to bless our great park to *the use and pleasure of future generations of all colors, creeds and customs*" ("His Worship" 1940, italics added). This is the first reference in the archives that attributes this utterance to Lord Stanley, and it is worth providing a little detail about Telford here. Before serving as Vancouver's mayor, he had been Vancouver East's Co-operative Commonwealth Federation (CCF) member in the provincial legislature from 1937 to 1939 (Elections British Columbia n.d.). He was a charismatic personality known throughout the province for his "spell-binding oratory" and as "the voice of the CCF." He published a socialist newspaper, the *Challenge*, from 1931 to 1933 and hosted a popular radio broadcast. Robert J. McDonald (2013) argues that his role should not be overlooked in the popularization of electoral socialism in British Columbia in the 1930s (92–3, 100). Some of Telford's own values seem to be imbued in the statement attributed to Stanley, as he demonstrated later during his term as mayor, which coincided with the internment of the Japanese in 1942. Patricia Roy in *The Oriental Question: Consolidating a White Man's Province, 1914–41* (2003) reports Mayor Telford's repeated efforts to quell general anxiety about the Japanese. Telford suggested that authorities should register *all* men between sixteen and sixty, not just those of Japanese heritage, and that they should only "investigate and intern Japanese who threatened Canada's war effort or safety" (22, 225). Although Matthews repeatedly asked early settlers for their memories of the day of Stanley's visit in 1889, none of them recalled Stanley's words in the park, and none of the newspapers of the day reported that he made a speech. This letter, by a socialist mayor in the context of the rise of fascism in Europe and anti-Japanese sentiment in British Columbia, is the first text recorded in the archives that reports Stanley as making his generous dedication to people of "all colors, creeds and customs."

Four years later, on 4 August 1943, while Matthews was preparing for the first of the "rededication" ceremonies, Frank Plante came to his office to inform him that he had driven Lord Stanley and Mayor Oppenheimer to the dedication in "the only two-horse hack in town." Plante described their clothes, the weather ("raining a little that day"), and the use of a bottle of wine to christen Stanley Park, and he claimed Lord Stanley made a speech, as did the mayor. He said that the ceremony lasted half an hour and that he was a few yards from the speakers, having pulled the carriage out of their way. He did not mention the laying of any stones for a cairn. He said he had his photo taken that day and allowed Matthews to copy it for the archives (Matthews, 1931–56, vol. 6, 1945, 119–20). Matthews reproduced the 1889 photo of Plante and added text that not only described the ceremony as happening beside Supple Jack's mausoleum[15] but also attributed the words "to the use and enjoyment for all peoples for all time" to Lord Stanley (123). Despite two subsequent conversations in the next few days that contradicted Plante's claim to have driven the carriage, Matthews had Plante reenact his driving in the rededication at the end of the month, and he published Plante's story in his books on the 1888–89 ceremonies (Matthews 1959, 1964a, 1964b).[16]

During the 1943 rededication ceremony (discussed below) and again in 1951 during a luncheon hosted at the Stanley Park Pavilion for Lord Stanley's great-grandson, the 18th Earl of Derby – where another reenactment of the ceremony took place in which Matthews, acting as Oppenheimer, presented a scroll to Derby, acting as Lord Stanley – Matthews used the phrase "of all colors, creeds and customs" as part of the dedication (Matthews, 1931–56, vol. 7, 1956, 123–4). Matthews constructed his reenactments, publications, and the monument of Lord Stanley from four documents preserved in the archives: the original welcome in 1889 by Oppenheimer to Stanley, which mentions the park as being for the "use and enjoyment for all time to come"; the 1937 report of Lord Stanley's arm gesture by the man supervising the waterworks; the 1939 letter from Telford to Derby, which includes the phrase "the use and pleasure of future generations of all colors, creeds and customs"; and the 1943 description by the driver of the "two-horse hack" of the ground being christened with wine and of speeches being made. It is important to note that Matthews put more value on the memories of the settlers than on the newspaper accounts. His innovative use of sources other than newspaper texts should not be discounted, yet I assert that because his work is received as history coming from the authority of an archive, its use of such sources needs to be explicitly acknowledged. In considering the creation of history using oral testimony, I would also like to be careful not to equate the conversations that Matthews had with settlers about their memories decades after events with Indigenous methods of orating history, which are used in the context of social infrastructures (i.e., ceremonies, witnessing, and the training of people in oration) that support the transmission of specific stories.

Other historians have used Matthews's construction of the event to describe the origins of the park. Barman briefly refers to the 1888 and 1889 ceremonies in her account of the imposition of the park in *Stanley Park's Secret* (2005). As sources for the details of the event in 1888, she uses the same newspaper accounts from the *Vancouver Daily News-Advertiser* of 27 September 1888 that Matthews published in his book *Naming, Opening and Dedication of Stanley Park Vancouver, Canada 1888–1889* (1959). As a source for the 1889 event, she uses a document Matthews wrote in 1958 that chronicles the events of the incorporation and dedication of the park, in which he recorded Lord Stanley speaking the "historic words" of his speech. She also uses the 1939 letter from Telford to Derby but does not realize that Telford is not quoting another source when he writes the words that Stanley speaks (Barman 2005, 93, 267nn17–18). Kheraj (2013) also quotes the phrase, commenting that its inscription on the statue at the entrance to the park "captured one aspect of the meaning of public space – it explained *who* could use the park, but it did not define *how* it could be used or who should govern its use" (63, italics original). Kheraj uses Matthews's 1959 book on the event and the monument itself as his sources (218n22). Renisa Mawani (2003), in her article on law, space, and the making of Stanley Park, conflates the 1888 opening with Lord Stanley's visit but does not discuss his utterance, mainly focusing on the choice of Supple Jack's grave as the site of the ceremony (109–10). Using Matthews's topical file on "Supple-Jack-Khaytulk," she discusses the event as though the grave were present during the ceremony (135nn15–16). Comparing these newspaper accounts of the events of 1888–89 with Matthews's archival records and published works, I assert that he constructed through *displaced transmission* what has become known as the 1889 park dedication ceremony featuring Lord Stanley. His efforts scripted a strong narrative that imbued both the *name* and the *space* of the park with a British, white identity while creating a space *around* which an unstable immigrant society could gather and connect over a local history. Once the narrative was established, he then moved on to further publications, reenactments, and a monument to create a habitual inheritance of whiteness. The original naming of the park and then Matthews's work over almost fifty years give some insight into the development of what Moreton-Robinson (2015) regards as the quotidian and ontological experiences of being in a variety of cities – including Vancouver – where "signs of white possession are embedded everywhere in the landscape" (xiii). She says that the "omnipresence of Indigenous sovereignties exists here too, but it is disavowed through the materiality of these significations, which are perceived as evidence of ownership by those who have taken possession" (xiii). The next section discusses efforts to create whiteness through performative reenactment, along with expressions of Indigenous continuing presence.

The 1943 Reenactment of the Dedication: *Around*

On 25 August 1943 the Vancouver Park Board, advised by Matthews, sponsored a "Rededication of Stanley Park" at Lumberman's Arch ("1889 Pageant Plans" 1943; "Foresight of Pioneers" 1943). The event was attended by over 15,000 people and was broadcast live on CKWX radio.[17] The archival file detailing the planning for the event includes four pages with Matthews's list of the names of people to be invited to the luncheon held at the Stanley Park Pavilion to honour the "pioneers," annotated to explain their genealogy and roles in early Vancouver.[18] Minutes from a planning meeting on 11 August indicate the "characters" who may be speaking and what stories they may tell. These invited guests included Maisie Armytage-Moore, identified as having "built up a sympathy and understanding for the Squamish tribe of the BC Indians,"[19] as well as August Jack Khahtsahlano, along with an explanation of his stories of a potlatch, the road built through his house, and his naming ceremony. His name is translated as "Man of the Lake, Lord of the Isles," and he is described as a medicine man. Repeatedly throughout the minutes, Matthews is identified as the one who will arrange and advise speakers and "instruct characters as to their duties." Since there is no archival record of a speech by Lord Stanley, Matthews composed one and included stage directions:

Your Worship, Ladies and Gentlemen: –

On behalf of Lady Stanley and myself, I thank you most heartily for the warmth and cordiality of your welcome. We <u>have</u> almost with amazement, observed the splendid progress which your citizens have made since that awful day of fire three years ago, when all, save the bare black earth, of which you were left possessed, was your courage, vision and faith. I am proud indeed, to accede to your request to dedicate this noble tract of forest as a park.

(takes the bottle of wine from his A.D.C. [aide de camp])

This seagirt expanse of primeval forest[.]

(throwing his arms to the heavens as though embracing the whole one thousand acres)

This seagirt expanse of forest; this marvel of natural beauty, which, since the dawn of time has stood, silent and still, awaiting this historic moment. I now solemnly dedicate to the use and enjoyment of peoples of all colors, creeds and customs for all time to come, and may the blessings of the Almighty rest upon those who here may come[.]

(pouring wine on ground)

I christen thee "STANLEY PARK."[20]

The agenda for the ceremony states that it will begin at 3:00 p.m. with Fred Bass, the host of CKWX's radio broadcast of the event, describing the scene and crowds while the procession makes its way to Lumberman's Arch, at which point the band will play "The Maple Leaf Forever." The agenda then states that the master of ceremonies, R. Rowe Holland, chair of the Park Board, will describe the original scene and that the characters Mayor Oppenheimer and Lord Stanley will perform their speeches (see figures 2.1 and 2.2). Afterward, there were to be a few events "tying in yesterday with today": a choir singing "old time" songs, awards for best costume and conveyance, a song and dance by August Jack Khahtsahlano and "accompanist" Chief Matthias Joe, and speeches by "old timers," all ending with a modern song and a speech by the current acting mayor.[21]

The timing of the event is curious since it was the height of the Second World War, it was not a special anniversary, and much of the perimeter of the park had been commandeered by the military for coastal defence, with installations of guns, searchlights, and observation posts (Kheraj 2013, 166). I also wonder why there was a need to rededicate. Had something undone the first dedication? Besides the war, another major upheaval in the coastal communities and the city of Vancouver had been the internment of all people of Japanese heritage. On 16 December 1941 the Park Board extinguished the light atop the Japanese Canadian War Memorial in Stanley Park, which is located near Lumberman's Arch, where this event was held; erected after the First World War, the memorial would not be relit until

2.1   David Oppenheimer, grand-nephew of Mayor David Oppenheimer, reading the original illuminated address presented to Lord Stanley in 1889.

3 August 1985 (Greenaway n.d.). By 1943 the internment was complete, and seized Japanese properties were being sold off, but as Patricia Roy (2003) has written, these actions were not without controversy (189–230). So perhaps this was an effort to reconnect with the British origins of the founding of the park at a time when the mother country was under assault as well as a way to unify a white identity after the turmoil of the Depression in the 1930s and at a time of great anxiety about the war. One newspaper account aligns with this connection in recounting Holland's speech to the pioneers, saying that "it was worthy of comment that in the midst of world turmoil Vancouver was taking time to honor its pioneers. 'It is the pioneer spirit that has made Canada what it is,' Mr. Holland declared. 'It is responsible for the courage and resistance being made by our soldiers on the battlefields today'" ("Foresight of Pioneers" 1943, 13).

Matthews took pains to find as many genealogical connections to the original event as possible. He invited Stanley's son, who was unable to come due to "ill health," so instead English Canadian actor E.V. Young played his part.[22] Mayor Oppenheimer was played by his grand-nephew, David Oppenheimer. The nephew of the first city clerk played the city clerk who

2.2   E.V. Young dressed as Lord Stanley addressing the crowd at the "Rededication of Stanley Park." Matthews's 1943 album caption read, "'Lord Stanley' (Mr. E.V. Young as Governor General) replies to 'Mayor Oppenheimer' according to request that he re-christen Stanley Park. 25 August 1943."

carried the copy of the illuminated scroll. The "old timers" represented themselves, including Frank Plante, whom Matthews identified in his album and subsequent publications as the man who drove Lord Stanley's carriage in 1889. The reenactment is based on Plante's story of the christening with a bottle of wine and Harris's story of the raised arms and includes some of the words Mayor Telford wrote to Derby in 1939.

Matthews also identified Plante as the "first white baby born here" (see figure 2.3) and in both of his publications on the original events as the "first baby of European parentage born on Burrard Inlet" (Matthews 1959, 42–3; 1964a, 42). However, a note dated 17 August 1943 details Plante's genealogy, in particular that his mother was the daughter of Kha-my, whose father was Chief Khat-sah-lanough. Her brother was Khay-tulk (or Supple Jack). Matthews concluded by saying that August Jack was present while he read this genealogy to Plante and that they were the "white great-grandson and Indian grandson of Chief Khahtsahlano" (Matthews, 1931–56, vol. 6, 1945, 123). Plante is quoted as saying that "he knew his grandmother was Squamish Indian, but added, 'That was not my fault. I had nothing to do with it'" (123). This exchange, transcribed by Matthews, is an example of the

2.3   Carriage driver Frank Plante delivering E.V. Young and David Oppenheimer to
Lumberman's Arch. Matthews's 1943 album caption read, "'Lord Stanley' (Mr. E.V. Young)
and 'Mayor Oppenheimer' (Mr. David Oppenheimer, grand nephew) are being driven
by Frank Plante over the same route as he drove Lord Stanley and Mayor Oppenheimer
54 years ago. He was the first white baby born here."

construction of whiteness through genealogical choices and the instability of
the identity. Genealogy itself, Ahmed (2006) suggests, "could be understood
as a straightening device, which creates the illusion of descent as a line"
(122). Matthews's documentation of Plante's and Khahtsahlano's heritage
and his further aid in the construction of Plante's identity through his photo
captions in his archival documentation, the 1943 reenactment, and his publications demonstrate Ahmed's process of genealogical white straightening.

    The 1943 event was documented through photographs, newspaper
accounts,[23] and possibly on radio, although I have not been able to find
a recording of the audio. Matthews then made two albums of the photos
and news articles – keeping one for the archives and sending one to the
17th Earl of Derby, Lord Stanley's son. The sixty-two-page album features
historical photographs (including one of Chaythoos discussed below) and
a few contemporary images with captions by Matthews as well as portraits of people in costume and pictures from the rededication procession
and ceremony.[24] Seven of the nineteen photos of the ceremony feature
Khahtsahlano (see figure 2.4).

2.4   August Jack Khahtsahlano and others at the "Rededication of Stanley Park."
Matthews's 1943 album caption reads, "Indian men and women dance separately;
never together."

I use these images of Khahtsahlano and Joe's performance to engage
with some concepts of performance and photography discussed by Philip
Auslander in "The Performativity of Performance Documentation" (2012).
He asserts that ideology is the only difference between theatrical and documentary modes of performance documentation: "*[T]he act of documenting
an event as a performance is what constitutes it as such.* Documentation
does not simply generate image/statements that describe an autonomous

performance and state that it occurred: it produces an event as a perform-ance" (53, italics original). He clarifies that his discussion of performance art documentation "participates in the fine art tradition of the reproduc-tion of *works* rather than the ethnographic tradition of capturing *events*" and that the presence of the initial audience is of no importance to our perception and analysis or "evaluation ... of its historical significance" (55, talics original). He says, however, that the decision to document shifts the assumption of responsibility from the initial audience to a subsequent one (55).

Despite his disavowal of discussing ethnographic documentation, I find this formulation productive in thinking about photographs of perform-ances that have an unstable status – in particular those that result from the ethnographic tradition of capturing Indigenous performance. This is the case partly because Indigenous performances that have been documented by settlers cannot be simply categorized as either event or performance but are unstable and often shift the assumption of responsibility for interpreta-tion to us as the present audience. The instability also allows us to be more aware of the aspirational and tenuous nature of the colonial project, or as Nicholas Blomley asserts in *Unsettling the City: Urban Land and the Politics of Property* (2004), "[b]oth dispossession and displacement *were*, and still *are* ... immensely powerful but also, to the extent that they are enacted, are partial and incomplete ... To that extent, displacement is open to con-testation and remaking" (109, italics original), and, he asserts, it relies on reiteration (50–1). The photos of August Jack Khahtsahlano dancing and Chief Matthias Joe singing and drumming could be categorized as archival and ethnographic but also, I suggest, may now be seen – by an audience that did not exist at the time they were taken – as evidence of two kinds of performance, one a settler colonial attempt at emplacement through the event's organization and its documentation and the other an Indigenous assertion of place, or what I have termed "grounded practice" in the context of that attempt.

An indication of the audience response at the time of Khahtsahlano's involvement with the rededication ceremony can be gleaned from a news-paper report of the event. In an article titled "Surveyors Came at Dawn: Corner Cut off House for Stanley Park Road" (1943), the *Vancouver Sun* recounted Khahtsahlano telling the story of the park's road workers chop-ping at the corner of his family's house. He concluded his story, "They say: 'You'll have lots of money.' That was more than 50 years ago and I'm still waiting for it." The only commentary in the article says that his address "amused the audience" (13). The same edition also features a large photo of Khahtsahlano and a man identified as William August, although Matthias Joe was the one who performed with him that day. The photo features Khahtsahlano, in a headband with a feather, drinking out of a mug. The man next to him wears a full feather headdress, and both have horizontal stripes painted on their cheeks. The photo's caption reads, "[A] touch of color is added by Chief Khahtsahlano (left) and his tom-tom beater, William August" ("Here's Key to Pictures" 1943). Despite their misguided reception by the audience at the time, Khahtsahlano's words "I'm still waiting for it" are an indication that he used the public forum to amplify the need for restitution.

I conclude my discussion of the 1943 interaction by pausing to consider what songs Joe sang while Khahtsahlano danced. His decision to dance publicly at a time when Indigenous ceremony and dancing were banned could be seen in terms of Taylor's (2003) concepts of "multiplication and simultaneity" (46). Although this was clearly an event meant to celebrate the settlement of land by the British, there may have been Indigenous people present to receive the knowledge transmitted through the repertoire enacted by Khahtsahlano's dance and Joe's song. Although his performance was interpreted by one newspaper article as his reenactment of "the dance he did for Lord Stanley in 1889" ("Foresight of Pioneers" 1943), Matthews's captions in the album demonstrate that Khahtsahlano informed him of some of the significance of the dances: that they belonged to him, that men and women danced separately, and that it was improper to copy them. Khahtsahlano's and Joe's actions can be interpreted as an intervention into the Indigenous-colonial relations of 1943 and/or as a temporal reach either to the past through his enactment of the dance or to the future as a method of knowledge transfer.

Correspondingly, Matthews and the Park Board were attempting to create a *temporal drag* from the past to the present in their attention to the genealogy of the enactors, namely Oppenheimer, Plante, the clerk, and even Young through his English heritage; their concern with spatiality, the proceedings occurring as close to the site of the 1889 event as the crowds and military defences would allow; their focus on text and objects in the form of the scroll and the wine bottle; and their emphasis on gesture, Lord Stanley's arms being raised to the heavens either to encompass the land or in victory. The reading aloud of letters from the first ceremony as well as the telegrams from Derby and from Oppenheimer's daughter and another one sent to Derby at the end of the reenactment are temporal and spatial interventions. Matthews's archival documentation of the event casts both to the future and across space to England, ultimately working to create a space where white bodies are comfortable. The inclusion of Indigenous people is consistent with observations by Margery Fee and Lynette Russell (2007) that "Aboriginality and settler invader 'whiteness' in Canada and Australia have a parallel history, that these identities were produced in the same discursive struggle over identity, and rely on each other for meaning" (194). The presence of Khahtsahlano and Joe needs to be seen within Ahmed's (2006) frame of white spaces that create comfort for white bodies but also include nonwhite bodies – which are not invisible. Perhaps in this case, they are hypervisible in a space that was being re-marked as one within the purview of white colonial power, and perhaps they were being used as bodies that the officials and audience could orient *toward*, creating whiteness.

Re/dedications by a Disappearing Mausoleum: *Toward*

I now move to the shifting and puzzling issue of what was present in the clearing at the time of the naming, opening, and "dedication" ceremonies in 1888 and 1889. In an earlier publication describing the site around χʷayχʷəy̓ and the Klahowya Village exhibits of 2010–14,[25] I describe the statue of Lord Stanley as standing in a clearing that once held the grave of a Skwxwú7mesh man, citing Barman's *Stanley Park's Secret* (Couture 2014, 243). However, the chapter that I cite, "The Imposition of Stanley Park," which discusses the displacement of the families living there, does not say that the statue is located on the spot of the dedication but that the cairn to commemorate the event *ended up* as a "one-ton statue of Lord Stanley" (Barman 2005, 93). My misreading may be an indication of my own willingness to employ the symbol of an Indigenous gravesite, but I also think it is based on a long-running ambivalence regarding the grave's status, which I examine in this section.[26]

In her chapter, Barman (2005) includes a long quote from Khahtsahlano explaining what happened to his family when the road surveyors cut off a corner of his family's house (92). This text is taken from Matthews's *Conversations with Khahtsahlano* (1955) and is cited as being from two different conversations, one in 1934 (although it seems from my reading to be from 1938) and the other in 1944 (35, 145–6). Barman's excerpt mentions Supple Jack's grave, but she does not include Khahtsahlano's comment from the 1944 conversation that the family left the grave there for a long time. She also edits out Matthews's parenthetical comment that "(It was beside this grave that the dedication of Stanley Park by Lord Stanley took place; the procession stopped there)" (35). Barman (2005) then states that as soon as Supple Jack's family learned of the plans for the ceremony, they removed the gravesite, which she deems "an action that only confirmed to city fathers that they were now in control" (93). She does not cite the source of this information, although it is consistent with some other statements made to Matthews (see below). Barman provides this account in the context of her effort to re-place the families on Brockton Point at the time and her comment on the disruption that the civic ceremonies caused them (93). It is clear from her citational choices that Barman is most interested in the story that the family removed the gravesite before the ceremony. There is reason, however, to attend to the multiple ways that this story has been told rather than choosing one narrative as the truth.

After the introductory letter by Matthews and a few pages of portraits and maps, *Conversations with Khahtsahlano* (1955) begins with a page of undated text that lays out a short biography of Khahtsahlano and his family, noting that he was born at Snauq and the significance of his father's burial place: "Khaytulk, [Chief Khahtsahlanogh's] son, known to early pioneers as Supplejack [*sic*], also lived at Chaythoos; he died in 1877, and, with much ceremony, was buried there, lying in a small canoe, covered with red blankets, placed inside a primitive mausoleum, a small shack with windows, raised on posts ... It was at this picturesque spot, *beside Supplejack's [sic] grave*, that the civic procession of Lord Stanley, officials, and citizens, after formal progress through the city streets, halted for the speech-making at the formal dedication of Stanley Park in October 1889" (9, italics added). In this one-page introduction to Khahtsahlano, Matthews uses one-fifth of the page to assert the location of Supple Jack's grave and the ceremony at the site. The status of the remains of Khahtsahlano's father at the time of the naming and dedication ceremonies is something to which Matthews returns repeatedly over the years of his conversations with Khahtsahlano and others. In addition to this assertion that the grave and remains were present during the naming, opening, and dedication ceremonies, there are five more assertions of the grave's status as present at the event in two conversations dated 1938 and 1944 (32–5, 145–6).[27] In the first conversation,

Matthews inserts both comments regarding the grave and ceremony. In the interaction in 1944, as they are discussing a painting of Chaythoos that Khahtsahlano has brought to Matthews, Khahtsahlano is quoted as stating, "[T]hey left the grave for a long time; until after Lord Stanley named the park. Then they took the coffin up to Squamish" (146). This painting, titled "Supplejack's [sic] Grave," which Khahtsahlano made in 1944 at Matthew's request, is included in the book, along with a caption that explains, "Khaytulk died here, and was buried with ceremony, in a small canoe within a mausoleum, *our first*,[28] of wood on posts ... Here, beside the tomb, on Oct. 1889, stood His Excellency Lord Stanley when he christened Stanley Park, and throwing his arms to the heavens, dedicated it to the use and enjoyment of peoples of all colours, creeds, and customs for all time ... Khaytulk's body remained for some years, then removed by canoe to Brackendale and finally to Po-kwi-la-sun, and tomb destroyed" (136D, italics added). Matthews also includes a photo of the site with a caption: "Here beside Hay-tulk's mausoleum, a canoe inside wooden tomb on posts, Mayor Oppenheimer opened park, Sept. 27, 1888; here Lord Stanley dedicated, Oct. 30, 1889" (24H) (see figure 2.5). His creation and captioning of the photo are undated. He also includes a sketch of Chaythoos made by Khahtsahlano "whilst sitting in my garden this evening" on 29 July 1937. Once again the ceremonies are located beside "Supplejack's [sic] mausoleum" (136E). These assertions are contradicted by other conversations, two of which are with Khahtsahlano in July and August of 1932. He says that his father's remains were "exhumed and taken to Squamish for reinternment" when the park road was put in (12). The next month, Khahtsahlano again mentions his father's grave but is less definite about when it was moved: "[M]ay be the time they were making the road, Stanley Park, they move him" (15).

In a conversation with Matthews in 1934, former city employee William Grafton clearly explains that the grave was moved. Grafton also comments that Supple Jack was "supposed to have been a 'bad actor,' supposed to have shot a lot of men coming through the Narrows." Matthews inserts a note that this is the clearing where the dedication ceremony took place but does not connect it to the grave being present. Matthews also comments in parentheses that Grafton's statement was "read to and assented to as accurate by A.J. Khaatsahlano [sic] May 31, 1934" (Matthews 1955, 272). He also includes a conversation with Frank Harris in 1937, who had lived in a cottage on Pipeline Road, saying that the remains were moved immediately

2.5 Prospect Point, Stanley Park, Vancouver. Matthews used this photograph repeatedly
in the 1943 album, in *Conversations with Khahtsahlano* (1955), in both editions of *Naming,
Opening and Dedication of Stanley Park, Vancouver, Canada 1888–1889* (1959, 1964),
and in *Stanley Park, Vancouver: The Rededication 19th May 1964* (1964). Until 1959 he
always included a caption that described this as the site of the opening and dedication
ceremonies in the presence of the grave of August Jack Khahtsahlano's father.

after the park road was put in (276). So if we follow a chronology, between
1932 and 1937 Matthews was told by Khahtsahlano as well as by two other
speakers that the remains had been moved by September 1888, when the
road was completed (Kheraj 2013, 95). However, in 1938 and 1944 the
gravesite and remains were inserted into the space during the naming and
dedication ceremonies. Only one of these statements is attributed clearly
to Khahtsahlano. After 1959 none of Matthews's writings or reenactments
references the presence of the remains.

Although it is impossible to know the status of the gravesite from the
contradictory statements recorded (and the privacy of the family should
be respected), analysis of the rhetorical use of the concept of the grave is
revealing. This fixation on the gravesite during the naming, opening, and
dedication ceremonies also demonstrates Ahmed's (2006) *toward*, which
determines both the subject's location (i.e., Lord Stanley in the present) and

the not-subject (i.e., the grave of the dead "Indian") with which one can extend the reach of the newly arrived subject, creating a space that is not an Indigenous home but instead a park for white people. Susan Roy in *These Mysterious People: Shaping History and Archaeology in a Northwest Coast Community* (2010)[29] discusses Indigenous gravesites and cemetery relocations in the context of the Musqueam people and the c̓əsnaʔəm village, which was used as an archeological site. She comments that for colonial society, the "passing of individual Native people in the early decades of the twentieth century represented the point of transition from ethnographic to historic, and from the supposed 'anonymous' to the 'named' Indian. In the narration of colonial history, the death of the 'last' Indian went hand in hand with the arrival of the 'first' white baby" (98). In this formulation, the placing of Supple Jack's remains at this site of the opening of the park makes perfect sense, along with the statement that the driver of the carriage was the first white baby. Roy then goes on to explain that when Aboriginal people began to engage with modern land claims, burial sites were both "real and symbolic expressions of ancestral ties to their lands" (99). The chronology of Matthews's placement of the grave during the ceremony and his subsequent removal of it coincides with the 1951 repealing of the legislation in the Indian Act that made it illegal for Aboriginal people to hire legal counsel (Hanson 2009a, 2009b). The inclusion in Matthews's narrative of the remains of an Indigenous man witnessing a British lord's dedication of the park no longer enabled whiteness but instead may have supported claims of Aboriginal title.

Joseph Roach (1996) asserts that European colonial projects included the spatial "segregation of the dead from the living" and that "modernity itself might be understood as a new way of handling (and thinking about) the dead" (48). Khahtsahlano's insistence that his father's remains had been moved may have been meant to ensure that his people were seen as behaving in modern ways. Renisa Mawani in "Imperial Legacies (Post) Colonial Identities: Law, Space and the Making of Stanley Park, 1859–2001" (2003) suggests that Supple Jack's grave – like the partial maps and the laws of governing technology that were used in the attempt to create Stanley Park – was also a "simultaneous presence and absence" at the moment of dedication: "[T]he celebrations that marked the opening of Stanley Park and brought together the city's largely British elite, did not only inaugurate the birth of a Park but the birth of a 'civilised' imperial city – a little piece of empire – that was imagined and constituted in relation to the perceived racialised 'primitiveness' and 'savagery' of Aboriginal peoples" (110). Mawani concludes that the grave's presence also foreshadowed the managed touristic use of the recognition of Aboriginality to celebrate the Canadian state's multiculturalism (110). The space of the "dedication" ceremony, whether or not it held the remains of Khahtsahlano's father, was known to settlers as the *clearing where Supple Jack's grave used to be*. Perhaps this could be considered a place name, and further inquiry might ask why this became a way to name the place and why it was then dropped? The timing seems to coincide not only with the changes in the Indian Act that permitted Aboriginal legal actions but also with Matthews's discovery of the mayor's promise to mark Lord Stanley's visit with a cairn, as well as his subsequent organizing through the 1950s to mark not just the clearing where they stopped in 1889 but the whole of the park with Lord Stanley's monumental presence.

The Lord Stanley Statue, 1952–60: *Around*

I will now delve into another manifestation of Matthews's seemingly inexhaustible desire to mark the space – but this time through monument. When "Lord Stanley Statue" is entered into the online search box for the City of Vancouver Archives, forty-four items are returned. Twenty-one of these are textual files, the rest being digital objects (or photos). The textual files contain numerous letters between Matthews and the English sculptor Sydney March, Matthews and the Park Board, and Matthews and contractors. They also contain flyers soliciting donations to pay for the statue, numerous newspaper articles, editorials, and magazine articles, an editorial cartoon by Leonard Norris, and photos of Matthews posing with his arms raised either to mimic the statue or in victory.[30] A version of this latter image appeared on the front page of the *Vancouver Sun* on 17 May 1960, the statue having been installed two days before it was unveiled by Governor General Georges Vanier,[31] as well as in *Maclean's* later that year (Garner 1960) (see figure 2.6).

The saga of Matthews and the Lord Stanley statue started in the early 1950s when he conceived of the need to create a marker in the park that would follow through with Oppenheimer's promise to mark the site of the dedication with a cairn. Instead of a cairn, however, Matthews designed the statue of Lord Stanley in the act of raising his arms and speaking the words of dedication he had cobbled together.

2.6   James Skitt Matthews imitating the Lord Stanley statue pose.

According to Matthews, quoted in an article dated 6 September 1952, "the statue would *commemorate an act*, not a man: the naming and dedication of Stanley Park on Oct. 29, 1889" (italics added).[32] Matthews recounted the story of the statue at a "private meeting" of the Park Board before the regular session on 25 January 1960, stating that in 1952 he requested permission from the Park Board to place a marker in the park commemorating its dedication in 1889, to which the board agreed but with the "stern admonition WITHOUT COST TO THE PUBLIC." He submitted a sketch to a "renowned sculptor" and paid him $200 to make a model. Matthews then displayed the model to the Park Board, which agreed it was suitable. He commissioned the sculpture for the cost of $4,500 – charged to him. He gathered donations from 200 "citizens of Vancouver and British Columbia," including $100 of his own money. The statue arrived in 1956 and was kept in storage, with the fees charged to Matthews. He then asked the Park Board for a grant of land 10 feet (3 metres) square on which to erect the base, and the board agreed. He commissioned a stonemason to make the base approved by the sculptor in London at a cost of $3,000 – again charged to him.[33] The contractor did not deliver the base but cancelled the contract after eight months. Matthews describes the interval of the next three or so years: "Next, at that time, the owners of the statue, who had paid for it, suffered a series of affronts and impertinences which caused for them to withdraw, and leave the statue in storage, where it has lain for several years. For good reasons, the owners are unwilling to surrender the statue to anyone; even after its erection they intend to remain custodians." At the time of this presentation to the board, he had finally agreed to begin planning for its installation in order to "permit a promise made by a Mayor of Vancouver to a Governor General of Canada to be kept, and bring to fruition an endeavour on which they have spent much time and money."[34]

Other versions of the story of the statue, likely what Matthews terms the "affronts and impertinences," involve objections to the lack of competition for the design, disagreement that Lord Stanley's dedication needed to be marked in any way, and Matthews's unreasonable desire for a prominent placement of the work.[35]

Despite these affronts and impertinences, the Lord Stanley statue still stands at the Georgia Street entrance of the park, near where Stanley Park Drive begins, frozen in the pose Matthews constructed. Etched on the base are these words: "To the use and enjoyment of peoples of all colours, creeds and customs for all time, I name thee Stanley Park." The manner in which the statue takes up space is very evocative: with arms outstretched and legs planted, this likeness of Lord Stanley is taking up as much space as a body can. The raised arms could be seen to signal victory, but the phrase etched on the base of the statue seems to disavow the victorious stance. An analysis of Canadian multiculturalism and the disaffiliation of racism that it employs explains multiculturalism's logic. Andrew Baldwin, Laura Cameron, and Audrey Kobayashi, the editors of *Rethinking the Great White North: Race, Nature and the Historical Geographies of Whiteness in Canada* (2011), define "disaffiliation" as a "practice by which white people distance themselves from the economy of signs that frame white hegemony. Its effect is profound: it allows the liberal majority to assert that racialization is something that *used* to occur but that no longer does, while the everyday embodiment of whiteness is simply absorbed into normative discourse" (14). When Matthews attributed to Stanley the statement on the base of the statue, he cast the disaffiliation backward into the year 1889, powerfully asserting the absence of racializing discourses and practices that would limit the privileges available to members of that society. In reframing the past, the statue also hails contemporary white passersby in order to recruit them into an admiration of the generosity of the British nobility.

Matthews's efforts to memorialize the event found another medium – that of the monument. Referring to Michel de Certeau's observation in *The Practice of Everyday Life* (1984) that "the passing faces on the street seem … to multiply the indecipherable and nearby secret of the monument" (15), Schneider (2011) explains that the monumental and the passersby "co-constitute each other in a relationship that can be as much about forgetting (bypassing) as commemorating (monumentalizing)" (7). The Lord Stanley statue can be seen as Matthews's effort to constitute the future people with whom it will achieve "inter(in)animation" (7), but he had no way of controlling the multiple responses, including the hockey fans who at various times have picked up on the victorious nature of the arm gesture and added a Vancouver Canucks jersey and a mock-up of the Stanley Cup[36] to his upraised arms. Schneider also speaks about the fact that the monument retains its secret – as it seems Lord Stanley's statue has done up until now – and about how *inter(in)animation* moves meanings "onto not only the 'spectator' or passer-by or reader (which would suggest only a one-way contingency in a linear temporal mode), but into chiasmatic reverberation across media and across time in a network of ongoing response-ability"

(163–4). With this new understanding of the *displaced transmission* that Matthews's monument represents, the reverberation back in time as we look at the statue will help white settlers to stay implicated in the privileges of whiteness, as Ahmed (2004) suggests. As long as this knowledge is not widely shared, however, we are left with the statue enacting the continuously constructed dedication and hailing of whiteness. Since the placement of the statue in 1960 – also with a ceremony and a dedication by another governor general – it seems as though reenactments of the 1889 dedication have ceased requiring the assembly of live bodies in costumes to make speeches; the reenactment never stops.

The 1964 Rededication and the Last Spike: *Around*

Nevertheless, on 29 May 1964, an eighty-six-year-old Matthews helped to plan yet another reenactment of the dedication of the park to mark the seventy-fifth anniversary of Lord Stanley's visit. This time the event took place at nearby Malkin Bowl instead of at Lumberman's Arch. The annual Park Board Pioneer Luncheon was held at the Stanley Park Pavilion, where Matthews gave his "traditional pioneer address." Afterward, the guests were invited to Malkin Bowl, where children took part in relay races and tumbling acts. The main theatrical event was former alderman Frank Baker's impersonation of Lord Stanley's arrival in a "surrey with a fringe on top" drawn by a horse down the centre aisle of the seating area. He then intoned the phrase and made the gesture, commented on the improvements to the road since his last visit, and urged the Park Board and staff to continue guarding the park as "jealously" over the next seventy-five years (Lindsay 1964, 30). Khahtsahlano did not perform, although Matthews (1964b) recorded that he and his wife, Swanamia, were guests at the rededication ceremony (37–8).[37]

At the end of the ceremony, the audience was invited to witness the "driving of the last spike" and the inaugural run of the newly built Stanley Park Miniature Railway, three-quarters of a mile (1.2 kilometres) in length, at which point those guests considered to be "Pioneers of Vancouver" were invited to have the first ride (Lindsay 1964, 30; Matthews 1964b, 18) (see figure 2.7).

There had been a small railway in the park since the 1940s, but after Hurricane Freda blew through Vancouver in October 1962, the Park Board used some of the cleared area to build a more elaborate attraction. This

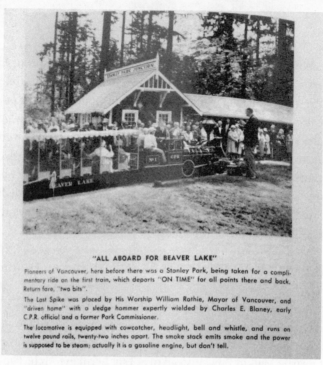

"ALL ABOARD FOR BEAVER LAKE"

Pioneers of Vancouver, here before there was a Stanley Park, being taken for a compli-
mentary ride on the first train, which departs "ON TIME" for all points there and back.
Return fare, "two bits".

The Last Spike was placed by His Worship William Rathie, Mayor of Vancouver, and
"driven home" with a sledge hammer expertly wielded by Charles E. Blaney, early
C.P.R. official and a former Park Commissioner.

The locomotive is equipped with cowcatcher, headlight, bell and whistle, and runs on
twelve pound rails, twenty-two inches apart. The smoke stack emits smoke and the power
is supposed to be steam; actually it is a gasoline engine, but don't tell.

2.7   "All Aboard for Beaver Lake" and "The Guests: Pioneers of
Vancouver" by James Skitt Matthews.

four-minute ride passed by "a prospector's cabin complete with water wheel,
a fire ranger's lookout, an Indian encampment, over a rustic bridge, along
the shoreline of a man-made lake and across the lake on a 140-foot-long
trestle into a windowed 60-foot-long snowshed, on through the blackness
of a 60-foot-long tunnel, around a view through the trees of Burrard Inlet"
(Lindsay 1964, 30). The train engine was also a replica of Engine 374, which
had pulled the first passenger train across the country (City of Vancouver
2013). At the 1964 rededication and opening of the railway, officials greeted
Baker acting as Lord Stanley when his carriage arrived at the Miniature
Railway station guarded by mounted police. Mayor William Rathie and
former CPR official and parks commissioner Charles Blaney then drove in a
golden spike to signify the completion of the railway (Matthews 1964b, 5).[38]
This rededication was different from the previous one in its *lack* of attention
to detail in reenacting the 1889 event. Perhaps such detail was no longer
necessary since the statue of Lord Stanley in the act of dedication was now
installed nearby.

Instead, this event focused on the opening of the Miniature Railway,
linking Lord Stanley's arrival to a Last Spike ceremony. In Canadian

history, much has been written about the Last Spike, which has been used
to symbolize the moment at which Canada became a nation. The photo
of Donald Smith[39] driving in the Last Spike is iconic. Margot Francis in
Creative Subversions: Whiteness, Indigeneity and the National Imaginary
(2011) interprets this moment differently, arguing that more than signifying
mere nation building, the photograph of the "'great men' of the railway
encapsulates the intersection of masculinity and technology" (60). She also
explains how the railway enabled Canada's claim to the immense territories,
"an audacious act of political imperialism" symbolizing from a Foucauldian
perspective "the decentred strategies of imperial rule and ... an emblem
of what Cole Harris calls the 'capillaries of colonial appropriation'" (62).
The completion of the CPR is also connected with the creation of tourist
promotions due to cost overruns, which drove the railway executives to
capitalize on the "spectacular scenery," eventually developing tourist sites
across the country (67–8). Francis also links the completion of the CPR
with the Canadian military's access to the plains, which allowed its soldiers
to put down the second Métis–First Nations uprising of the North-West
Resistance of 1885 (66).

The image of the Last Spike that was invoked through reenactment at the
opening of the Miniature Railway was one of an aspirational success, which
was also memorialized triumphantly by E.J. Pratt's long poem *Towards the
Last Spike* (1952). Yet it was an incomplete aspiration of a united nationhood. F.R. Scott's poem "All the Spikes but the Last" (1966) responded to
Pratt with a question:

> Where are the coolies in your poem, Ned?
> Where are the thousands from China who swung
> their picks with bare hands at forty below?
>
> Between the first and the million other spikes
> they drove, and the dressed-up act of
> Donald Smith, who has sung their story?
>
> Did they fare so well in the land they helped to
> unite? Did they get one of the 25,000,000 CPR acres?
>
> Is all Canada has to say to them written in the Chinese
> Immigration Act? (64)

The Vancouver Park Board had not included any actors impersonating Chinese railway workers, nor had it invited any of their descendants to this event. The Khahtsahlanos may or may not have attended the Last Spike ceremony, but the impact on Indigenous lands and people that the railway (and its miniature replica) had was certainly not being considered. The only reference to Indigenous peoples was the train ride passing by an "Indian encampment." The rest of the features were replicas of railway infrastructure like tunnels and bridges, along with the spaces that hold people who are involved in resource extraction or protection, namely the prospector's cabin and the fire ranger's lookout. Despite this illusion of an empty land of resources – across Canada and within Stanley Park – the railway continues to be on Indigenous land, as Cree-Métis poet Marilyn Dumont forcefully explains in her poem "Letter to Sir John A. McDonald" (1996): "[T]hat god-damned railroad never made this a great nation ... [W]e were railroaded/ by some steel tracks that didn't last/ and some settlers who wouldn't settle" (52). Her reference to settlers who "wouldn't settle" resonates when thinking of Matthews and his reiterations of naming, dedicating, and gathering together an archive *around* which settlers and newcomers might find comfort.

Conclusion

In this chapter, I have argued that James Skitt Matthews intervened in and manipulated the archive that he almost single-handedly created and maintained for forty years. I have noted the lack of a critique of his work by Vancouver historians and provided evidence that he constructed a Stanley Park dedication event to suit a retroactive *disaffiliation* with racialized policy and actions by early Vancouverites. Not all observers, however, have been oblivious to the unlikeliness of Stanley's utterance. Stó:lo poet, scholar, and educator Lee Maracle picks up on it in her story "Mink Witnesses the Creation of Stanley Park" (2014), which ends, "'Stanley Park, named after John Stanley. All races welcome in this park.' All races welcome, humph, good idea" (1). Matthews's work on the reenactments of 1943 and 1964, along with his creation of the archive of the events, served to provide an orientation *around* a construction of whiteness that favoured a British imperialist view of resource extraction and dispossession of Indigenous people. This undertaking was aided by an emphasis on the presence of both the live and dead Khahtsahlano family *toward* which a white identity could offer recognition, a type of politics that has been criticized by both

Renisa Mawani and Glen Sean Coulthard. Mawani (2004) asserts that public recognition can mistakenly be read as the redistribution of material resources and of economic, social, and political power (52–4), whereas Coulthard (2014) argues that it actually works to reconcile "Indigenous assertions of nationhood with settler-state sovereignty" (3).

The reiterations of these orientations through the institution of the archive, publications, reenactments, and the monument have created an inherited habit of whiteness in Vancouver. It is a phenomenological inheritance of whiteness, in Ahmed's (2006) framing, as well as a literal inheritance given that Matthews willed his collection to the City of Vancouver. I suggest here that this habit of whiteness is an addiction that must be broken. The narrative that Matthews constructed about Lord Stanley through "surrogation" and "displaced transmission" (Roach 1996, 2, 59) may seem harmless; the statue stands in the park, welcoming all people for all time. Yet due to Matthews's disaffiliation of the British invasion and settlement of this area, contemporary city dwellers are able to comfortably continue in their inheritance, using the statue and the Stanley dedication narrative as evidence that this city was built on an openness to all. But what if this narrative, instead, is a creation of a disoriented society, one that is nauseous and horrified by its own contingency (Ahmed 2006, 157–8). In the previous chapter, I asserted that place names hold knowledge, wisdom, and identity for hənq̓əminəm̓-speaking people; I have now expanded this understanding to include awareness of the settler knowledge and aspiration to white identity held within the place name "Stanley Park."

The loss of this knowledge has been one that, as Schneider (2011) has asserted, the archive regulates, maintains, and produces (103). Derrida in *Archive Fever: A Freudian Impression* (1996) also notes that the archive is a "place of election where law and singularity intersect in privilege ... becom[ing] at once visible and invisible" (3). Matthews's control in the selection of the archive is itself worthy of note and critique. His further performative activities involving the archive align even more closely with Schneider's (2011) description of it as a "house of and for performative repetition, not stasis" (110). In the next chapter, I return to performative interventions in Vancouver history, but this time I offer an example of how Indigenous people exerted control over colonial archival impulses. First, however, the following section examines how a theatrical performance of an iconic Canadian playwright's work has been able to reinsert an Indigenous woman into theatre history.

Michel Tremblay's
For the Pleasure of Seeing Her Again

To continue seeking understanding of the construction of whiteness, and to respond to contemporary theatrical interventions into the disappearance of Indigenous women, I now engage with Western Canada Theatre's (WCT) 2012–14 production of Michel Tremblay's *For the Pleasure of Seeing Her Again* (1998), which is not *textually* engaged with the place-based issues that are the focus of this book but, through the performers' bodies, demonstrates an embodied transfer of historical knowledge. This approach allows us to consider how in this production the performance of Nana, the fictionalized mother of Tremblay, by the "mother of Canadian Aboriginal theatre," Cree-Saulteux actor Margo Kane, has an impact on our understanding of both Tremblay, who is a major figure in Québécois and Canadian theatre, and his oeuvre. Much of his work, including *Les belles-soeurs* (1968), was inspired by his mother and her sisters. Yet, although Tremblay had been writing about his mother's Cree heritage since the 1990s, this production was the first to cast Indigenous actors in the play. This short section therefore aims to bring into conversation the two solitudes of Indigenous and Québécois theatrical culture.[1]

The production opened in January 2012 in Kamloops, British Columbia, before touring to the annual Magnetic North Theatre Festival in June 2013. I attended a performance staged during the Talking Stick Festival in Vancouver in February 2014 at the York Theatre. My interest in responding to the play here is connected to director Glynis Leyshon's (2014) decision, based on evidence in Tremblay's text, to cast Indigenous actors and change the final imagery to connect with Indigenous life in Saskatchewan. I assert that this decision, while emphasizing the Cree heritage of Tremblay's mother and opening a line of inquiry into many of his works that were inspired by his mother, also illuminates the gendered nature of the colonial process. This production was both a vehicle for a virtuosic performance by Margo Kane as Nana and one where the representational mode of performance of Nana as a Cree woman

connected with what Mi'kmaw scholar Bonita Lawrence (2004) has
called a "metanarrative about encounters with genocide" (xvii).

Tremblay wrote *For the Pleasure of Seeing Her Again* as part of the
thirtieth-anniversary celebration of *Les belles-soeurs*. The play features
only two characters, Nana and her son, the Narrator. It takes place in five
scenes during which the Narrator, sitting in an armchair, interacts with
his mother at five different ages between ten and twenty. She chastises
him, they discuss books and television shows, she gossips about family,
and she eventually succumbs to cancer. Tremblay has stated that this play
was his effort to go back to how he was formed as an artist, to the woman
with whom he "apprenticed" as a dramatic storyteller, his mother
(Tremblay and Wachtel 2000). The play, although full of appreciation, is
also tinged with sorrow given that Tremblay's mother died before he was
successful; he has stated that he regrets not having been able to share his
success with his parents. He has also acknowledged, however, that
his mother's early death allowed him to write *Les belles-soeurs* without
self-censoring. He says, "[S]he would have hated every word I wrote in
that play because she would probably have thought I was laughing at her,
or at her sisters, or at these women" (Tremblay and Wachtel 2003). The
two plays could be said to respond to each other, demonstrating how
deeply Tremblay's career is intertwined with the figure of his mother.

For the Pleasure of Seeing Her Again was first produced in August
1998 as *Encore une fois, si vous le permettez*[2] by Théâtre du Rideau
Vert and featured Andre Brassard and Rita Lafontaine, whose careers
were launched along with Tremblay's by *Les belles-soeurs* (Charlebois
2013). Two months later, in the quickest performance of Tremblay's
work in translation up to that point, the Centaur Theatre in Montreal
produced the play in English, starring Nicola Cavendish as Nana and
Dennis O'Connor as the Narrator (Borgstrum 1999, 324). There have
been numerous productions since that time. In 2002 the American
Conservatory Theatre in San Francisco opened the play on Mother's
Day, with Olympia Dukakis and Marco Barricelli in the roles of Nana
and the Narrator, describing it as a "French-Canadian comedy about
the relationship between a supportive mother and her gay son" (Ehren
and Simonson 2002). In 2004 W!ld Rice Theatre (2004) in Singapore
produced a version with Neo Swee Lin as Nana and Ivan Heng as the
Narrator, describing it as a "celebration of the magic of theatre as well
as maternal love." Stratford Festival's 2010 production, directed by Chris

Abraham with Lucy Peacock as Nana and Tom Rooney as the Narrator, emphasized the autobiographical nature of the play and the "world view that charts a way of living that leads to joy, redemption and harmony" (White 2010, 3). The director noted how extensively Tremblay has written about his mother, saying that in this play he "shows us that 'The Mother' is the most universal character" (Abraham 2010, 3). In the entry about the play in the online *Canadian Theatre Encyclopedia*, Gaeten Charlebois (2013) calls it a "refreshingly uncomplicated and lucid work." Although the play has been received this way, I argue that the WCT production complicates the work in a necessary and even more refreshing manner.

As early as 1994, Tremblay published details of his mother's Cree heritage. In his 1994 memoir, translated into English as *Birth of a Bookworm* (2003), Tremblay explains his mother's roots. He says that her mother (his grandmother), Maria Desrosiers, was a Cree woman from Saskatchewan and that her father (his grandfather) was a sailor from Brittany. They met in Rhode Island and had children. His mother was then sent back to Saskatchewan and raised by her Cree grandparents. Eventually, she ended up in Montreal, where she met his father, Armand Tremblay (9–12). In his dedication to *Twelve Opening Acts* (2002), he also describes his mother, "Rhéauna Rathier, half-Cree, half-French." He had identified his mother as having Cree heritage even before he wrote *For the Pleasure of Seeing Her Again*, but WCT was the first company to have picked up on this part of her character, even though there are references to it in the text itself. In the middle of the play, when the Narrator is a young teenager, he and Nana engage in a discussion about the creation of nobility, or "blue blood," in the context of a French novel, *Patira*. The Narrator asks whether the rich girls who go to the Mount-Royal Convent School have blue blood. Nana replies, "Of course not! Nobody has blue blood in America! Only in Europe!" She cannot explain why only Europeans have nobility, and the Narrator asks about her family: "[Y]our grandparents were Cree from Saskatchewan – ... they'd settled here a long time before the Europeans arrived – how come the Good Lord never appeared to tell them they had blue blood? How come he just appeared in Europe? I don't think that's fair! There must've been a Cree somewhere who deserved to be declared noble like those guys on the other side" (Tremblay 1998, 39–40). Nana agrees that this is not fair and suggests that it was because the Cree did not know the Lord.

A few minutes later, however, after discussing the many nationalities of nobility in Europe, she says, "I'm beginning to wonder, you know … I never thought about it that way. When you get right down to it, there must've been a Cree who deserved it, too" (42).

Leyshon (2014) calls the Cree element the heart of the WTC production. Besides casting Kane and Cree actor and director Lorne Cardinal in 2012–13 and Kane and Nlaka'pamux actor and playwright Kevin Loring in 2014, she also changed the ending from the original, which had Nana ascending to heaven in a wicker basket with angel wings in front of a tromp-l'oeil backdrop of Saskatchewan plains and a lake (Tremblay 1998, 77–9). Instead, the WCT backdrop was a northern Saskatchewan scene of snowy birch trees and a frozen lake in front of which Nana rode a silver-winged canoe to the skies on a set designed by Pam Johnson, with lighting by Gerald King. Nevertheless, although these changes were noted in media discussion of the original Kamloops production in 2012, few of the reviewers of the 2013 or 2014 productions mentioned the additional focus of the play. Mike Youds (2012b), arts reporter for the *Kamloops Daily News*, discusses the implications of the casting in his preview to the Kamloops production, commenting that both Cardinal and Kane are of Cree descent, like Nana, but calls this coincidental to their roles. Kane is quoted as saying that having Aboriginal heritage is a fact of Canadian existence, and "I think people in Quebec also have a lot of mixed blood. That's part of who we are in this country." Youds (2012b) also notes that "Nana's love of storytelling reflect[s] the tradition of oral narrative in Aboriginal culture and is central to the plot." Youds's review of the production (2012c) and a subsequent article (2012a) mention the Cree content but state that it is not central to the plot. He acknowledges, however, that this production is part of a gradual good change for Aboriginal actors. Nevertheless, when the play was restaged in Ottawa for the Magnetic North Theatre Festival, little of the Cree interpretation was noted. Patrick Langston's (2013) *Capital Critics Circle* review of the show comments extensively on Kane's performance but makes no mention at all of the new interpretation, nor does B.M. McNally's (2013) *Ottawa Tonight* review. Alvina Ruprecht's (2013) *Capital Critics Circle* review comments on the types of structure in the play text that reflect Tremblay's oeuvre and is critical of the lack of variation in Kane's performance. Ruprecht concludes that neither Leyshon nor Kane was "properly tuned to the nuances of Tremblay's 'score,'" while

not considering that the play could have been instead attending to
an unacknowledged Cree underscore. An unattributed response in
the *Ottawa Citizen* does note the Cree heritage of both Tremblay and
Cardinal and addresses the differences between their life experiences,
quoting Cardinal as saying that whereas Tremblay's parents wanted him
to become a printer like his father, his own parents, because of their
residential school experiences, only wanted him to be happy ("Loving
Tribute" 2013). When the production arrived in Vancouver as part of the
Talking Stick Festival, reviewers still did not comment on the significance of this restaging (Jane 2014; Oliver 2014). One reviewer does call it
an adaptation through casting, saying the production changed the characters "from Catholic French Canadians to a First Nations mother and
son" and recast the play with Aboriginal actors based on one line in the
text, but he does not mention how this might be significant (Jones 2014).
Neither the major Vancouver newspapers nor other online theatre sites
reviewed the production. This lack of thoughtful response in reviews is
not necessarily surprising, as the form requires a quick turnaround and
is not conducive to extensive research or reflection. It also, however, can
be seen as part of the attempted erasure that Aboriginal women continue
to endure as part of Canadian colonial processes, which began officially,
as Lawrence (2004) explains, even before Confederation in 1867.

Bonita Lawrence's *"Real" Indians and Others: Mixed Blood Urban
Native Peoples and Indigenous Nationhood* (2004) is useful to us help
understand why Tremblay's Cree mother and grandmother were distanced from their families and how this experience is part of the much
larger context of Canadian colonial processes and policies. Lawrence
traces the patriarchal definitions of Indianness from 1850 when the
first legislation was passed declaring that Indian status depended on
either "Indian descent or marriage to a male Indian" (50). "Indian
status" refers to a historical and legally significant Aboriginal identity
in Canada, which forces the government to acknowledge its obligations
to Aboriginal peoples. Status, although inherently problematic since
the criteria for its determination were derived from the paternalistic
colonial relationship, confers the right to live on reserves, share and
inherit band resources, and vote in council elections (Crey and Hanson
2009). It also, as Lawrence (2004) argues, can be a way to affirm identity
and belonging. Thus the loss of status carries material, cultural, and
emotional consequences. In the Gradual Enfranchisement Act of 1869,

Indigenous wives of non-Aboriginal men lost inheritance rights and
were automatically enfranchised with their husbands, and section 6
stripped Indigenous women of Indian status if they married anyone
without status (50). By 1874 the term "Indian" was defined by descent,
which flowed solely from the male line, and the superintendent of Indian
Affairs was given power to stop payments to women who had no children or left their husbands (52). In the 1951 revision of the Indian Act, the
limited rights that entitled deserted or widowed Indian women to shares
of treaty money or informal recognition of their band membership were
removed (50–1). Lawrence also argues that the backlash against the
1969 White Paper intensified the division between status and nonstatus
Indians, noting that the latter category, due to the previous 119 years of
legislation, includes a disproportionate number of Indigenous women
(60). In 1985 Bill C-31 attempted to remedy this gender discrimination by
restoring status and membership to "eligible people" and by passing control of recognition to bands (65). When Bill C-31 was passed, there were
350,000 status Indians; by 2004, 127,000 people had regained status,
although 106,000 applications were denied (65). Lawrence then lists
the mind-bogglingly myriad ways that status can be applied or denied
through marriage, childbearing, and generational flow (65–9). She also
pauses to consider not just the individuals who lost their status but
also all of their descendants, counting between 1 and 2 million, which,
when compared to the presence of only 350,000 status Indians, begins to
show the scale of cultural genocide (56). Lawrence concludes with a call
to recognize the ambiguity in Native identity rather than trying to solve
it (187). Therein lies the significance of both wct's production of *For the
Pleasure of Seeing Her Again* and the continuing lack of recognition with
which it was received.

I now arrive at my response to the performance. This show was one
of the mainstage features of the thirteenth annual Talking Stick Festival,
organized by Full Circle First Nations Performance (fcfnp); it was
also the first time in many years that Margo Kane, who is the artistic
managing director of fcfnp, had performed at the festival other than
at a cabaret night or as the host of an event. For Kane's fans, the title of
the play, while ostensibly referring to Tremblay's mother, also referred
to our chance to see her in a role that seemed written for her comedic
physicality and stage-filling presence. Kane's casting also echoed
Tremblay's acknowledgment of his mother as an influence and artistic

mentor. Kane's career in theatre (onstage and in administration) has now spanned over forty years. Her first prominent role was as Rita Joe in Prairie Theatre Exchange's mounting of the first production of *The Ecstasy of Rita Joe* to have an all-Aboriginal cast. George Ryga's play had been an important part of Canadian theatre since its first production in 1967, but it took fifteen years for a company to cast it with Aboriginal actors (Couture 2011, 11–17). Since that time, Kane has toured the country, performing in cities, towns, and on reserves, and as Renate Usmiani (2013) says, she "is widely considered the 'mother of Canadian native performance arts.'" Both her work with the National Native Role Model program and her one-woman show *Moonlodge* (1990) were influential in inspiring many younger artists, including Marie Clements, Lisa Ravensbergen, and Yvette Nolan. Kevin Loring also credits her with helping him to learn a practice of self-exploration in the FCFNP Ensemble program ("Talking Stick" 2013).[3] Kane's presence onstage at the York Theatre, to use Bert States's terms (2007, 28), was not merely the "frontside" (onstage) performance of an actor portraying the character of Nana but also included the "backside" (offstage) context of her place in the history of Indigenous theatre in Canada.

Kane's performance was fun, being full of the dramatic exaggeration of words and the full-body expression of emotions, such as Nana's fury at her son in the first scene for throwing a chunk of ice at a car. She paced the stage quickly, moving away from him and back again as she remembered her moments of fear and shame. Loring, as the Narrator, had the difficult task of acting from an armchair. Tremblay has described the Narrator's opening monologue as his theatrical credo, which states essentially that tragedy can be about ordinary people like this woman (Tremblay and Wachtel 2000). Loring opened the play by filling the stage with his embodied allusions to works throughout Western theatre history by William Shakespeare, Anton Chekhov, Euripides, Sophocles, Henrik Ibsen, Eugène Ionesco, Jean Genet, George Bernard Shaw, Samuel Beckett, Tennessee Williams, and more, and then he sat in the armchair for the duration of the action until the final few minutes of the show. The blocking was purposeful: he was her audience, mesmerized by her. It was a challenge, however, to make him interesting, although he acted as our proxy (or perhaps we were his) as we watched and enjoyed Nana's antics. Opening with the references to great characters throughout theatre history put Nana in the continuum. The most enjoyable scene of the night was Kane's imitation of Nana's fifteen-year-old niece with an eye twitch at a ballet recital. She moved her aging body gracefully about the stage, both executing ballet positions with the skill of a lifelong dancer and allowing herself to hesitate as a young girl learning to dance might. It seemed almost like a part written for her, one in which she could stretch out in a self-expressive virtuosic performance mode.

The final scene of Nana's illness and ascension was extremely sad after witnessing her vibrant personality up to then. Tremblay wrote it as a retroactive gift he wished to give to his mother for all she had given him. The WCT production's change in the staging at this point introduced another performance mode by having a canoe descend to take Nana away, invoking her Cree heritage. This insertion added on a representational mode of performance, making Nana a historical persona: a Cree woman who, through the policies outlined above, had been separated from her heritage. The gift of a painless separation that Tremblay invokes through his use of the phenomenological apparatus of the theatre was at this point expanded through Leyshon's directorial choices and the actors' performances in order to also stage the recognition of what Lawrence (2004) regards as the ambiguity of Native identity (187).

As Nana ascended, she promised to come back to haunt her son if he did not live his life to suit her, and we were reminded that her son had conjured her through a theatrical haunting. But in this production, the haunting was expanded from the type of ghosts that populate a stage to those of Indigeneity that also haunt the nation, as Margot Francis (2011) has suggested, and perhaps also haunt what we conceive of as modern Canadian theatre history. Tremblay's career began during the Quiet Revolution, and as the "redefinition of Quebec's political identity intensified, the articulation of its culture played an increasingly important role in the ferment of the times. Michel Tremblay was right in the midst of that ferment" (Wasserman 2012, 59–60). Tremblay's role in the creation of Québécois and Canadian culture and his status as one of the foremost dramatists of the country have been widely accepted. I note, however, that in European settler Canadians' eagerness for a definition of a distinct (white) Canadian culture, there had been no theatrical uptake of his acknowledgment of his mother's Cree identity prior to the WTC production. This show, an example of a collaboration between Indigenous and non-Indigenous theatre artists creating an eddy of influence in the existing narrative of Canadian theatre history, indicated a way forward through a critical reconsideration of the women characters inspired by Tremblay's Cree mother that have populated his plays throughout his influential oeuvre.

Vancouver's 1946 Diamond Jubilee: Indigenous Archival Interventions

The City of Vancouver Archives are held in a building set in a beautiful natural environment. A few hundred metres back from a rocky beach with a seaside bicycle route, it is built into a small hill covered with rolling green grass and has a view of the downtown skyscrapers across Burrard Inlet and the North Shore Mountains looming behind them. For a city that prides itself on being the birthplace of Greenpeace and mixing urban life with unspoiled nature, this is in many ways an appropriate setting to house the archives. The physical space is also entangled with another less publicly promoted part of the city's heritage, that of the dispossession of Indigenous peoples. Nearby the unceded Coast Salish land on which the archives are housed is the site of the village discussed in the introduction called sən̓aʔqʷ in hən̓q̓əmin̓əm̓ and Sen̓ákw in Sḵwx̱wú7mesh. The meaning of this place name, "direct the head there," is derived from this action (Suttles 2004, 571). Although the name perhaps indicates movement to a destination, as in to direct the "head" of a canoe toward the area, there is a certain kind of irony that the land now houses an archive, which, in Western historiography, is thought of as the repository of rational knowledge, or the "head" of the social body. There is a further layer to this space, as discussed in chapter 2, which is that the creation of the archives was also the result of James Skitt Matthews's stipulation in his will that within a year of his death the city must construct an archival building to hold his collection. He did not choose the area, but as it was down the road from his home in Kitsilano and was also formerly one of the homes of August Jack Khahtsahlano's family, he might have approved. The village was part of a network of communities used by Musqueam, Tsleil-Waututh, and Squamish people throughout the Lower Mainland until, in 1869, 37 acres were set aside as an "Indian reserve." In 1877 the federal and provincial Joint Indian Reserve Commission expanded the reserve to 80 acres and allotted it to the "Skwamish Tribe" alone (Roy 2011, 87–8). In 1913 provincial officials coerced residents of the reserve into selling the land. Some of the families and their belongings were taken by barge to Squamish reserves in Howe Sound, with others returning to Musqueam and Coquitlam; all the buildings were burned after they left (Barman 2007, 17; Roy 2011, 89). As documented by Susan Roy (2011), the sale was illegal under the terms of the Indian Act, and the land remained an Indian reserve until April 1946 when the Squamish Council surrendered it to Indian Affairs (89). In 2002, after a twenty-five-year court case that included counterclaims from the Musqueam and Tsleil-Waututh First Nations, the Squamish Nation was awarded control over a fraction of the area, namely the railway right of ways (89). This entanglement of space, so much part of the layers of history throughout Vancouver, is an example of the ways that the recorded and unrecorded history of the city, the archives, and the lived embodied experience of Indigenous peoples resonate in Vancouver.

Since the arrival of European settlers on the West Coast in British Columbia, there has been a consistent effort at erasure of First Nations villages from the land that has become the city of Vancouver. Certain locations have been part of the public narrative of Indigenous displacement and settler emplacement on the land, most particularly during times of civic celebrations. I use here the concepts of displacement and emplacement from Nicholas Blomley's *Unsettling the City: Urban Land and the Politics of Property* (2004). Blomley makes a distinction between *dispossession*, the process by which settlers acquired title to Indigenous lands, and conceptual *displacement*, the process by which Indigenous people were removed from the settler-city space to allow for the *emplacement* of settlers. He argues that the dual process of *displacement-emplacement* is a social and political project: "[T]hey are both immensely powerful but also, to the extent that they are enacted, are partial and incomplete. For a settler society, displacement is a social achievement, but also an aspiration; it is an accomplishment, and also an assertion. To that extent, displacement is open to contestation and remaking" (109). Archival records of two performance events during Vancouver's Diamond Jubilee in July 1946, *The Jubilee Show* and *The Indian Village and Show*, present the settler vision of Vancouver's history and future that was crafted by a citizens' committee, yet at the same time the absences in the archives, which at first seem to be part of the colonial ignorance about Indigenous people, may actually be Indigenous assertions of power through cultural restriction. These archival absences as well as *The Indian Village and Show* itself and the publicity surrounding it are examples of the Native Brotherhood of British Columbia (NBBC) employing grounded practices to create a lasting eddy of influence.

Diana Taylor's (2003) focus on the tension between the archive and the repertoire is useful here. She cautions against polarizing the two methods of knowledge transmission, instead asserting that "the archive and the repertoire exist in a constant state of interaction" (21–2). The reasons for this caution can be demonstrated by examining the records of the Vancouver Citizens' Diamond Jubilee Committee (VCDJC), with particular focus, briefly, on *The Jubilee Show* and then, in more depth, on *The Indian Village and Show*.

The Jubilee Show and *The Indian Village and Show*: Settler Assertion, Indigenous Contention

Near the site of χ̌ʷaẏχ̌ʷəẏ, *The Jubilee Show* was performed at Brockton Point in 1946. The city archives hold extensive textual and visual records of this show. There are files of correspondence, records of meetings, the original script and two revised versions, as well as dozens of photos depicting the building of the stage, backstage preparations, audience members, lighting equipment, and scenes during the show. The show was an ambitious event: it ran from 1 to 17 July and remarkably included 4,200 performers on the purpose-built Timber Bowl outdoor stage, which seated 15,000 spectators (see figure 3.1). Advertised as a "dramatic pageant of Vancouver's history," the production can be considered an attempt to use a large-scale physically embodied narrative to reinforce a dominant colonial history (and future) for Vancouver. The scale of *The Jubilee Show* is itself almost a caricature of settler *emplacement* on Indigenous land. With the number of performers and spectators converging each night at Brockton Point, it amounted to approximately 7 per cent of the city's population gathering in the small area.[1] The opening act, the "Indian Sequence," consisted of 125 Vancouver settler citizens cast as Indigenous characters on a site of unceded land, which was still inhabited by Indigenous people.[2] This was a performative and physical *emplacement* of settlers in the land and narrative of the city. In contrast to the characters they played, the settler bodies asserted their modernity and ownership of the future, symbolically displacing Indigenous people who were physically still there. The use of ballet dancers in redface to perform a potlatch ceremony was a particularly complex mingling of performance traditions. Ballet, considered one of the highest forms of art in

3.1   Brockton Point during *The Jubilee Show*, July 1946.

Western civilization, was being used to express this "uncivilized"[3] ceremony. In addition, the pleasure for the audience would have been enhanced by the costumes of the performers. Redface performance in revealing costumes allowed for a heightened viewing of dancers' muscular bodies (see figure 3.2). Although it is unclear how much of the script was actually performed after opening night, following which three hours were cut,[4] it is clear that somehow, in the script revision process, the writers decided to include more Indigenous people as part of the labour of the founding of the city and as somewhat engaged with modern life. They are mostly silent presences; nevertheless, they are there.

A contentious response to this attempted erasure of Indigenous people was running concurrently as *The Indian Village and Show* at Kitsilano Park (now called Vanier Park), the site of sənaʔqʷ/Senákw and the former reserve and currently the site of the City of Vancouver Archives. The covers of the programs for the events provide a visible contrast that shows the difference in intent. *The Jubilee Show* organizers were looking to the future, imagining the potential of the city, and although seemingly open to acknowledging the Indigenous presence during the founding of the

3.2 "Potlatch Ballet" opening sequence of the *The Jubilee Show*, July 1946.

city, they were ambivalent about inclusion of Indigenous people in the future of the city. This sentiment is most evocatively suggested by the front and back covers of *The Jubilee Show*'s souvenir program. The front cover depicts a view of the city of Vancouver with the ocean in the front and the snowcapped mountains behind the downtown city skyscrapers. Floating prominently in the immediate foreground is a totem pole, to the right of which a ghostly image of Captain George Vancouver has materialized in the clouds. The back cover, titled "Tomorrow's Vancouver," pictures the city with much higher buildings cradled in a massive hand with no Indigenous iconography in sight (see figures 3.3 and 3.4). The program for *The Indian Village and Show* signals a continuation of Indigeneity, featuring artwork on the cover that is both modern and influenced by Northwest Coast Indigenous form and line (see figures 3.5 and 3.6). *The Jubilee Show*'s program is clearly a souvenir of the event and features ten full pages of advertisements – out of twenty-four pages. *The Indian Village and Show*'s program, however, is a mixture of information about the performance and about Indigenous people's endurance of settler colonialism. This fusion of themes is accomplished through poetry, essays, and photos of Indigenous people and their allies. It is important to contextualize this event by recognizing not only the significance of the site but also the changes in its status according to Indigenous responses to colonial procedures. Three months

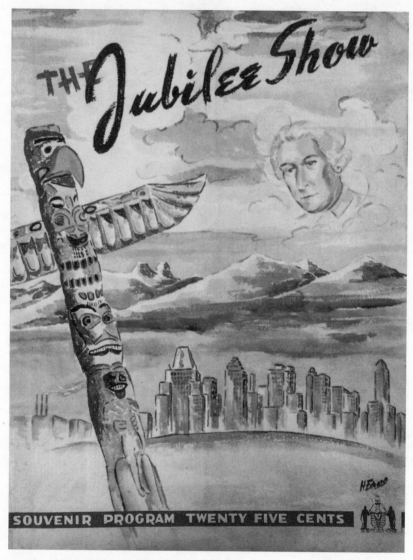

3.3   Front cover of *The Jubilee Show*'s souvenir program.

earlier, in April 1946, the Squamish Council had officially surrendered
the land to Indian Affairs (Roy 2011, 89). Although residents had been
removed thirty-three years earlier, a decision had recently been made by
some Squamish leaders to sell the land for $250,000;[5] it was sold in sections
to various parties over the next twenty years (89). *The Indian Village and
Show* of 1946, run by a pan-tribal provincial organization with the support

3.4   Back cover of *The Jubilee Show*'s souvenir program.

of at least one Squamish man, re-placed Indigenous bodies and culture at a site where there had been continuous pressure to eradicate them.

The dominant narrative of Indigenous art and culture in British Columbia is that it was devastated upon first contact and revived through the work of Haida artist Bill Reid (1920–1998). Tsimshian and Haida art historian and educator Marcia Crosby in her essay "Haida, Human Being

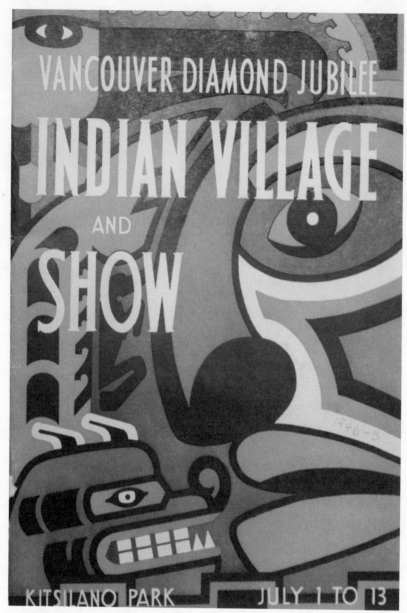

3.5　Front cover of *The Indian Village and Show*'s program.

3.6   Back cover of *The Indian Village and Show*'s program.

and Other Myths" (2004) asserts that there was not a simple revival of Indigenous culture in the 1960s but rather that there has always been continuing contention with colonialism. The story of the NBBC and *The Indian Village and Show* of 1946 helps to show a lack of tidy endings and beginnings, while filling in the continuous "middle" to which Crosby wishes to bring awareness (117). The somewhat extensive archives of the event include correspondence between Indigenous allies such as Maisie Armytage-Moore and the citizens' committee, the richly detailed program, and mainstream media coverage not only of the tensions between organizers and Indigenous performers but also of the ceremony to make the governor general of Canada an honorary chief. Not held within the city archives but available through the University of British Columbia's Special Collections is the Indigenous media coverage of the ceremony with the governor general. There are also, however, notable absences from the city archives respecting *The Indian Village and Show*, particularly when contrasted with the materials available related to *The Jubilee Show*. There are no photos of performances or any reviews of or responses to them. The only photos that exist are of the ceremony with the governor general. At first, this lack of visual or textual evidence of the performances was frustrating to me, as I was able to read about the plans for the event but nothing about what actually happened. This seemed yet another example of colonial bias until I found a document assigning the copyright for photos of eleven "Indian Ceremonial Dances" to Chief William Scow, president of the NBBC.[6] In the end, what is present in this archive and what is absent led me to believe that, when they are considered together, interacting as Taylor suggests, we can see differing methods of settler colonial and Indigenous knowledge transfer and a trace of one Indigenous leader's contention with the dominant culture's desire for access to restricted Indigenous knowledge.

The Indian Village and Show: Allies in the Archive

The poster for Vancouver's Diamond Jubilee celebration advertises the sporting events, shows, and parades happening from 1 to 13 July 1946 in honour of the city's sixtieth anniversary; in the bottom right hand corner, it reads, "As an Added Attraction, Be Sure to See the INDIAN VILLAGE ... Tribal Rituals ... Fire Dances ... The Pulse-stirring THUNDERBIRD DANCE!! and many other wonders of Indian lore and customs that White Men have not yet been privileged to see!"[7] The citizens' committee commissioned *The*

Indian Village and Show and hired former US reservation teacher Ralph E. Hiltz as the producer-director (Hawker 2003, 117). Archival records show that performers and hosts were acquired through connections with Maisie Armytage-Moore (later known as Maisie Hurley)[8] and the NBBC (Fortney 2010, 74–9). Examining the details of the creation of a working relationship between the VCDJC and the NBBC through Armytage-Moore partly illuminates the operations of the lost "middle" of continued political resistance that Crosby (2004, 117) describes.

By 1946 the NBBC had consolidated its power with that of other pan-tribal organizations. The NBBC had been formed in 1930 in an attempt to "raise the standards of living, education and the general social structure to an equivalent of the white population … [It was also] recognized as the bargaining agent for all Indians on the coast."[9] Armytage-Moore was inducted into the NBBC in 1944 as an honorary member for the advocacy work that she had been doing since the 1930s with lawyer Tom Hurley (Fortney 2010, 82). Her connection to the project was instrumental in bridging the cultural gap and creating working relationships between the VCDJC and the NBBC. An undated and unsigned memo in the city archives' file on the Diamond Jubilee celebrations describes her as knowing "all about the North Shore Indians," noting that she had "studied them for a long time" and gone prospecting with them. It says that she was "very keen on having the Canadian Warriors Pageant."[10] It mentions her preferences for working with August Jack and the NBBC over Andy Paull and a man called Mathias (perhaps Mathias Joe). It also notes her associations with local politicians. The final page of *The Indian Village and Show*'s official program gives a further trace of Armytage-Moore's importance to the project. It lists the firms that helped with the project, gives a general thanks to all who contributed, and then specifically states, "And to Mrs. Maisie Armytage-Moore, Life Member of The Native Brotherhood, for her untiring effort toward the success of the Village."[11]

These archival records of the Vancouver Citizens' Diamond Jubilee Committee show their legitimizing of Armytage-Moore as a source of information and a bridge to creating working relationships with certain Indigenous people. These various positionings of Armytage-Moore show the importance of cross-cultural relationships and of broker figures – who could just as easily be Indigenous, as will be shown through Chief William Scow's actions. It is important to note, however, that her relationships are with "North Shore" and Northwest Coast Indigenous peoples but not, according to these documents, with Musqueam or Tsleil-Waututh peoples. Sharon Fortney's description of Armytage-Moore's work and legacy, "Entwined Histories: The Creation of the Maisie Hurley Collection of Native Art" (2010), confirms she had reciprocal relationships with many key Indigenous organizers (74).[12] As a Scottish woman who could also access class privilege through her heritage, who had the respect of local political figures through her legal work, and who was a member of the NBBC, she helped to connect the NBBC with a civic power source, the VCDJC.

Aaron Glass in his introduction to *Objects of Exchange: Material Culture, Colonial Encounter, Indigenous Modernity* (2010) recognizes the opportunity that such encounters – although acceptable to authorities because they were a "carefully circumscribed, aestheticized, and commodifiable production of the past ... [enacted] as one minor step toward modernization" – offered to First Nations people struggling with colonial modernity a "gap in colonial policy (however contradictory) may have created a space (however marginal) for social and cultural reproduction under new conditions of material flexibility and artistic freedom" (30). Armytage-Moore helped her Indigenous allies to exploit this gap in 1946 by co-organizing *The Indian Village and Show* and funding the publication of the *Native Voice* newspaper five months later (Fortney 2010, 82).[13]

A careful consideration of both *The Indian Village and Show*'s program, which had a print run of 10,000 and was sold at the site, and the printed set-design for the dance performances shows how the organizers alternated between satisfying the existing objectification of Indigenous cultures and accessing artistic freedom through performance choices, ultimately using this gap to create more space for First Nations people as subjects in their own right. The writing in the program alternates between invoking the salvage paradigm and emphasizing the living Indigenous people of Canada. Hiltz states in his foreword, "The Indian Village represents a dying culture of a truly great *Canadian* people. If it is allowed to disintegrate into an oblivious past it will be a great and irreplaceable loss to our *national* social structure. We then, are attempting to place these cultural arts on a basis of a *national individualism* as is enjoyed by *other nationalities in Canada* in the form of their traditional dances, songs and arts. Let us enjoy and appreciate these talents of an original people, respect their heritage and assist their hopes. THANK YOU, MR. AND MRS. CANADA" (italics added).[14] Hiltz's opening words configure this civic celebration as salvaging a dying culture within a nationalist framework. The next two pages immediately introduce the reader/viewer to the NBBC and the Native Sisterhood of British Columbia. The NBBC's history is reviewed as well as its aims, which as stated above mainly concerned standards of living and education. After an affirmation of these unobjectionable aims, there is also an assertion that the NBBC is the bargaining agent "for all Indians on the coast." Also introducing the NBBC are photos of Secretary Herbert Cook, President William Scow, and business agent Guy Williams, each dressed in a suit jacket and tie (see figure 3.7). Although there are no photos of the women, the next page of the program includes an acknowledgment of the Native Sisterhood, which acted to support the NBBC through "feeding and lodging during annual conventions," and mentions that its members did not, as yet, vote at the conventions. Next is a welcome reported as being from August Jack Khahtsahlano, also pictured, who is not in modern dress but wears what looks like a beaded headdress with one feather at the back. He has his arm raised to shade his face from the sun (see figure 3.8). He is described as the "host chief" of the event, and this greeting is printed in the program:

Welcome, my friends, this village *set once again upon the soil* where my Grandfather, Great Chief Khahtsahlano, did stand upon the shores of the blue sea beneath the snow-capped peaks of the mountains to behold the visiting Chiefs approach.

Welcome to where I did as a boy play with my Indian brothers and at the early age of nine became their Chief.

Welcome I now give you, as did my Grandfather give to his guests in ages not too distant past.

Let our White Brothers behold our friendship. Let happiness fill our hearts and theirs. Let us enjoy the beauty that abounds.

This was our land and now we share it with you. Feel secure there is enough for all.

I speak for my people and of my people. Welcome.[15] (italics added)

The salutation is a reminder of the Indigenous people who lived on the land where *The Indian Village and Show* was now set, although if read carefully,

Native Brotherhood of British Columbia

HERBERT COOK
Secretary

WM. SCOW
President

GUY WILLIAMS
Business Agent

The organization known as the Native Brotherhood of British Columbia is sixteen years old. Since its inception by four natives who stirred within themselves with conditions that existed which were withholding the progress of the Indian people, it has grown to be a powerful organization chartered as an incorporated group and recognized by the government as representing the native population of British Columbia.

ORIGIN

It was first given birth by Ambrose Reid, William Beynon, Heber Clifton and Alfred Adams. The latter, Alfred Adams, a Christian gentleman with high ideals and good principles, became its first president, which he remained until his death. He was followed in the presidency by William Scow, who at this time is carrying his organization forward in a manner which is a credit and example of leadership and good business. Previous to the

3.7   "Native Brotherhood of British Columbia" in *The Indian Village and Show*'s program.

the greeting does not state a specific nation's claim to the land. As noted in the previous chapter, Khahtsahlano's mother was Musqueam and his father was Squamish. Therefore, the use of the first-person plural possessive in the phrasing of "our land" could be interpreted as containing multiple nations. The program remarks attributed to Khahtsahlano make this point in a nonthreatening manner: "This was our land and we share it with you." Khahtsahlano was already a well-known public figure by this point. He had performed three years earlier at the Stanley Park rededication event detailed in the previous chapter and had been featured in newspapers.

Your Host

CHIEF KHAHTSAHLANO

Welcome, my friends, to this village set once again upon the soil where once my Grandfather, Great Chief Khahtsahlano, did stand upon the shores of the blue sea beneath the snow-capped peaks of the mountains to behold the visiting Chiefs approach.

Welcome to where I did as a boy play with my Indian brothers and at the early age of nine became their Chief.

Welcome I now give to you as did my Grandfather give to his guests in ages not too distant past.

Let our White Brothers behold our friendship. Let happiness fill our hearts and theirs. Let us enjoy the beauty that abounds.

This was our land and now we share it with you. Feel secure there is enough for all.

3.8   August Jack Khahtsahlano's welcome in *The Indian Village and Show*'s program.

The use of this site must also be contextualized within the Canadian history of land claims. Section 141 was added to the Indian Act in 1927, making land claims illegal, and would not be repealed until 1951. At the time of the Diamond Jubilee event in 1946, none of the local Indigenous peoples could legally engage in a dispute over the taking of the land, but marking it with their presence could serve other social and educational aims, once again creating an eddy through which intercultural communication had to flow.

Following this welcome is a poem by Blanche Muirhead Howard, "To My Indian Brother," which expresses the guilt of a settler enjoying "such loveliness which rightfully / Belongs to my Indian Brother" and calls for "equally sharing" the joys of the land in the future. Over the page from Howard's poem is a short, unsigned essay called "Word Sketch of the Indians of B.C.," which first positions the former dignity of "the Indian" and then creates a contrast: "Stripped of his hunting ground and his heritage we may see him labouring with pick and shovel in a modern trend alien to his ancestry ... [He] readily accepted [white man's] vices but acquitted few of their virtues." The author then moves on to describe a "modernized Indian" who is "willing to accept more of the responsibility for his own welfare. *The call to arms of two wars has not passed his ears unheeded* and from reports they made good soldiers and good citizens." The author then finishes, saying, "however they feel toward the *invaders of their land* ... one thing seems certain: that we stand before the dawn of a new era, a free people, democratic and sincere, in a land of hope and plenty" (italics added).[16]

A number of pages feature illustrations depicting a visual art exhibit at the site called "The Circle of Legends." Images illustrate what the organizers called the "pictorial word records" from Pauline Johnson's *Legends of Vancouver* (1911), including the place name stories of "The Two Sisters" and "Siwash Rock," discussed in chapter 1.[17] These images once again illustrate the grounded practice of using place names to assert Indigenous connection to land during a mega-event.

A little further are two pages that comprise a listing of the names of performers, dances, and the "visiting bands of the coast." The names are written using English-language orthography and do not correspond to current spellings.[18] The only names that are recognizable among the "Southern Dancers" are possibly Haatshalano and Swanomia, who may have been Khahtsahlano and his wife Swanamia. This could be an area of further inquiry that someone with better knowledge of the sounds of peoples' names and the genealogy of southern groups may be able to undertake.[19] There is, however, also an interesting note written on the inside front cover of the program by Matthews that comments on the spelling of the names as "all wrong" and urges the future researcher to "place no reliance in it whatever" (see figure 3.9). He calls it "awful 'stuff,'" saying that it was "got up by a scatterbrain."[20] The names, therefore, were not recognizable to a knowledgeable (and opinionated) contemporary settler either. The designer of the program may have been a settler appointed by the VCDJC who lacked the knowledge, resources, or relationships to represent the names accurately. The program editor is not credited, so it is

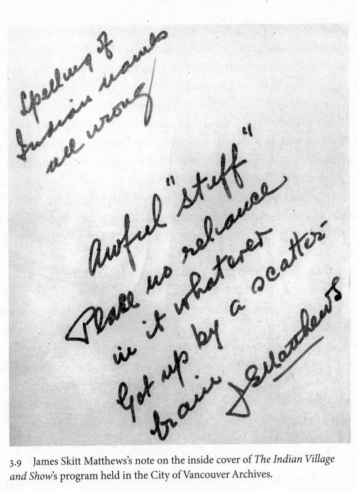

3.9　James Skitt Matthews's note on the inside cover of *The Indian Village and Show*'s program held in the City of Vancouver Archives.

unclear whether this is the case. It may also be that the names were given to the organizers by the NBBC, who were accessing knowledge that was not available to Matthews. Matthews's insertion of a note on the inside cover of the program in the archives, however, indicates once again the significance of naming, the type of knowledge that can be lost using English-language orthography to express Indigenous language names, and the archivist's willingness to insert his opinion in the archives. The NBBC was founded by northern Indigenous communities. However, by the 1940s there were a few branches in Coast Salish communities (O'Donnell 1985, 45). It is unclear, however, other than Khahtsahlano, which people from Musqueam, Tsleil-Waututh, and Squamish may have been involved in this event.

Overall, the program was working to disrupt settler assumptions. The NBBC organization, with its clearly identified officials in business attire, packaged its work in an understandable way. Placing this information about the organization between the nationalist salvaging of a dying culture in Hiltz's foreword and Khahtsahlano's clear visual and literary signification of Indigeneity and space, followed by settlers acknowledging wrongs done to Indigenous people and expressing hope for equality in the future, created a rupture in the dominant narrative of the "vanishing Indian" that was being expressed at *The Jubilee Show*. This program, with its large print run, acknowledgment of dancers and tribes, and careful preservation in the archives, was produced by the NBBC and its allies to document the events as an eddy of influence enhancing intercultural communication.

The Indian Village and Show: Media Coverage

Articles in the *Vancouver News-Herald* helped to publicize the event, naming the chiefs attending, focusing on the secret tribal dances and the "vague worries accompanying breaking the tradition of the elder chiefs," and explaining that the performers were missing out on their fishing season.[21] Misunderstandings involving the citizens' committee and the performers were also eagerly reported in the press. The VCDJC received a postcard written by Mrs Alice Colclough of View Royal, Vancouver Island, on 5 July after hearing a Vancouver news broadcast. She reported,

> Chief William Scow, the agent of the Indians attending and taking part in the Diamond Jubilee celebrations, had stated they were keenly hurt at the treatment they had received as for – standards of transport [and] accommodations. The clamour of the public – breaking into their village grounds instead of paying admission etc. That they had sacrificed by trading this for fishing at home. That they were playing on only because of their promise to make the governor general their Chief. I do beg of you to see that is an outstanding ceremony – Thus do all you can to make up to them for such serious [mistakes].[22]

The problems continued, and on 9 July a headline in the *News-Herald* read, "Disgruntled Indians May Quit Show."[23] The performers found that the transportation and accommodation costs were taken out of the pay they were expecting. This left them with almost nothing and no ability to return home. They also explained that "unless a more equitable settlement is reached, plans to make Viscount Alexander an honourary chief will have to be abandoned." The next day, the *News-Herald* reported that a settlement had been reached, the northern performers had returned home, and the show and ceremony would continue.[24]

The media surrounding the event are discussed in relation to art and resistance in Ronald Hawker's *Tales of Ghosts: First Nations Art in British Columbia, 1922–61* (2003):

> The local media appeared ready to follow a predictable pattern in promoting the village, but Scow and others led them in another direction. Thus, while Scow tantalized the public with the statement, "I can assure you the things our people will be bringing down with them have never been seen by white people," he also made certain that band names such as Owakalagalis, Pilnaquwilwakwas, Humchitt, Owad, and Nagaeselaq received top print billing. Scow, as a member of the Native Brotherhood leadership, was determined to make and control the First Nations presence at the jubilee. (117)

Hawker also notes that the dances were being performed at a time when the potlatch ban was still in effect, "prohibiting First Nations people from dancing off their own reserves." He theorizes that wearing modern urban clothing enabled the dancers to assert both their continuity with the past and their participation in contemporary life and that their presence "suggested that modernity and First Nations integrity were not mutually exclusive and that First Nations identities were more than touristic" (120). Hawker concludes that through this event, as well as the founding of the *Native Voice*, "First Nations art became attached to the Native Brotherhood's attempt to present First Nations individuals to the non-Aboriginal public as dignified, organized, and professional people" (121–2).

Hawker does not consider the implications of the physical bodies of performers at the particular site of Kitsilano Park. For my analysis of the event, the media uproar is also notable partly because of the awareness it brings to the physicality of the performers. It shows a transition. The performers were initially being treated as art objects that would not need anything beyond secure transport and a safe space to be viewed. Following the public voicing of their concerns, they were understood as people with the immediate needs of comfortable transport, accommodation, and food as well as the long-term needs of recompense for their expertise that would offset any time lost from their regular work. Their threat to abandon the ceremony for the governor general and the response – by at least one member of the concerned public, as demonstrated by Colclough's letter – show that the civic organizers of the Diamond Jubilee were also invested in the ceremony for Governor General Harold Alexander. The ceremony, which I return to later, was to serve multiple needs of legitimation. Moving on from the ways that the media record of the event shows the movement between object and subject, I now consider more carefully how the space of the performances, both the set design and the land itself, was also used to enact this shift.

Embodiment: Grounded Practices at səńaʔqʷ/Sen'ákw

The village site was open during the day for people to walk around and view "a traditional Indian way of life." In a letter to the vcdjc, Hiltz described the setting for *The Indian Village and Show* as well as the intended effects:

> A giant tom-tom measuring twenty (20) feet in diameter will be constructed in front centre of the Grand Stand, a narrow lip about the rim will conceale [sic] the lighting effects of various colors which will fold over the surface of the tom tom. [T]he side will be covered with giant masks and totem design painted in luminous paint, a circle of light four feet from this will flood these figures.
>
> Six thirty foot totem poles lean on an outward angle around the tom tom surmounted by giant Thunderbirds. These will also be painted in luminous paint, these should be visible from many parts of the city (an advertising advantage).
>
> ... Then will follow the fire dance[,] the mask dance and feature of features "THE INITIATION OF THE DANCER". These dances have never before been performed before white men. They are tribal and secret, but on this very special occasion will be presented.[25]

Hiltz's letter is notable for its description of the viewing opportunities that would be possible.[26] First, the description of the stage as shaped like a "giant tom-tom" effectively miniaturizes the performers. "Tom-tom" is a British word for a child's toy drum and could be considered part of a derogatory colonial perspective minimizing the importance of an Indigenous drum

(Native Languages of the Americas 2015). Making the stage a giant drum enables the performers to be viewed as portable souvenir objects seen as though from a distance – both through space and time. Hiltz is also aware of the dramatic opportunity of using light and darkness to highlight the secret nature of the dances. He describes using lights hidden on the interior lip of the stage as well as lights placed 4 feet (1.2 metres) out to illuminate the totem poles. The footlights illuminating the performers from below would add to the mysterious nature of the dances being performed, creating unusual shadows while focusing the viewer on the lower part of the dancers' bodies. The poles leaning at an outward angle could be seen as ancient poles that were deteriorating and about to fall or, particularly with the lighting effects, as looming and threatening to the spectators. Hiltz also envisioned the event in the context of the city skyline, wanting to create it on a scale that would be viewed from afar, attracting further attention as well as helping to brand the city.

The "giant tom-tom" is pictured in the program with four small dancers on it and described as a space where the "authentic" and "tribal secret" dances were enacted (see figure 3.10). Again, it emphasizes the restricted nature of the dances but highlights the power of the NBBC by explaining that they were being performed "on behalf of the efforts of the Native Brotherhood." It also notes that "the masks surrounding are copies of genuine museum pieces."[27] The reader – who may also be the spectator of the dances, although not necessarily – is briefly taken away from contemporary political concerns outlined in the preceding pages of the program and oriented instead toward the attraction of the restricted and authentic, before being returned to the political dimensions through the legitimization by the NBBC via museum culture.

The well-publicized ceremony involving Governor General Alexander planned for the final day of the installation at 9:30 p.m. was the climax of the legitimization of the NBBC at this event. The newly appointed governor general of Canada, who was a British field marshal and Second World War hero (Hillson 1952, 2), was made an honorary chief in a ceremony involving eighteen Indigenous Second World War veterans and twenty-five chiefs. The ceremony is described in full detail in the program and in the first edition of the *Native Voice*. Here, I quote at length significant elements of both descriptions and then suggest how they could have affected the viewers. In describing the ceremony, the program says,

The Giant Tom-Tom

On the Giant Tom-Tom are enacted the authentic dances of the Indians. These dances have never before been witnessed by the public. They have been tribal and secret and held very dear to the Indian. On behalf of the efforts of the Native Brotherhood they have agreed to do these dances at this time.

The masks surrounding the tom-tom are copies of the genuine museum pieces.

3.10   Description of the stage in *The Indian Village and Show*'s program.

His Excellency, on arriving at the Village, comes to the east gate. From behind a raised dais at the south side a procession consisting of eighteen torch-bearers, chosen braves[28] of the tribe who have served in World War II, followed by twenty-five chiefs in their full regalia, proceed to the east gate. A proclamation (upon their arrival at the east gate) is read by the Ceremonial Chief stating the desire that he become an Honorary Chief and the reasons for which he has been chosen. Then escorted by the chiefs, he advances to the dais. While the procession returns, Indian maidens rejoice and dance on the Giant Tom-Tom. Then, standing before the dais, His Excellency is robed and receives his headdress, ascends the dais to his seat, flanked

3.11   Chief William Scow and party confer an honorary chieftainship on Governor General Harold Alexander, 13 July 1946.

by all chiefs ... The entire ceremony is in native tongue. An interpreter will be supplied to analyse the entire procedure of the ceremonial dance and translate the Indian tongue.[29]

There are multiple photographs in the City of Vancouver Archives of Chief William Scow, president of the NBBC, presenting Alexander, in his military uniform, with ceremonial dress. In the photo of Scow reading the declaration, we can see that the NBBC prepared the declaration to be visible (see figure 3.11). It is written formally on a large piece of paper and decorated; it can be seen as a prop as well as the text of a political speech. Also, significantly, in light of my earlier assertion of the miniaturizing and distancing power of the "giant tom-tom" as a performance space, this political ceremony did not take place on that platform. Instead, the organizers built a raised dais on which their bodies would be seen as occupying coeval time and space with the governor general of Canada, who, as a war hero and a federal official representing the king of England, had a larger-than-life presence. The "Indian maidens," in rejoicing and dancing on the "giant

tom-tom," are marked as being of the past and having less status. The decision to use an Indigenous language[30] and have it translated would also have
an effect on the spectators. Why use two languages? A number of reasons
could have been at play: some of the attending Indigenous participants
might have been unilingual speakers of this language, so using it would
have been a mark of respect for them; it would also have initially distanced
the members of a settler audience, forcing them to concentrate on the
visuals, before moments later giving them an intelligible understanding;
or it could have been intended to highlight the attraction of the restricted,
which the NBBC had been employing in its publicity materials. This split-
ting of attention creates a moment when disruption of stereotypical views
can happen. The use of an Indigenous language and its translation could
also have operated as an opportunity to speak aloud in public one of the
languages that were being suppressed in residential schools; therefore, it
may also have been a method of knowledge transfer in line with Taylor's
(2003) conceptualization of repertoire. This ceremony was clearly carefully
organized for multiple purposes.

To understand some of the purposes more clearly, it is important to note
the social and political context of this event. The Second World War had
just ended, and postwar prosperity was beginning, along with a growing
belief in universal human rights due to the Allied powers' fight against
fascism. This belief resulted in a new willingness by the federal government to consider the plight of Aboriginal peoples in Canada. Moreover,
the Indigenous people who had fought in the war returned "with much
more sophistication about the ways of the world" (O'Donnell 1985, 47). In
1946 a special joint committee was appointed to revise the Indian Act, and
a delegation from the NBBC, including William Scow, appeared before the
committee in May 1947. The summer of 1946, however, had been marked
by discontent regarding unfair treatment of Indigenous war veterans, who
were not accorded the same benefits as white veterans, such as off-reserve
farmland or $2,300 grants to start a fishing business or build homes
(Government of Canada 1996). The multiple notes in the program about
Indigenous veterans as well as their physical participation as torchbearers
in this ceremony enabled the NBBC to bring their existence to the awareness
of the thousands of visitors to the site.

Later that year, in December 1946, Armytage-Moore and the NBBC
published the first edition of the *Native Voice*. The ceremony involving
Governor General Alexander is covered on the second page. A large photo

of Scow putting the Thunderbird headdress on the governor general's head accompanies the article summarizing the ceremony. The unidentified writer mentions that the ceremony was witnessed "by thousands of spectators, many of whom had waited hours" ("Governor General" 1946). The newspaper's description of the ceremony is similar to the one in the program: the "specially prepared dais" is noted, as are the tribal torchbearers. This unnamed writer mentions, however, that the governor general knelt before Chief Scow (see figure 3.12). The translated text of the speech that Scow gave is included at the end of the article, noting that eight BC chiefs had signed it:

> I hereby declare before the people assembled, the desire of the Indian people of the Brotherhood of British Columbia to confer the title of Honorary Chieftainship upon one –Viscount Alexander ... Governor General of Canada: whereby Viscount Alexander did conduct himself and proved himself as a great leader and a great warrior for the causes held dear to peaceful and democratic nations and *win the respect of the Indian peoples over which he did hold command in His Majesty's armed forces during World War II*, and did out of winning the gratitude and respect of the Indian peoples, earn for himself this, the highest honor the Indian Nation can give. From this thirteenth day of July, one thousand nine hundred and forty-six, you shall be known as Chief NAKAPUNKIM, "Great Warrior," and we, the undersigned, set our hand to witness that these things are so. Concurrent with the above, His Excellency – Viscount ALEXANDER, Governor General of Canada is duly registered with the Native Brotherhood of British Columbia as First Honorary Life President. ("Governor General" 1946, italics added)

This speech was read in an Indigenous language and translated, so even if any of the spectators had not read the notes in the program about the Indigenous veterans participating as the torchbearers, the words of the speech would have focused attention on the veterans, and if Scow chose to, he could have gestured to the men surrounding him.

Although it is not mentioned in either the program or the article, the governor general was presented with a totem pole carved by Mungo Martin over the duration of the event at the site (LeBlanc 1997, 2).[31] Hawker (2003) does note this gift in his analysis of the naming ceremony, calling it a

3.12   Governor General Harold Alexander being made an honorary chief named Nakapunkim by Chief William Scow at Kitsilano Beach, 13 July 1946. This is the same photo that accompanied the article reporting on the event in the *Native Voice* 1, no. 1 (1946): 2.

"physical reminder" that the honorary chieftainship, like the name Chief Nakapunkim, "was Martin's own prerogative" (118–19). Martin's physical presence while he carved, not just the fact that his work was presented to the governor general, also emphasized the continuing contemporary culture of which he was a part. But as a 1946 article shows, his presence could also have been viewed through the salvage paradigm: "As the eyes of hundreds of citizens at Kitsilano Indian Village Saturday night were fixed on the robed figure of the Governor General Alexander on the chief's dais or on the garish masks of native dancers on the giant tom-tom stage, a craftsman of a dying art was working within a few yards of them unnoticed."[32] It is possible that this observation was meant to praise Martin's work by contrasting it with what the writer (and perhaps others) considered the kitschy show biz of the "giant tom-tom."

Returning to the ceremony and dance performance, the *Native Voice* article contextualizes the nature of the dances being performed slightly differently: "The newly installed Chief, and incidentally the thousands of spectators, were treated to the spectacle of famous Indian secret dances never before performed before the eyes of white men. In fact, some of the dances were of such a secret nature that even many of the hundreds of Indians present had not witnessed nor had any previous knowledge of the stories or legends behind them as no written record in any language has ever been made" ("Governor General" 1946). This text supports John Comaroff and Jean Comaroff's assertion in *Ethnicity, Inc.* (2009) that "the producers of culture are *also* its consumers, seeing and sensing and listening to themselves enact their identity – and in the process, objectifying their own subjectivity, thus to recognize its existence, to grasp it, to domesticate it, to act on it and with it" (6, italics original). Likewise, Jennifer Kramer in her study of the contemporary Nuxalk engagement with the commodification of their art in *Switchbacks: Art, Ownership, and Nuxalk National Identity* (2006) identifies activities engaged in cultural tourism as a form of strategic essentialism and asserts that this tactic leads to regaining control, self-definition, and self-display. She concludes that "self-objectification can serve not only as a powerful force when reappropriated by Native peoples but also as an indispensable tool for identity construction and culture making – the prime ingredients in the cultural revival process" (50–1).

This text of the declaration and the events surrounding *The Indian Village and Show* helps to explain the NBBC's involvement. By bringing the Indigenous veterans into the chieftainship ceremony, the organization reminded the general public that these men had fought in the war under the governor general's command. By bestowing a chieftainship on him, the NBBC positioned itself as a political body that could give honours. And as Susan Roy (2002) suggests in her article on Musqueam culture and British Columbia's celebrations in 1966 to mark Canada's approaching Centennial, "Perhaps making White dignitaries 'Indian' was a way to symbolically incorporate non-Aboriginals into the Aboriginal community, transforming White politicians into pseudo-kin or inter-villagers with certain obligations and responsibilities" (83). These public performances of language, dances, and songs could also have helped to maintain the cultural continuation of the repertoire at a time when ceremonies were illegal. They may also have signalled that despite the ban on ceremony, Indigenous cultural activities were still strong.

Using available resources, the NBBC was searching for ways to have a large audience engage with issues of veterans' rights, living conditions, and more subtly, control of land. The founding of the *Native Voice* was one such attempt, as was the NBBC's decision to work with the VCDJC on the installation and performance as well as on the ceremony with the governor general. By agreeing to work within a cultural event and performance framework, the NBBC had more room to advance its agenda. In a performance, set design and translated speech can influence spectators in subtle ways, as can the presence of live performers. Among the living artists here were Mungo Martin as he carved, the performers of the "secret dances," and the war veterans as torchbearers. Recent theoretical work on Indigenous performance and cultural tourism informs considerations of these activities. Fred Myers in his introduction to *The Empire of Things* (2001) notes that the discussion of intercultural performances "ignore[s] the power of the exhibitionary gaze to impose identity, and the resulting stance still tends to dismiss intercultural productions of identity as complicitous ... Critics seem ambivalent about such practices, reflecting a continuing view of colonialism as absolutely determinative and of native peoples as merely victims or passive recipients of the actions of others" (52–3). Also arguing against a simple view of colonialism as "absolutely determinative," Paige Raibmon notes in "Theatres of Contact: The Kwakwaka'wakw Meet Colonialism in British Columbia and at the Chicago World's Fair" (2000) that "[s]urvival under colonialism *required* compromises. These compromises were not necessarily symptoms of cultural decline, and they could often be signs of cultural resiliency" (187, italics original).

Present but Incomplete:
William Scow's Copyright Assignment

Although a great deal is present in the city archives regarding *The Indian Village and Show*, the absence of photographs and responses to performances of the dances seems to be a gaping hole. As mentioned above, however, while researching *The Jubilee Show*, I came across a document assigning copyright of "Indian Ceremonial Dances" to Chief William Scow, as well as copies of the photos themselves.[33] At first I was stunned to find them in what I thought was the wrong file. The photos depict a multi-age gathering of exclusively Indigenous people in a wooden structure (perhaps a Big House). There are photos of masked performers on the ground and up on a raised platform as well as photos of spectators. They seem to show that the "giant tom-tom" was not used as the site of performance and that there were more Indigenous spectators than settlers. In investigating the photos, I learned from Karen Duffek (2012), curator of Contemporary Visual Arts & Pacific Northwest at the University of British Columbia's Museum of Anthropology, that the masks and gestures shown indicate that they were of a Kwakwaka'wakw dance, the Atłakïm. She also suggested I read Chief Robert Joseph's account of dancing the Atłakïm as a child in *Down from the Shimmering Sky: Masks of the Northwest Coast* (1998). His essay recounts his experience of the dance that was interrupted at Gilford Village: "My memory fails me somewhat, for I was then a little boy. My next recollection is that we reassembled in the Big House, still in full dress for the Atłakïm, posing for photographs. I remember a policeman in uniform being there. No charges were laid, even though the anti-Potlatch statute was still in effect. My people were operating covertly to sustain their traditions, values and beliefs to which the mask is so integral" (26). This account is illustrated by two of the photographs taken that night. One of them, from the British Columbia Archives, is exactly the same as one of the "Indian Ceremonial Dance" photos that Chief Scow purchased from the VCDJC. Clearly, the photos I had found were not of *The Indian Village and Show* but instead of the interrupted dance at Gilford Village, which also took place in 1946. Further correspondence with Martha Black (2012), curator of Ethnology at the Royal BC Museum, revealed more information on the photos from their description in the archives: "copy of a print owned by William Scow of Alert Bay. He claims that it was taken by a policeman at a dance at Gilford in 1946. This is not a potlatch, but rather a public dance program ... Photographs taken inside Scow house." The question now arises, why did the VCDJC own the copyright to these photos? Had someone from the citizens' committee gone to see the dances and taken the photo? Had they been given to the committee as an artifact? Had they been part of the display during the installation? It makes sense that Scow wanted the copyright in order to be able to control the circulation of the photos, particularly since the dances may have had Kwakwaka'wakw cultural restrictions and were also still outlawed by Canadian federal law. The assignment purchase price of $1 indicates that it was a legal formality, not a commodity purchase, and also indicates a degree of acknowledgment of his rightful ownership by the VCDJC.

Conclusion: Decolonization through Imaginative Space

As a result of this copyright assignment, I began to reconsider the absences in the city archives regarding *The Indian Village and Show*. Perhaps there are no records of the script or photos of the performance due to an exertion of restriction orchestrated by the NBBC leadership. This consideration would tell a very different story of the colonial archive and of the knowledge that passes through the repertoire. The "secret dances" so promoted in publicity materials had been outlawed and were therefore under stress because it was more difficult to pass on the knowledge. They may also not have been "secret" dances but instead some that were allowed to be performed at intercultural public events. The dancers may also have used the gathering as an opportunity to exchange knowledge while they were not publicly performing. Perhaps the NBBC chose to organize performers for the dances in order to continue to pass on the repertoire of ceremonial dances, while working with non-Indigenous allies in the citizens' committee to uphold cultural restrictions through the control of photos. Textual evidence for public consumption was produced and preserved through the program, but either visual evidence through photographs was not produced or, if it was, the preservation has been restricted. Another clue that the NBBC was interested in promoting the dancing is the identity of the dance announcer, Chief Dan Cranmer.[34] Cranmer was the host of the infamous potlatch held twenty-five years before this event, in 1921, at which many participants were arrested and some were imprisoned for their unwillingness to surrender their dance regalia. The relinquished items were then sold to museums in the United States and Canada (Hawker 2003, 17–33).[35] Cranmer was a

Kwakwaka'wakw leader and also a public figure who embodied a public defiance of the potlatch ban.

Taking time to consider the absences in the city archives regarding this event is intended to create a pause in my analysis in order both to focus on what is absent from the archive of *The Indian Village and Show* and to think creatively about why some things might not be there. My aim is not to discount what is available in the archive but to acknowledge the biases that helped to create it (as detailed extensively in chapter 2) and the powers that may have kept things from inclusion.

As a performative event that celebrated the sixtieth anniversary of the city of Vancouver, *The Indian Village and Show* contrasted greatly with *The Jubilee Show* by featuring Indigenous people who were not only modern, politically engaged cultural producers but also knew that settler curiosity about their culture could be a source of power for them. Alongside the narrative of Indigenous *displacement* and settler *emplacement* that was being performed in *The Jubilee Show* at Brockton Point nightly, there was a counter-narrative being performed twice daily during the same period to the south around the peninsula and across the bay in Kitsilano Park. Thus the VCDJC failed to create a single large-scale narrative of the city's history in *The Jubilee Show*. That the citizens' committee revised the script and commissioned the NBBC, a mainly northern-based pan-tribal organization, to put on *The Indian Village and Show* suggests that it already had some doubt that such a historical narrative could exist. A further initiative three years after the Diamond Jubilee also shows this ambivalence. In 1949 the new mayor, Charlie Thompson, who had been part of the VCDJC, formed the Totem-Land Society with members of City Council, former committee member Harry Duker, Maisie Armytage-Moore, and members of the NBBC to work on branding Vancouver as "Totem-Land."[36] The sole surviving document from this society is a letter regarding finding the exact location of a midden and posting signage,[37] an attempt to re-place Indigenous history within the urban landscape (Phillips 2000, 51–4).[38] The municipally controlled VCDJC, while staging a colonial narrative of the city that glorified settlers in Stanley Park, also attempted to work with an Indigenous political organization that strategically performed some elements of its members' cultural heritage in order to maintain a presence and to influence the future. It is notable, however, that the citizens' committee did not ask local Indigenous people from Musqueam, Tsleil-Waututh, and Squamish to host the show. That may have been because their claim to the land, although

not legally recognized, would have been too legitimate. The NBBC may also
have been chosen because of the size of this organization and its ability to
gain support from across the province.

The land on which *The Indian Village and Show* was staged has continued to be a space of historical performance in many ways. It is the
location of the City of Vancouver Archives, the Planetarium and Museum
of Vancouver, the Maritime Museum, and the summer Bard on the Beach
Shakespeare Festival. It is also a space that has electrified the discussion of
Indigenous land use in urban space. Since the 2002 decision that awarded
a fraction of it to the Skwxwú7mesh Nation, the people of that nation have
had to decide what to do with the valuable land. A few months before the
2010 Winter Olympics juggernaut descended on the city, the Skwxwú7mesh
Nation erected a massive double-sided electronic billboard on the west
side of the Burrard Bridge, which, along with three other billboards on
their North Shore lands, will generate millions of dollars over multiple
years ("Electronic Billboards" 2009). The outcry from neighbours was
predictable, mainly concerning the blocking of expensive views by the
unsightly advertising, yet the project went ahead. Of more interest to me,
particularly given *The Indian Village and Show*'s use of art for political
intervention, is the *Digital Natives* (2011) project that made use of the
electronic billboards near Burrard Bridge. For one month, interspersed
with the ads for large corporations and appearing for ten-second intervals
were 140-character messages, some in Skwxwú7mesh, Kwak'wala, and
hən̓q̓əmin̓əm̓. These numerous messages glowed either in white text on a
red illuminated background or in red text on a white background against
the grey Vancouver sky. One of the messages, "Dukwida'masixwa 'kikw? /
Can you see the Totem Pole?" is attributed to Kwakwaka'wakw artist and
scholar Marianne Nicolson. She explains that it was an effort to play with
ideas about the existing copy of a Mungo Martin totem pole outside of the
Maritime Museum and about the billboard itself as a mimicking of the
"Pacific Coast Aboriginal public declaration of rank and ownership traditionally expressed by the 'totem pole,'" as well as an effort to acknowledge
the awkward and disputed practice of having "Kwakwaka'wakw art in Coast
Salish territory" (quoted in Brown 2011, 53). Nicolson's message also seems
appropriate to consider as a reference to *The Indian Village and Show*, a
briefly luminous performative intervention of strategic grounded practices
organized by the NBBC on Indigenous land and conducted within textual
and visual parameters.

That the work of the NBBC continues to be an inspiration to performers is discussed in the following section about Marie Clements's *The Road Forward* (2013). In chapter 4, I also revisit the work that performers do in forging connections with land, only this time with reference to more explicit cooperation between a provincial Indigenous organization and local Indigenous peoples, returning to the site of xʷay̓xʷəy̓.

Iterations of Marie Clements's
The Road Forward

Indigenous performances staged for large-scale spectacles or international festivals and those that circulate as film on the Internet can
be ripe sources of information about embodied performance and
heritage transmission that are concurrently expressive of local voices
and intended to influence global cultural flows. In this section, I explore
some iterations and phenomenological dimensions[1] of a performance
event that has circulated in each of the aforementioned formats, Marie
Clements's *The Road Forward*.

At the Aboriginal Pavilion on the final day of the 2010 Winter
Olympics in Vancouver, *The Road Forward*, a musical performance
installation created and directed by Clements, composed by Jennifer
Kreisberg, and choreographed by Michael Greyeyes, was performed
six times for the international audiences attending this mega-event.
The technical rehearsal for this performance was also filmed. Clements
then developed it into an award-winning music video, which circulated
to sixteen film festivals in North America and Europe (PuSh 2013, 2).
In February 2013 at Vancouver's PuSh International Performing Arts
Festival, Clements and Michelle St John's company, red diva projects,[2]
developed a full-length "Aboriginal blues/rock multi-media musical"
(PuSh 2013, 2) that was performed one night only at Club PuSh and
subsequently remounted for a three-night run during the 2015 PuSh
Festival.[3] Clements then worked with the performers of these events and
the descendants of the earlier activists to produce the musical documentary film *The Road Forward* (2017).[4] A full analysis of all five iterations
is beyond the scope of this intervention, and although I refer to the 2010
music video, I mainly discuss the 2013 live performance.

The program for this event, designed as though it were a replica of
the Native Brotherhood of British Columbia's newspaper, the *Native
Voice*, explicitly connects the performance with activist work done by
the Native Brotherhood and Native Sisterhood of British Columbia from

the 1930s to the 1970s.[5] The program also links their activist work with
that of the grassroots Constitution Express of the 1980s and the contemporary Idle No More movement.[6] In her program notes, Clements says,
"*The Road Forward* was <u>and</u> is an opportunity to create something that
can *sing* inside an audience – the possibility to place this little known
history inside *our collective voice* ... not just so we get to know it, but so
that we get to understand it is a part of ourselves ... so that it can make
us stand taller, appear bigger, move forward understanding that creating
change for the better is a long tradition" (PuSh 2013, 3, italics added).

The events and film present the singers and musicians in a self-
expressive virtuosic performance mode as they sing compositions that
integrate traditional and contemporary music while also performing in
a representational mode as historical personae to bring attention to local
Indigenous histories. Projections of archival documents also aided in the
re-presenting of these histories. During the PuSh Festival, the projections expanded to include a live streaming of video and a Twitter feed.
These elements allowed for a collaborative performance mode, asserting
the contemporary connections to the heritage of the absent activists
and ancestors. All iterations use "frontside" characters along with both
simultaneous and alternating exposures of the "backside" singers, actors,
and activists, which Bert States (2007) has described as deliberate
phenomenological frames of perception whose combination demonstrates theatrical collaboration through the "the drama of presence and
absence" (28). I assert that Clements's *The Road Forward* responds
to pressures of globalization to package one-dimensional historicized
Indigenous characters by instead circulating uncontained, continuing
identities presented through the use of modalities of performance that
insist on affective connections and historical "inter(in)animation[s]"
with the present and future (Schneider 2011, 7).

Before I begin my analysis of the 2013 performance, I would also like
to link this work with some of Rebecca Schneider's ideas of performativity and historical reenactment, referred to in chapter 2's discussion
of James Skitt Matthews's rededication reenactments in Stanley Park.
Schneider (2011) explains the significance of affect, noting that it usefully
resists the binary in which performance studies still gets mired (e.g., text
versus embodied gesture or live versus recorded performance). Affect (or
feeling/emotion) is situated in between; it is sticky and jumps between
bodies and time, moving us. She connects this phenomenon to the

Deleuzian "assemblage" used "to unsettle the rootedness of identity, to gesture not only to mobility but also to the always already *crossingness*, or *betweeness*, or *relationality* of the sets of associations that make up something resembling identity" (35–6, italics original). Attention to affect then leads to a notion of "temporal drag" (14) and temporal reach, the idea that time is flexible, not linear, and that the past can be dragged into the present even as the present also reaches into the future, which contributes to the "interaction or inter(in)animation of one time with another" (31).

Although *The Road Forward* is not exactly a historical reenactment, these terms are useful for thinking about how the performance revives history and connects it with the present. In the music video, the performance includes women dressed in 1950s-style costumes, evoking The Supremes, and combines the *frontside* (onstage) view with the *backside* (in the darkened room). The glowing orb that floats throughout the song showing archival images also haunts it. As the song progresses, the viewer can see that during the 2010 performance the archival images were projected on the dome of the Aboriginal Pavilion and that these images are what the performers are singing and raising their hands to.

I first isolate moments of the various performative modes in the 2013 production and then identify how they each contribute to the *temporal drag* that cross-constitutes the present artists/activists with their ancestors. I use this to connect with the significance of the music in the reenactment of the past through the archival images.

The singers in the 2013 production had a strong self-expressive presence. The ensemble sang eighteen songs, ten of which had lyrics by Marie Clements and were mainly composed by Jennifer Kriesberg and/or Wayne Lavallee. Two songs were covers. One was the Native American band Redbone's 1974 hit "Come and Get Your Love," described by band leader and contributing composer Mwalim (Morgan) James Peters as "a tribute to REDBONE and Vegas Lolly, as well as a statement about Idle No More being all about NDN [Indian] and [F]irst Nation People getting our love/ what we are entitled to!" (Peters 2013). The other cover was of Labelle's 1975 disco hit "Lady Marmalade." These songs allow the singers, St John and Kreisberg along with Cheri Maracle, to soar and show off a range and vocal power that makes me aware of their presence as supremely talented people. As Peter Dickinson (2013) wrote in his blog, *Performance, Place, and Politics*, they were the "vocal soul" of a "galvanizing evening."

This focus on the women's voices also underscored the intention to honour the women activists of the Native Sisterhood, to memorialize missing and murdered Aboriginal women, and to connect with the powerful women of Saskatoon who had spurred the Idle No More movement and with Chief Teresa Spence, whose six-week hunger strike had ended only a week prior to this performance. The strength of all these women's voices was represented in St John's, Kriesberg's, and Maracle's performances. The artistry of these women singers and the other musicians overtly commanded the audience's attention, and the performers did not fully disappear into their roles. So although they were costumed to evoke a past era, with some of the musical choices as well as the projected archival materials also supporting this pastness, their self-expressive *presence* kept asserting *the present*.

Another way that we were kept aware of the present moment was through the use of the multiple collaborative performance elements by which Clements shifted awareness back and forth between the audience and performers. The Club PuSh performance space was set up cabaret-style, and most of the audience space was made up of chairs surrounding small tables, encouraging audience members to be aware of each other and to interact. The show opened with people coming in through the audience while singing and drumming. Chief Ian Campbell (aka Xàlek or Sekyú Siýam), of the Squamish Nation, sang a canoe journey song, and then an unidentified older man spoke words of welcome in hən̓q̓əmin̓əm̓, which he also translated into English. Thus, following welcoming protocols, the opening made a direct connection to our presence on Coast Salish lands and indicated that this intra-nation Indigenous performance was also a grounded practice. The performative mode here was one of direct connection between the speakers and witnesses.

In a further effort to unsettle the usual performer-audience viewing perspective, after the musicians entered and started an instrumental opening to the show, a projection of three women in a dressing room lit up a large frame-style hand drum propped up at the front of the stage. At first, it was unclear whether this was recorded footage or live-streamed. The women were fixing their makeup in a mirror and putting finishing touches on their costumes. The music mounted as they got ready, left the dressing room, and made their way through the building to the backstage area with their images still projected on the drum. We started to hear them singing, and then finally they burst onto the stage. Like the placement of the seating and the opening welcome songs, this detail focused us on the stage as a space of performance and then, as the singing started, folded us back into our roles as audience members.

The closing images returned to this mode. As the evening started to wind up, ushers circulated through the audience giving out 3D glasses. The images were then projected in 3D as more performers came onstage – and everyone sang some unidentified West Coast–style traditional songs.[7] While this was going on, the drum, which had been used as a screen on and off throughout the show, now had a live Twitter stream projected onto it. It took me a while to understand that the tweets were from other audience members. I was distracted by the tweets at first, and then I realized that, like the 3D archival and contemporary images that floated behind the professional and amateur performers as they sang traditional and contemporary music, the tweets were another assertion of live continuity. It is also significant that this was happening at a time when #Idle No More was all over the twitter-sphere and given that the movement had been mentioned repeatedly during the evening, connecting the current activism with the historic work. This use of projected images also brings to mind Schneider's (2011) assertions, quoting Walter Benjamin, about the "'future that subsists' in the condition of the still" (161). Schneider suggests that the "future subsists not only *in* the photo but *through* the 'we' who look to 'rediscover it' as 'still' – 'still' in the sense of the term that signifies remaining, more than silence and motionlessness" (162). These layered moments of performance as the event concluded brought the collapse of the present and the historical to a crescendo.

Just before this finale, there was a moment that made particularly powerful use of the representative performance mode, which had been balanced with the self-expressive and collaborative modes throughout the night. A major focus of the work, as mentioned, was to represent historical archival material through the use of costume, images, and most significantly for the next example, song lyrics.

Ronnie Dean Harris (aka Ostwelve) sang a song based on the words of a speech by George Manuel, a šəxʷepməx leader influential in Canadian

and international Indigenous organizing. Manuel was instrumental in the
national organizing against the 1969 White Paper,[8] and internationally
he was involved in the creation of the United Nations Declaration on
the Rights of Indigenous Peoples, adopted in 2007.[9] He also coordinated
support to ensure the protection of Aboriginal rights within the Canadian
Constitution as a major organizer of the Constitution Express (Hanson
2009c; Manuel 2015, 65–75). Ostwelve's song was called "If You Really
Believe." It was a hip hop iteration of a 1979 speech by Manuel (Union of
British Columbia Indian Chiefs 1979); the song lyrics repeatedly asserted
Manuel's words: "If you really believe that education for our children (or
health care, or housing ...) is our right ... you don't ask for it ... [Y]ou
take it." Ostwelve's performance was riveting, aggressive, and emotional.
He held his lower body still and stared straight out at the audience,
and then with the hand that held his drum, he slowly gestured at the
group of people watching him as he addressed us directly. His skill as a
self-expressive performer was on display as he presented Manuel's speech,
thereby connecting our present with this past through affect.

As Clements herself points out in the program, the event was a "fusing
of ink and voice" (PuSh 2013, 2). She is playing with words here as she
discusses the influential newspaper the *Native Voice* and the voices of the
singers and artists encountered at the event. Her choice of the musical as
the form through which to express this history is significant. Song and
music, as Helen Gilbert and Joanne Tompkins point out in *Post-Colonial
Drama: Theory, Practice, Politics* (1996), can be "'detached' from the theatre event by the audience to live on after the performance's conclusion
when the audience retells or resings parts of the theatrical presentation
as an act of memory" (194). Music can also be a powerful transmitter of
intense emotional affect. And even more significant to my consideration
here of the chiasmatic meeting of the present with the past when playing
music, Schneider (2011) points out that playing music is not only a form
of mimetic representation but also a *making* of music. It is both action
and representation, being "the beloved and often discussed conundrum
of theatricality in which the represented bumps uncomfortably (and
ultimately undecideably) against the affective, bodily instrument of the
real" (41). So as the musicians, singers, and artists performed, inspired
by the Native Brotherhood and the Native Sisterhood, whether they were
performing original compositions or those based on texts of activist

ancestors or even covers of 1970s pop songs, they were always in the present tense, expressing emotion in a way that had the potential to travel with audience members out of the venue and into the future.

The various iterations of Marie Clements's *The Road Forward* have garnered global attention, including now their discussion in this book. The dense layering of self-expressive, collaborative, and representational performance modes in a musical format successfully *inter(in)animates* the activist continuum of Indigenous peoples – those alive, working, and performing right now, along with generations of their ancestors and descendants to come. The significance of this layering lies not just in its assertion of a continuing presence against the uninformed view that Indigenous peoples of the Americas have tragically vanished; rather, although this assertion is (unfortunately, tiresomely) still necessary at times, the layering evident in Clements's *The Road Forward* is also significant for demonstrating the effectiveness of using various phenomenological performance modes to fold time. The 2013 production of *The Road Forward* briefly opened a place where the people posing and looking at the camera in old photos or the writers who committed their ideas to paper could be understood to have been active in their own time even as their eyes and words were reaching toward the future, ready for the audience's gaze to reanimate them. The presence of these archival works floating through the air (in 3D!) while the singers performed history through songs passed on by a physical repertoire blended Indigenous and Western historiographic methods, layering and balancing them in such a way that neither the present nor the past took precedence. Times co-existed, depending on which mode audience members chose to access.

Besides being an entertaining and inspiring evening that brought people together to collaborate, *The Road Forward*'s reenactment of the past through the archival images in the context of the Idle No More movement also demonstrates how this kind of *inter(in)animation* can be part of a revolution. In this time of resurging activity and strength, connecting with the power of those who have passed, not merely by understanding the historical facts of their activities but also by summoning their presence, will contribute to the forward momentum through *temporal reach*. To complete my discussion of this work, I return to the song "The Road Forward" and quote a few lines:

I feel you beside me, I know your name.
I hear your voice becoming ours, it is the same...
I feel your breath, I know your pain, I hear you cry.
We carry the load together, you and I.

The words themselves are powerful, and I feel a bit of chill as I write them out, responding to the summoning to carry the load together. I hope that my reader is also similarly affected.

Indigenous Performative Interventions at Klahowya Village

On a hot day in late July 2010, I walked through an area of Stanley Park, the 1,000-acre public park in downtown Vancouver, with some youth participants of an exchange program I was co-hosting between East Vancouver and Fort Good Hope, Northwest Territories.[1] We had stopped on our way to a picnic lunch at the beach for the northern youth to have a chance to see some huge West Coast trees. After we passed the aquarium, the sign for Klahowya Village caught our attention. Just behind it, Coast Salish iconography decorated the entranceway, a false wall of a longhouse made up of cedar planks with two large cut-outs of red hands upraised in a gesture of thanks and welcome – the logo of the Aboriginal Tourism Association of British Columbia. I had heard of the recently opened tourist attraction, but we had not planned to bring our visitors to the site. However, they were interested, so we walked through, stopping to rest beside a carver working on a tree stump. He engaged some of us in conversation, and when he learned that our group was participating in a youth exchange, he decided to perform a ceremony with us. He had us join hands in a circle around the stump he was working on and explained that he wanted us to help him connect with the spirit of the wood. A singer in costume danced and drummed as we circled and sang along. As the song ended, he asked us all to lay our hands on the wood. Then we packed up and went on our way.

I was left feeling ambivalent. I did not understand what I had just experienced. I am wary of much of the cultural tourism that happens in Vancouver's public spaces and suspicious of the commodification of Indigeneity. We had not been asked to pay any money for our experience, but offered for sale were artisan-made cedar bark hats, dreamcatchers, and bentwood boxes, as well as tickets to ride the Spirit Catcher Train. I did not know where the performers and artists at the village had come from or who was paying them to be there, yet our interactions with them were positive. I felt uncomfortable and wanted to know why.

This chapter is a result of my trying to understand the source of this discomfort.[2] Here, I argue that the presence of performing artists at this culturally significant site in Vancouver –metres from χʷay̓χʷəy̓ and, as detailed in chapter 2, a diligently assembled public archival site – asserts a limited form of what Seneca film scholar Michelle Raheja (2010) terms "visual sovereignty." Raheja has described this practice in the context of Indigenous filmmaking as one that addresses settler populations through the use of stereotypical self-representations while connecting to aesthetic practices that strengthen treaty claims and more traditional cultural understandings by revisiting, borrowing, critiquing, and stretching ethnographic conventions (19, 193).[3] Encountering the stereotypes employed in this process could have been one source of the discomfort I felt, as could my venturing into an unsettling space inflected by colonial conventions. Expanding on Raheja's analysis of *visual sovereignty* in Indigenous filmmaking to consider the performative aspects of a live event, I show how the grounded practices of the performers at Klahowya Village created eddies of influence within the layered archival architecture of this tourist space.

Diana Taylor (2003) distinguishes between the archive, which she argues is generally misconceived as unmediated records that work across distance, space, and time to preserve memory, and the repertoire, which "requires presence: people participate in the production and reproduction of knowledge by 'being' there, being a part of the transmission" (19–20). She asserts that the repertoire is equally important as "a system of learning, storing, and transmitting knowledge," noting that the archive and the repertoire exist in a constant state of interaction, thereby expanding what we understand as knowledge (16, 21). To access this knowledge, Taylor develops a methodology of focusing on the "scenario," which draws attention to the repertoire by emphasizing the power of performance to transmit knowledge, social memory, and identity (28–33). As stripping away knowledge containing social memory and identity has been one of the methods employed in the colonial process to eliminate Indigenous people's culture – a process exemplified by the Indian residential school system in Canada – the use of the repertoire to transmit that knowledge is an important means of recuperating Indigenous subjectivities. My intention is to explore not only how Indigenous people resist colonialism in the present but also how Indigenous knowledge is transmitted through performances that do not depend on the colonial archive. I also contend that the *visual sovereignty* asserted in this space creates a new archive to interact with this repertoire.

Focusing on multiple modes of performance observed over seven site visits in the summer of 2012, I examine the *scenario* of touristic encounter layered into the village, taking into account the physical location and historical context of Indigenous performance in this region. This focus on the *scenario* illuminates the knowledge transmission that occurs through the embodiment of social actors and the use of formulaic structures that predispose certain outcomes while also allowing for reversal, parody, and change. I also consider the implications of what non-Indigenous people might consider "aberrant" cultural practices during a live performance as opposed to a film (Raheja 2010, 204). Following Taylor's (2003) emphasis on the repertoire and the archive as not being sequential or binary (22) and using Raheja's notion of *visual sovereignty* to analyze the site design of the tourist village as an intervention in the colonial archive, I demonstrate how Klahowya Village presents an enterprise that asserts sovereignty while enabling some intra-nation Indigenous transfer of knowledge, although it is also structurally limited as a site of Indigenous critique of settler society due to its status as a touristic spectacle.

A Coast Salish Genealogy of Cultural Performance

Settler government policy in Canada and British Columbia has a long history of funding cultural projects to capitalize on Aboriginal tourism, dating back to the early days of European settlement. One commentator asserts, "Young people today are not able to find employment because they are not trained for new fields in business life ... Indian young people, by reviving old native arts, will find a profitable trade in the tourist industry" (quoted in Dawn 2008, 12). These words could easily be from a recent news conference, but they are not. The speaker is R.A. Hoey, head of Welfare and Training at Indian Affairs, who came to Vancouver in 1938 to announce the federal government's new policy regarding First Nations art. Whereas the government had outlawed traditional *ceremonial* practices in the late nineteenth century, it began at this point to encourage traditional *artistic* practices for economic uses. Although not explicitly articulated in government policy, the fact that performances were banned whereas visual arts were encouraged is an indication that performance had the power to unsettle colonialist operations. As discussed above, the potlatch ban was enacted in 1884, thirteen years after the colony of British Columbia joined Confederation, and it remained in force until 1951 even though Indigenous groups publicly resisted its strictures through petitions such as the one signed by Coast Salish people in 1910 (Shaw and Campbell 2013a, 165). As Dawn (2008) explains, the 1938 policy has been considered the spur that started a postwar revival in Indigenous art production, but it was already flourishing. Instead, the policy helped to change the audiences for that cultural production from Indigenous to non-Indigenous people and recontextualized its tangible creations within museums as aesthetic objects that were consumable commodities, "divorced from cultural meanings" (43).

This policy may have been influential in the Native Brotherhood of British Columbia's involvement in the 1946 celebrations of Vancouver's Diamond Jubilee, discussed in chapter 3. Centennial celebrations have also been a recurring site of Indigenous cultural performance. Susan Roy (2002) positions the Musqueam people's involvement in British Columbia's 1966 celebrations to mark Canada's approaching Centennial, including their enactment of a warrior dance at a totem pole raising in Tsawwassen, south of Vancouver, as performing resistance to settler efforts to culturally homogenize all BC First Nations people. She also examines their decision to use sχʷayχʷəy dance in a ceremony making a mayor into a chief, which she reads as strategic: "[I]f we understand politics to encompass the strategies employed by Aboriginal communities to further their existence, visibility, and recognition as nations, then other activities (such as the display of expressive culture) can also be understood as political strategies ... Cultural performance makes the connection between people and place visible, tangible, and, it is hoped, memorable" (90). Roy's observations support the idea that performances were banned because of their usefulness as political strategy and their ability to unsettle. Indigenous cultural performances continued to be supported by governments and used strategically by First Nations groups in this region throughout the twentieth century and into the twenty-first, the most internationally visible taking place during the opening ceremony of the 2010 Winter Olympics and in the accompanying Cultural Olympiad.

As discussed briefly in chapter 1, a significant element of the plans made by the Vancouver Organizing Committee for the 2010 Olympic and Paralympic Winter Games (VANOC) was the negotiated involvement of some Indigenous groups and the creation of the Four Host First Nations (FHFN) organization to officially represent the Lil'wat, Musqueam, Squamish, and Tsleil-Waututh people on whose territories the events were being held. Their involvement and representation were intended to ensure economic benefit to these First Nations groups, while legitimating the Olympic movement's social impact (Silver, Meletis, and Vadi 2012, 294). Christine O'Bonsawin (2010) asserts that the 2010 Winter Olympics influenced the modern treaty process by motivating the government to settle with First Nations on whose land a major ferry dock would be built in order to avoid disruption in transportation, adding that the process also "encourage[d] First Nations communities ... to develop tourist centres with the purpose of promoting Indigenous cultures" (151–2). Her assertions make explicit the connections between land, political negotiations of power, and performative events at this time and in this space.

During the opening ceremonies of the Winter Olympics, members of the FHFN entered immediately after the national anthem in full regalia, speaking words of welcome in their own languages while four massive welcoming statues with arms outstretched rose from the stage. The spectacle then expanded to include hundreds of Aboriginal people from across Canada who danced in the arena throughout the hour-long parade of the athletes (olympicvancouver2010 2010). The games also featured an Aboriginal Pavilion that showcased 232 performances,[4] as well as the film *We Are Here*, projected on the inside of the dome (VANOC 2010, 85, 82). Of the hundreds of events staged during the Cultural Olympiad, twenty-one were categorized by VANOC as Aboriginal, including two original plays. Bruce Ruddell's musical *Beyond Eden* dramatized Canadian artist Bill Reid's 1957 expedition to recover totem poles in Ninstints on Haida Gwaii, and Marie Clements's *The Edward Curtis Project* recontextualized the work of renowned photographer Edward Curtis by imagining him in dialogue with a contemporary Indigenous journalist who is trying to deal with the traumatic deaths of two young children (Couture 2010). The work done by the FHFN organization during the Winter Olympics was in keeping with the genealogy of ongoing federally and provincially funded projects (mentioned above) to increase Aboriginal tourism. Since 1997 a closely related organization, Aboriginal Tourism of British Columbia (ATBC),[5] has been offering training, resources, and networking to First Nations entrepreneurs and communities working in the tourism business (Aboriginal Affairs and Northern Development Canada 2009; "Shaping the Future" 2019). For five years, Klahowya Village was one of ATBC's projects and clearly a genealogical descendant of governments' past promotions of Aboriginal tourism for economic stability and its use as a political strategy for First Nations groups, which includes performances of grounded practices.

Archive: Context, Site, Naming, and Space

One part of the strategy was the rebranding of the site on which Klahowya Village was located. In his broad-ranging study of Pacific performances, Christopher Balme (2007) draws from Taylor's concepts when he describes the buildings of Hawaii's Polynesian Cultural Centre as an archive (186). Similarly, the site of Klahowya Village is an archive in the process of a politically motivated mediation, a concept upon which Taylor (2003) elaborates in discussing the myths of the archive (19). In 2009 the Vancouver Park Board, facing a budget shortfall, decided to close the Children's Farmyard in Stanley Park. It had been losing money for years, and the city chose not to subsidize it further. In May 2010 the board approved a motion that AtBC open Klahowya Village, using the existing Stanley Park Miniature Railway at the site as an Aboriginal cultural tourism attraction and renaming it the Spirit Catcher Train (Vancouver Park Board 2010).[6] Klahowya Village was run at the site until the end of the summer of 2014.

There was no admission fee to get into the site, but a small amount was charged for the train ride. The village was layered over the various other signifiers of farm life left from the Children's Farmyard. In the summer of 2012 a teepee structure was set up in the middle of a yard that was surrounded by two barns, livestock pens, a red cast-iron water pump, some split-rail fencing, and rough stone walls (see figure 4.1). The former ticket booth to the farmyard was now a BC Métis Federation exhibit of information and artifacts. The Miniature Railway, which winds through the forest around plastic replicas of livestock and various remnants of farm life, including a farmhouse, covered wagon, wooden waterwheel, and woodshed, has been transformed into the Spirit Catcher Train ride with the addition of two tunnels: when I visited, the entrance tunnel had poster-sized photos of a teepee, a child in dancing regalia, and a man drumming; the exit tunnel had glow-in-the-dark fluorescent masks. The farmhouse roof was adorned with a cut-out of an eagle, and oversized bentwood boxes were placed as props throughout the forest for the use of the costumed performers acting out the "Legend of the Sasquatch." As previously discussed, the Miniature Railway is itself a particularly significant example of archival architecture, the engine of the train being a replica of Canadian Pacific Railway Engine 374, which pulled the first Canadian transcontinental passenger train into Vancouver in 1887 (City of Vancouver 2013). Although some European settlement had occurred in the area for sixty years, the arrival of the railway consolidated the incorporation of the existing settlement into the city of Vancouver.

4.1   Teepee in farmyard, Klahowya Village, July 2012.

The name of the village installation, Klahowya, was explained with signage at both entrances: "Prior to European contact, the Aboriginal people
of BC spoke Chinook, a trade jargon that was spoken between several First
Nations and was made up by many First Nations languages which allowed
communication and trade of resources that were not typically found in
one zone territories. The Chinook language was used from Baja to Alaska
and into Montana. In Chinook, Klahowya means Welcome." The use of
the Chinook word for "welcome" to name the village was diplomatic. As
a language developed for intercultural communication, Chinook signified
the cross-cultural contact that was expected to happen between tourists
and Indigenous representatives at the site. It also signified, however, that
this site of χʷay̓χʷəy̓ as well as Stanley Park and Vancouver in general are
on unceded and overlapping territories of Coast Salish nations. Each host
nation, the Musqueam, Sk̲w̲xwú7mesh, and səlil̓wətaɬ, was represented by
signage at the entrances. The Musqueam sign emphasized the continuing
presence of Musqueam people "on this location where you now stand,"
explained the meaning of their name to be "People of the River Grass,"
recounted their origin story, and stressed the importance of runners in

protecting their land. The sign also explained the orthographic system of the hən̓q̓əmin̓əm̓ language and depicted the Canadian hockey team's 2010 Winter Olympics jersey, which was designed by Musqueam artist Debra Sparrow. The sign displayed by the S̱kw̱x̱wú7mesh incorporated text in their language, as well as a map of their territory identifying Klahowya Village as the site of the S̱kw̱x̱wú7mesh village of X̱wáy̱x̱way. Modern and historical photographs of S̱kw̱x̱wú7mesh people were also included. The sign of the səlilw̓ətaʔɬ was printed in hən̓q̓əmin̓əm̓ first and then translated into English; they identified themselves as "People of the Inlet," described their traditional lands, mentioned their creation story, and emphasized their knowledge of the land and the connection between the health of their culture and the health of the environment. The sign depicted famous leader, poet, and actor Chief Dan George – who starred in Arthur Penn's film *Little Big Man* (1972), among other screen and stage works – and it displayed recent images showing səlilw̓ətaʔɬ involvement with the Winter Olympics' opening ceremony and torch run. Each host nation, as well as the Sts'ailes from farther up the Fraser River and the BC Métis Federation, also had a weekend set aside during the summer when its performers were featured. These signs were an important part of the *visual sovereignty* being asserted. Their representations of traditional culture along with performers, leaders, and images from the recent Winter Olympics marked the Klahowya Village project as part of the ongoing political strategy both to increase recognition and connection to the land and to ensure cultural continuation.

The rebranding of the site was a conscious choice. Each of the major reports on the project that AtBC published during the first three years emphasized the brand, noted and enumerated its use in all creative designs and signs on-site, and stated that branding Klahowya Village as an integral part of AtBC was an important strategy and had marketing potential (AtBC 2010, 17; 2012a, 14; 2012b, 21). Such branding can be seen as a method of creating a visible public archive, just as the City of Vancouver has attempted to brand itself with Indigenous signifiers over the years. In particular, this part of Stanley Park is a space where, I contend, the settler city of Vancouver also performs itself – and has for many years.

Not far from this site is the remnant of an attempt by R.C. Campbell-Johnston[7] and the Art, Historical and Scientific Association of Vancouver, starting in 1915, to purchase and move a Kwakwaka'wakw village from

Alert Bay to Stanley Park. The association's plan was interrupted in 1925 when a Skwxwú7mesh representative, Andrew Paull, met with its members and Indian Agent C.C. Perry to explain that the "Squamish did not want a Kwakwaka'wakw village. They had no objections to a mixed village ... but they wanted the living Squamish to be recognized" (Phillips 2000, 28; Hawker 2003, 44). Currently one of the most visited tourist sites in Vancouver, the Stanley Park totem pole collection is a leftover from this effort. The City of Vancouver updated (and rebranded) the site before the 2010 Winter Olympics to include a commissioned series of three Coast Salish "gateways," called *People amongst the People* (2008), by Musqueam artist and carver Susan A. Point (Wilson 2016b; City of Vancouver 2019).

In such proximity that I could ride around the area on my bike within ten minutes are well-known destinations like the Vancouver Aquarium and Lumberman's Arch, the latter being an arrangement of four large rough-hewn logs that celebrates the logging industry. The area is also home to an open-air performance venue, Malkin Bowl, where the summer company Theatre Under the Stars operates, as well as Brockton Oval, which was the site of the Timber Bowl outdoor stage, where *The Jubilee Show* was performed in 1946. Nearby, visitors can also find the Shakespeare Garden, in which all the trees mentioned in William Shakespeare's plays and poems have been planted. Another kind of settler performance can be seen every evening with the firing of the 9 O'Clock Gun, a decommissioned British naval cannon installed on the point in 1894 when a community of Indigenous people was still living on the site (Barman 2005, 109). Matthews's monument to Lord Stanley's 1889 imagined act of dedicating the park is just over 500 metres south of the tourist village.

Keeping these past and present settler uses of the site in mind while also noting the ATBC interventions in the area helps to clarify the dynamics of performance, history, and spectatorship that were evident at Klahowya Village. This part of the city, which masquerades as a natural park, is actually a carefully constructed public archive that contains many layers of history, performance, tourism, commodity exchange, and intercultural communication. Klahowya Village was only the most recent one to be added as settler and Indigenous people continue to contend with the task of establishing respectful relations. Touristic spectacle, in order to be most accessible to a general public, often aims to avoid the difficult truths inherent in the settler-Indigenous relationship; however, any encounters that occur here are nevertheless embedded in this context.

Repertoire: Knowledge Transmission, Inversion, and Critique

Touristic spectacle mainly aims to entertain, yet this does not preclude an educational function. Spectacle can overlap with a necessary part of resurgence, namely knowledge transmission, within an Indigenous culture in order both to enable recovery and to correct cross-cultural misunderstandings. The dances at Klahowya Village enabled one prominent means of cultural transfer. Each of the six dance groups that I saw perform over the summer was multi-aged and included young children who were clearly being instructed to model the skilled performers. Two of the youngest were less than two years old; they were dressed the same as the other dancers and were free to come and go onstage. One toddler was given a drum to play. The speaker for the Kwakwaka'wakw group, when introducing his toddler grandson, explained that this was part of the practice of passing on knowledge of song and dance.

The Sts'ailes Nation dance group engaged in both kinds of knowledge transmission. Of all the groups I saw, they were the most multigenerational. The adults sang and drummed while a teenage youth led about six boys through the dances, with the younger children rarely looking away from him to the audience and the older boy watching each of them in turn as he danced. One dance was about the Sts'ailes creature Sasq'ets. The Sasquatch, aka Bigfoot, is well known all over North America as an elusive creature of the woods. The 2012 Klahowya Village's event space, website, and promotional videos on YouTube were branded with images of the Sasquatch. The Sts'ailes Nation, however, reclaimed the story, explaining that the name "Sasquatch" was thought to be a mispronunciation of "Sasq'ets." Their dance troupe performed in mid-July, singing their Sasq'ets song and explaining the story's origin. While reclaiming the story for themselves and passing on the dance skills, the group also transmitted knowledge across cultures. A spokesperson for this Sts'ailes group emphasized that the dancers were following protocol by sharing only some of their songs, and they ended their performance by opening up the touristic encounter and inviting spectators to join in the last dance, which many people did. In the recorded narrative that accompanied the Spirit Catcher Train ride, the Sasquatch, usually cast as a mysterious and somewhat fearsome monster, was instead presented as a protector of the environment who punished only greedy people. The puppet show performed in a barn also featured the Sasquatch as a protector of the land who taught an urban Indigenous girl where her food came from and the importance of not polluting the earth.

The Sts'ailes group functioned confidently and generously, transferring knowledge through generations and across cultures while performing and modelling resurgence. When a woman in the audience interrupted the spokesman to ask whether the name "Sasq'ets" was related to the name of the Canadian province of Saskatchewan, he patiently explained to her that Saskatchewan was very far away and derived its name from a different First Nations language, and then he returned to his performance. His patient response to a seemingly obtuse question (rudely asked) was yet another Indigenous demonstration of the kind of generosity employed for inter-cultural communication during performance events. The Sts'ailes group also approached the story in dynamic ways. In traditional accounts, the Sasq'ets creature is viewed as fierce, very bad smelling – usually smelled before he is seen – and male. There is also a female counterpart, who steals children found out after dark. The Klahowya Village adapted the story to connect it with environmental concerns of contemporary life, thereby demonstrating that knowledge is transmitted not from a static archive but from an active repertoire that can incorporate change because it is responsive to context.

Another significant element to note about the dance performances was their location on the site. One of the major alterations to the Children's Farmyard in 2012 was a stage built into the fenced area by the barns. A large courtyard surrounds this stage, along with a few viewing platforms, although they are all separated by a large pond directly in front of the playing area. The stage also has a striking sculptured eagle made out of cedar shingles that serves as an overhang. Despite its appealing design, this area was rarely used over the summer. Balme's analysis of performances staged at the Polynesian Cultural Centre in Hawaii is helpful in under-standing the performing space chosen by the dance groups at Klahowya Village. Balme (2007) contrasts the Maori and Hawaiian performances staged at the centre with those of the Samoans and Tongans, noting that, submerged in a majority colonizing culture, both the Maori and Hawaiian groups staged "performance traditions which fulfilled the double function of presenting an image of cultural vitality to the colonial gaze and finding new functions for performance within a new cultural situation" (185). Balme describes the Hawaiian hula performances as "entirely didactic," happening within the village without a raised stage as tourists gather around informally, with the performers acting as cultural demonstrators (185). Balme's insights into this didactic tourist spectacle help to explain why dancers at Klahowya Village did not favour the dramatic stage. Rather than displaying themselves at a distance, which could have made them seem far away and of the past (perhaps a reprisal of the "giant tom-tom" of *The Indian Village and Show*, discussed in chapter 3), they chose to dance on the same ground as the spectators. This positioning emphasized both their presence in the present and their connection with the land on which they danced.

One method of asserting strength is to elicit a formulaic expectation and then refuse to fulfil it. The storyteller, who was on-site telling stories twice daily, did just that. He would call people to his area, which comprised a number of logs arranged as seats in front of the stump of a tree carved out with enough space for a person to stand inside. He was usually dressed in everyday clothing, although sometimes he would wear his dancing clothes. He did not introduce himself on any of the days that I attended. His performance integrated drumming, singing, and telling stories. One story he told, first in his own language and then translated into English, was about an industrious beaver who carries a lazy porcupine up a mountain to force him to find a new shelter. In another story, presented as a way of explaining how the plants and animals are talking to us, an old man learns from a spider web how to make a fish net. These narratives, however, were only part of the storyteller's performance. He mainly initiated a dialogue with the people who attended, asking them where they were from and inviting questions. He was incredibly patient with people as they came and went, often asking him to pose for pictures – sometimes even in the middle of his performance. He spoke about the term "Indian," explaining that it was a government word and important to use in order to hold governments to their responsibilities. He spoke of Aboriginal title, demonstrating with a newspaper and his credit cards how it underlies all other titles and cannot be extinguished. He also showed – by lifting up a log from the ground and carrying it – what it was like to carry hatred around with you. The advertised storytelling session thus became a space for sharing insights and experiences. At each session, he also shared his drum with visitors and would sing to whatever beat they played, always making sure any children present had a turn.

These performances went on for much longer than the scheduled half-hour. At one session, when the storyteller explained that there would be no more First Nations people by 2048 (I think he meant those with

government-recognized status), a white man who identified himself as a
Mormon from Japan was moved almost to tears and asked for suggestions
about how to help Indigenous people. I was struck by this interaction; it was
so unlike the anthropological staging of culture in museums, what Andreas
Zittlau (2014) calls an "encounter without ever meeting" (100). Instead, the
performer had created a safe environment for conversation and meeting.
He often commented that he did not mean to offend people and once
mentioned that ATBC had hired him and given him leave to say whatever he
wanted. The choreography of his performance also inverted expectations.
As he moved from the defined performance area in front of the stump
into the adjacent forest behind the audience and sometimes out of view to
gather plants to use as illustrations for his stories, the spectator-performer
arrangement dissolved into a space of dialogue for sharing insights and
life experiences. This use of shared space echoed the movement of the
dance groups away from the stage with the sculpted-eagle overhang and
onto the grass field behind the vendors and seemed to indicate an overall
effort by the performers to create ambiguous encounters that could also be
cross-cultural interactions without the barrier of theatricality.

One element of the Klahowya Village site was particularly puzzling.
A red and white beaded and feathered headdress had been placed on a
manikin head with an invitation for visitors to take photos of themselves
wearing it next to the totem pole (see figure 4.2). The bedraggled headdress
was not identified as representing any BC First Nations people, and no
staff attended to it. I observed many visitors who took photographs of
themselves wearing it. This item was incongruous, playful yet unsettling;
it invoked a Hollywood stereotype of the "Indian" in a space that seemed
to be making an effort to undo such conceptions. As an empty headdress
available for visitors to put on, this prop recreated the settler vision of
what Daniel Francis (2011) calls the "imaginary Indian," a colonialist construction. Many people interacting with the headdress seemed surprised
and laughed.

Such moments can be illuminated by a concept that Philip J. Deloria
develops in *Indians in Unexpected Places* (2004). Deloria makes the point
that people respond to images of Native Americans in modern situations
with a "chuckle" (3). He believes this patronizing chuckle has to do with
the anomaly of an Indigenous person engaged with modernity but argues
that settler expectations actually create the anomaly (4). Perhaps by
placing an object that signifies stereotypes of the "Indian" within a site

4.2   Headdress at Klahowya Village, July 2012.

where Indigenous peoples were asserting both their modernity and the continuation of their traditions, the Klahowya Village organizers inverted the chuckles. Inviting visitors to perform expectations from the past as well as to indulge in the desire to "play Indian" in the context of the exhibition created even more of an emphasis on the present. Not everyone accepted the invitation, however, and some passersby dismissed the headdress as a discomforting relic. Discomfort and ambiguity, although not conducive to a simple entertaining touristic experience, are part of the decolonizing process, a chaotic and unclean break from colonialism not answerable to concerns regarding settler futurity (Tuck and Yang 2012, 20, 35). In that respect, this strange and unexpected object was among the most compelling elements of the installation. Balme (2007) calls this "reverse colonial mimicry": "instead of imitating the colonizer and developing forms of subversion by holding up a distorted image of the European," Indigenous people mimic "European projections of themselves" (182). However, Anishannabe-Ashkenazi theatre scholar and artist Jill Carter in "Repairing the Web: Spiderwoman's Children Staging the New Human Being" (2010) cautions against a simple reading of moments of mimicry as resistance or as a "*reaction* to the perverse metonyms which have inhabited the colonial imagination for centuries now" (176, italics original). Instead, she emphasizes engaging with these moments as proactive instances of survivance through which Indigenous people centre their artistic expressions and decentre coloniality, adopting and adapting non-Native metonyms of cultural genocide to their own purposes (180). With Carter's warning in mind, this unattended headdress that invited the tourist to "play Indian" for a two-dollar donation may in the end have been about making pocket change.

In her discussion of *visual sovereignty* in Indigenous filmmaking, Raheja (2010) notes that some directors deliberately show the aberrant – for example, the eating of raw meat or polygamy – as a method to disrupt dominant narratives and create debate (204). In my analysis of performances at Klahowya Village, I looked for representations of what non-Indigenous audiences might consider aberrant practices. I could not find any, leading me to think about the difference between live performance and film. Aberrant acts displayed on film can affect an audience strongly and provoke reactions. No matter what the reaction, however, the actors in the film are not in immediate danger during the shared moment of screening. This is not the case with live performance, especially where the boundary

4.3   Safety fencing and burnt trees after arson on 21 June 2012 at the Miniature Train Station, Klahowya Village, August 2012.

between the audience and performers is so permeable that the dancer can pose next to the spectator in the headdress or that the dancers and singers can stand on the grassy lawn surrounded by spectators. Raheja also discusses the potential for violent retribution for critical self-representations, noting that the "threat of violence explains how early Native American cinematographers ... [worked] primarily within the bounds of hegemonic discourse out of fear of violent reprisal, while also subtly critiquing Indian images" (231). Klahowya Village was well staffed and supported in a very public space in Vancouver; the potential for violence in some ways seemed very remote.

However, on 21 June 2012, the opening day of that summer's enterprise, an act of arson burnt down the Spirit Catcher Train Station and Info Booth (see figure 4.3). The fire was set in the night and completely destroyed the building, which was in the middle of the site, as well as $40,000 worth of artists' supplies, tools, and products (Harry 2012). The arson has never been attributed to any person or group. Klahowya Village's organizers held a healing ceremony a few days later in order to respond to the incident and carry on; however, throughout the summer the burnt site, with its safety fencing and singed trees, remained a constant reminder of the violence.

Even if the arson was completely unconnected to ATBC's work, in the context of past and contemporary acts of violence toward Indigenous people, it must be recognized as constituting part of the milieu within which Klahowya operated. For this reason, it is not surprising that the performers avoided shocking or aberrant cultural practices during the live events.

Conclusions and Continuing Plans

At the ceremony opening Klahowya Village on 1 July 2010, Chief Ian Campbell (aka Xàlek or Sekyú Siỷam), of the Skwxwú7mesh Nation, made note of the site's connection to the historic Coast Salish village and suggested that perhaps Stanley Park should be renamed Xwáyxway. The ensuing media storm, with comments both in support and virulently dismissive of the idea, was put to rest only when a federal Cabinet minister with the governing Conservative Party declared that it would not happen (Stueck 2010). This statement highlighted the layered colonial history of this area: the park is federal land because it was considered a strategic military position by the original colonial land surveyors and is only leased to the City of Vancouver, although no records exist to support this federal claim (Barman 2005, 25–7).

I now recognize the source of the discomfort I originally felt upon entering Klahowya Village. The enterprise, which seemed like an easily dismissible touristic spectacle, was actually what Raheja (2010) describes as "the space between resistance and compliance" (193). In the summer of 2012, dance groups and the storyteller used tactical grounded practices to transmit their knowledge in a way that inverted the stereotypical expectations occasioned by the repertoire of performance enacted repeatedly over the weeks, and the village's interventions in the archival landscape design had the same effect. Each of the groups mentioned at some point during its performance the proximity to χʷaỷχʷəỷ; indeed, the spokesperson for the səlil̓wətaʔɬ pointed out one of their group's young dancers, saying that his great-grandfather had lived there and fished nearby. As discussed in chapter 1, the place name "χʷaỷχʷəỷ" reflects knowledge regarding the continual performing that has occurred there as well as, possibly, the shifting dynamics of affect between performers and spectators/witnesses. The name of the original village therefore reinforces the notion that the current use of this space by Coast Salish groups is a continuation and adaptation of cultural practice and thus is not without precedent.

Klahowya Village in the summer of 2012 was still in development. It represented a cooperative project for an Indigenous group that was promoting an economy based on tourism while working collaboratively with other local Indigenous nations and three levels of government. That summer's incarnation offered some opportunity for knowledge transmission, dialogue, and unexpected humorous critiques of stereotypes, while still needing to be somewhat neutral in order to attract tourists and create a safe space for interactions. The ironic visual layering of an "Indigenous village" on top of a "settler farm" offered a rich metaphor for the possibilities of restitution. The tourist village operated until the end of 2014, and ATBC has since changed its tactics. The train station that was destroyed by fire was rebuilt in 2015, and the farmyard now sits empty, its gates locked except during seasonally themed train rides, such as the Ghost Train in October and Bright Nights in December. Since the summer of 2017, it has been running as the Urban Forest Train, with a recorded narrative that emphasizes the plants and animals, both "native and introduced," that are present in "one of the largest urban parks in North America." Although the ATBC tourist village is no longer in existence, performances by Indigenous people have continued in this space, taking multiple forms that promise the continued use of grounded practices in this long-swirling eddy of influence that exists on the edge of Vancouver, is named after a British Lord who visited briefly in 1889, and is built on top of and in the midst of an Indigenous archive now kept alive through an ongoing repertoire.

Before moving to the book's conclusion, which outlines eleven significant policy changes taken up by the Vancouver Park Board in response to the Truth and Reconciliation Commission of Canada's *Calls to Action* (2015) and the United Nations Declaration on the Rights of Indigenous Peoples, agreed to by Canada in 2016, I offer one more reflection on the use of performance as a method of historiography, this time by Inuk throat singer and artist Tanya Tagaq.

Tanya Tagaq and Robert Flaherty's *Nanook of the North*

The York Theatre was set up with a large, towering screen positioned stage left and slightly angled toward stage right, where Inuk throat singer and artist Tanya Tagaq, violinist Jesse Zubot, and drummer Jean Martin stood crowded together among electrical cords, microphones, visual monitors, and amps. This recently renovated hundred-year-old proscenium-style theatre seemed unlikely to be able to contain this "concert for film" wherein Tagaq, Zubot, and Martin would create a soundscape set to Robert Flaherty's film *Nanook of the North* (1922).[1] The vertical looming screen brought to mind Diana Taylor's (2006) formulation of the past, conceived not only linearly with a disappearing horizon but also as a "multilayered sedimentation, a form of vertical density" that is stored within performance as what is already here and "made present and alive in the here and now" (83). The screen would hold the knowledges sedimented within the images of the Inuit who had performed as well as collaborated with Flaherty in the production of the film by operating cameras, developing film, and suggesting scenes, as Michelle Raheja discusses in *Reservation Reelism: Redfacing, Visual Sovereignty, and Representations of Native Americans in Film* (2010, 195). Raheja argues that *Nanook of the North* is used as a repository of both knowledge and method by contemporary Indigenous filmmakers who recognize "the imprint of Indigenous people working in various capacities as intellectual and cultural advisors and technical assistants ... [to] draw from this early motion picture material to frame their own projects that engage with notions of the traditional in order to think about how the past informs the present" (196). She also asserts that film technology permits filmmakers to "stage performances of oral narrative and Indigenous notions of time and space that are not possible through print alone" (196). In this performance response, I contend that Tagaq's interaction with this archival film was an embodied performance of a historiographic method. And, like the production of Michel Tremblay's

For the Pleasure of Seeing Her Again (1998) discussed in the intervention following chapter 2, although this performance did not take up issues directly concerning Coast Salish lands, her method and affective impact were crucial to the argument I have been building throughout this book regarding performance and knowledge transfer.

Jacky Bratton in *New Readings in Theatre History* (2003) discusses the concept of the performer as historian in an effort to move away from a literary-based theatre history. She considers how comic actor Charles Matthews, who performed on the London stages in the early 1800s, embodied and performed a version of theatre history through his mimicry of others in his "monopolylogues" (114–15).[2] She also points out that imitation is not conservative stasis, arguing that Matthews's creations of elaborate syntheses of performers imitating performers "suggest that there is in these recuperations ... an intention to build upon memory, an appeal to organic growth" (118). In a similar vein, Tagaq's response to her ancestors' creation of *Nanook of the North* involved both mimicry and a dynamic building upon memory that used her body, breath, and voice to make present a history onstage.

All live performance responses require attention to details of actions onstage and a consideration of how these create responses in the audience. The effect of this performance was astounding in so many ways, yet the details are difficult to put into words for two reasons: the nature of the throat-singing form and Tagaq's manifestation of it as well as the immense presence of the film onstage. Peter Dickinson (2014), in his review of this performance, responded to both of these elements, saying that Tagaq breathed new life into the film and that his gaze shifted continually between Tagaq and the film, creating a "constant and conscious perceptual adjustment that forced me to recalibrate, in the moment, my reading of each." I begin by examining Tagaq's interpretation of the throat-singing form and the content of the film. I then articulate a response to two particularly evocative moments of Tagaq's performance.

Nine months after this performance at the York Theatre, Tagaq's album *Animism* (2014) won the Polaris Music Prize for best Canadian album.[3] While introducing her, musician Geoff Berner (2014) exhorted the audience to listen to her music: "If you listen, you will careen through a panorama of the contradictions of existence. You can hear the living land, and the land under assault. You can hear children being born and conceived. You can hear the torture of the innocent, and the glory of the tenacious, unstoppable force of life. If you listen you can actually hear the sound of a people defying genocide to rise, wounded but alive, strong, and ready to fight." Her subsequent performance and acceptance speech garnered a great deal of international attention, and in many newspaper and magazine profiles she has spoken openly about her history of sexual assault, substance abuse, and a suicide attempt, drawing attention to these issues in order to destigmatize them (Nelles 2015). Many of these profiles have attempted to put into words what Tagaq does onstage: "she is almost demonic. Her face contorts in fury or ecstasy; her hands slice the air; she hunkers down and crawls across the stage, stampeding through the songs without stopping ... [and] what we hear is something like her insides – guts, heart – trying to escape her body" (Nelles 2015); she "sings about what it feels like to be an Inuk woman today – a lot of hurting about abuse, pain" (Chapman 2014); and her performance is a "jaw-dropping forty-five minutes of guttural heaves, juddering howls, and murderous shrieks" (Seabrook 2015). In a video made for the Open University, Tagaq demonstrates how she makes the sounds of throat singing. She sings a deep note on exhalation and a high note on inhalation, making noise high up in the nasal cavity and then down by her epiglottis. While exhaling, she also splices the notes from high to low. She uses her mouth to shape sounds further. Some songs are only deep tones, during which she inhales quickly for a continuation of the low sounds. Her advice to people who are learning the technique is to spend a year trying to sound like their dog (musicisayer 2009).

Tagaq is described as an Inuk throat singer, but she explicitly states that although her singular practice is based on tradition, it is a creative interpretation of it. She taught herself how to throat sing while at art school in Halifax from a cassette recording of Inuit women that her mother sent her. Past practice of the form has been taken up mostly by women in pairs as part of a joyful competition, with an emphasis on imitating the "soundscape of northern life," including the syllables of words, names of ancestors and places, or something present where the women are singing (Diamond 2008, 52, 49; Nelles 2015). Tagaq does link her contemporary practice very explicitly to her experiences of the land, telling Inuk journalist Malaya Qaunirq Chapman (2014) that she is "yelling about the land, the experience of the Nuna [land] and the peace on it. The peace – the most deepest, perfect, amazing peace I've ever felt in my whole entire life and the whole root of who I am." An analysis of her work on *Animism* also makes this link to a personification or amplification of the land, particularly with the song "Fracking," in which she makes the sounds of the earth undergoing this oil extraction process (Polley 2015). This explanation of the form as well as Tagaq's use of it connect with what I have termed the "grounded practices" of Indigenous performance while also demonstrating imitation used as historiographic method. Unlike Charles Matthews in Bratton's example of embodied performative historiography, Tagaq's mimicry is of human as well as other-than-human life.

The other part of the performance onstage at the York Theatre was the projected film *Nanook of the North*. Although the film is iconic in Canadian and documentary film history and was used in schools to teach about "Eskimo" life for years, this was the first time I had seen it. However, I had read about it in Raheja's (2010) book, and I had attended a panel discussion earlier in the day. Therefore, unlike most people who first see the film, I was well aware of the collaboration of the Inuit people with Flaherty, which led to my staggering appreciation of this remarkable film. After establishing the character Nanook (Inuk actor Allakariallak) as a respected and skillful hunter and introducing his extended family, which includes two wives, Nyla (possibly Alice Nuvalinga) and Cunayoo (an actor whose name is not known) (Emberley 2007, 86),[4] the film moves on to tell the story of the family's life over a few seasons. There are scenes on the water with small and large boats, scenes on the ice with dogs and sleds, and demonstrations of how to melt ice, build shelters, and use numerous technologies needed for life in the northern environment. Flaherty uses a staged narrative and continuity in his editing to give a realistic sense of being in the space with this family. There are scenes of humour, including their arrival at a trading post in a small covered boat out of which five people and a dog emerge as well as Nanook's playful interaction with a gramophone when he bites a record while laughing at the camera.

The gramophone scene has often been read as one that seeks to place Inuit outside of modernity, although Raheja (2010, 190) argues that the actor's laugh can be read as part of an Inuit cultural code, one that can confront non-Inuit spectators with the absurdities of their assumptions and flag complicity in structures of dominance and stereotype, somewhat akin to Philip J. Deloria's (2004, 3–4) "chuckle," discussed in chapter 4 with reference to the headdress at Klahowya Village. It is also

a scene that Tagaq's performance brought into sharp focus, as I discuss
below. The film stages numerous scenes of tension and danger when
characters are hunting as well as when they are seeking shelter as a
storm approaches.

Additional scenes include the use of the aberrant, which Raheja
(2010) regards as one of the methods of *visual sovereignty* in Indigenous
filmmaking: a child enjoying castor oil, polygamy, the nonchalant display of women's bare breasts, the killing and butchering of animals, and
the eating of raw meat. The skills sedimented in the film, such as killing a
walrus with a harpoon, building a shelter out of snow and ice, and catch-
ing a seal through a small hole in the ice, display knowledge that Tagaq
has described as provoking a sense of "pride" and the awareness that
her "ancestors were basically superhuman to live in that environment"
(quoted in Werb 2014). My intense interest in the film during the York
Theatre performance was due to a mix of my respect for the Inuit actors'
abilities and the tension that came with knowing that they were skilled
collaborators in the filmmaking process even while, throughout the film,
the ethnographic gaze seeks to separate them from the present moment.
So, despite Tagaq's riveting performance and presence, like Dickinson, I
was equally mesmerized by the recorded performances and shifted my
attention back and forth between Tagaq and the film, missing parts of
each element, although I used my peripheral vision to keep myself alert
to significant changes.

The show was sold out, the small venue having only about 350 seats,
but the design of the house made it feel like the audience was crowded
around the stage. Tagaq opened by introducing the other musicians
and inviting her family to come backstage afterward. Then she peered
out into the audience and said that she thought she could see someone
she just wanted to hug. She talked about the film, saying it made her
feel proud of her ancestors and the Inuit science that had enabled them
to live in such an extreme environment. She mentioned that the film
is from the 1920s and that there is a racist element in its portrayal of
"happy-go-lucky Eskimos." She said that they were happy but that they
were also "hardcore."

The opening credits of the film rolled and the music started. Tagaq
set a regular rhythm that matched a resting heart rate. She changed the
microphone from hand to hand, depending on which way she was sway-
ing. At times her hips moved from side to side, her shoulders moving

the opposite way, and sometimes she thrust them front to back. Her head and arms traced diagonals. She bent her knees and raised her hand above her head.

On-screen when there was footage of the family on the water in a big boat, Tagaq moved her hips front to back, almost as if she were the boat on the water. One hand held the microphone to her mouth, her face was tilted up, and we could not see her expression. Then she lowered her head, face, and shoulders, her arms floating down in front of her. One arm made circles around her side; as she screamed, she held the microphone farther away from her mouth. Her head tilted to the side and she held her arm out in front of her.

During the scene in which Allakariallak as Nanook talks to the white trader and examines the gramophone, eventually biting the record to understand and then laughing, Tagaq repeatedly sang the only English word she has ever throat sung: "colonizer." Although this moment could be read as an indictment of the film, her commentary on it connects it even more closely with Raheja's (2010, 190) analysis of the laughter. When asked at a panel discussion about her decision to sing that word, she explained that she was making fun of herself, the film, and the colonizers (PuSh 2014).[5] She discussed her work with the film as an effort to facilitate change without laying blame or sounding like a victim, adding that she wanted to present anger in a loving way. Nevertheless, as a descendant of settlers, listening to her growling the word made me hold my breath.

When the film moved on to scenes of a walrus hunt, Tagaq stomped her feet and swayed her shoulders from side to side as though she were walking through a substance that was thick and heavy. Her hands traced a half-circle and her breath was going in circles; as she lowered her voice, she lowered her hand as well. During the longer sounds, she stretched her arm out in front of her. In the film, the actors sneak up on a group of sleeping walruses, spearing one of them. The rest of the walruses swim offshore and wait while the Inuit hold the sinew attached to the spear, keeping the captured walrus close to shore. The most intense fusion of sound and visuals happened when Tagaq screamed for the walrus that was trying to lock horns with her captured mate. The combination of visual and aural stimuli created goose bumps all over my arms. Eventually successful, the hunters pull the dead walrus ashore and begin to skin it; Tagaq's voice softened and went into a higher register, cyclically intoning four regular syllables. I was sitting beside a friend, Skye Maitland, who understands a bit of Inuktitut, and she leaned over to tell me that Tagaq was now singing another word. It was *qujannamiik*, or in English "thank you." With this utterance, she demonstrated the appreciation shown to the hunted animal by the Inuit on-screen while also keeping knowledge of the word's significance for only those audience members who had access to the language. As the show progressed (the film is sixty-seven minutes long), Tagaq's rate of singing slowed and quickened depending on the events depicted, but she never stopped. Her performance was a feat of endurance that connected her to her ancestors on-screen. She seemed superhuman herself. While expending so much energy so intensely, she demonstrated a live version of the strengths of the Inuit in the film, making present what was already there. Tagaq repurposed this archival footage, which was originally partly a result of the salvage paradigm of ethnographic history, by reverberating and imitating the footage into a new contemporary understanding of Inuit historical events.

At the panel discussion, Raheja termed Tagaq's work with the powerful film a "repatriation" and an "intervention" into the violence of ethnography (PuSh 2014). Her use of the term "repatriation" is telling. It refers to the return of people or valuable objects to their point of origin and is often used to describe the process by which a museum returns an artifact to an Indigenous group. Often this action is taken only when the group is able to demonstrate the ability to care for it; until that point, the museum keeps possession, even while it acknowledges the rightful ownership. Tagaq's engagement with the film acknowledged and claimed its fullness as an Inuit historical artifact, which she then made present and alive through her voice and body.

Conclusion

In recent years, much has taken place that relates directly to the topic of *Against the Current and Into the Light*. In Vancouver alone, there have been the actions to protect the Musqueam village site of c̓əsnaʔəm and, as I have discussed, the subsequent initiative to stage the tri-museum exhibit about this village co-curated by Musqueam people; Vancouver City Council's official declaration in 2014 that the city sits on the unceded territories of the Musqueam, Tsleil-Waututh, and Squamish peoples (City of Vancouver 2014); and ongoing actions to protect the coast from the Trans Mountain Pipeline, which is intended to carry bitumen from Alberta. In British Columbia at large, there have been the historic Tsilhqot'in decision on Aboriginal title[1] and widespread opposition to the Enbridge Northern Gateway Pipelines project, which was eventually denied permits in November 2016. Across Canada, from 2008 to 2015, the Truth and Reconciliation Commission (TRC) held events to document and inform people about Indian residential school experiences and abuses, resulting in its ninety-four *Calls to Action* (2015), and an Indigenous resurgence has emerged publicly, one expression of which is the Idle No More movement, which began in the winter of 2012–13. It seems a bit strange, perhaps, to detail a performance history of a place where so much continues to go on in the present. Although histories have been written already that narrate how Canada became a unified nation and Vancouver a city settled by Europeans, there is room for a history that contends with these narratives. This book has been an effort to demonstrate the need for a history conceived through the use of performance that argues that this space called Vancouver, despite the nationalist invading settler forces that have aimed to define it, nevertheless continues to be Indigenous.

I began this book by describing the process of working with place-based knowledge held within in a language that is many thousands of years old before tracing the performative activities of Indigenous people and settlers throughout the twentieth century and into the early years of the twenty-first. I have argued throughout that grounded practices expressed through performance have caused reciprocally affective intercultural influence akin to the action of a swirling eddy in the water. At times, especially during the early era of British colonial projects overseen by James Skitt Matthews, it may have been difficult to imagine that the white space being created in "Stanley" Park could ever be countered. However, through the continuous actions of local and international Indigenous activists, scholars, and performers, we have come to a time when the City of Vancouver, and many more of its citizens, acknowledge the park as Indigenous land. This understanding has not come without struggle, and the city is still in the early stages of establishing a respectful relationship with local Indigenous nations in order to make reparations and move toward finding a way to share the land.

It also must be said that this recent turn in municipal politics in Vancouver is a direct result of the strength and perseverance of the survivors of the Indian residential school system. Their work bringing lawsuits against the federal government and church organizations eventually became the largest class action suit to date in Canada, resulting in the federal Cabinet's approval of the Indian Residential Schools Settlement Agreement of 2006. This agreement in turn led to court-enforced Common Experience Payments, services for health and healing, and the funding of the five-year Truth and Reconciliation Commission. As the TRC began its work, some shifts began within the Vancouver municipal government, eventually resulting in an intricate link between the TRC's *Calls to Action* and the future of Stanley Park. In 2012 the city established the Urban Aboriginal Peoples' Advisory Committee,[2] and in early 2013 – after two presentations, one by the grassroots Indigenous organization Reconciliation Canada and another about the Idle No More movement, which was then spreading rapidly across the country – the committee unanimously approved a motion to direct the City of Vancouver to recognize the United Nations Declaration on the Rights of Indigenous Peoples, adopted by the General Assembly in 2007 but not by Canada until 2016. The City of Vancouver adopted it on 26 February 2013. On National Aboriginal Day, 21 June, the City of Vancouver declared the next twelve months to be "The Year of Reconciliation," and the TRC's hearings in British Columbia were held that September, with Mayor Gregor Robertson as one of the honorary witnesses. In June 2014, City Council formally acknowledged that the city "is on the unceded traditional territory of the Musqueam, Squamish and Tsleil-Waututh First

Nations" (City of Vancouver 2014). Realizing that reconciliation could not be accomplished in a symbolic year, the city subsequently declared itself a City of Reconciliation, and City Council directed staff to respond to the TRC's *Calls to Action*. These initiatives led to mistakes by some city staff, who were not yet equipped to handle new job expectations.[3] On 29 June 2015, the Urban Aboriginal Peoples' Advisory Committee requested that the Vancouver Park Board (a governing body separate from City Council) also adopt a motion regarding the TRC's *Calls to Action*. Six months later, the Park Board approved eleven strategies to respond to the *Calls to Action*. jil weaving[4] "noted that the Park Board response is based on responding to the principles and areas of potential action and not restricted to those calls directed specifically at the municipal level of government" (Urban Aboriginal Peoples' Advisory Committee 2016a).

This policy document, adopted in January 2016, is one that needs to be known – both because of the wisdom contained within the directions to staff and because it holds the Park Board accountable to these new directions (see figure c.1). The preamble states that the eleven strategies are in response to the TRC's *Calls to Action*, and it directs staff to adopt the United Nations Declaration on the Rights of Indigenous Peoples as a framework for reconciliation initiatives, to conduct cultural competency staff training in collaboration with Indigenous peoples, to take a holistic approach to all parks and recreation programming both by increasing public awareness of reconciliation and by providing support for Indigenous people of all ages, and to align partner and business contracts with the TRC's *Calls to Action*. All of these directions to staff are relevant to the establishment of better relations, but some of the other directions quite eloquently speak to issues of history, land, and knowledge that have been discussed throughout this work. The direction to continue the practice of not charging for name changes on Park Board recreation passes, called the OneCard, "especially in relation to Indigenous people reclaiming names changed by the residential school system," recalls the scene that Matthews described when he assisted August Jack Khahtsahlano to officially change his name – but refused to fix his birth certificate to reflect his birth place at Chaythoos. The direction to engage with archeological protocols on park lands in order to ensure respect for Aboriginal cemetery sites or middens on park lands also speaks to much of the settler development of the park – and to the disrespectful use of the belongings and remains unearthed at χʷaÿχʷəÿ during the construction of the first park road. The strategic direction to integrate "Indigenous history, heritage values, and memory practices" into future monuments, memorials, and pubic art also speaks to so many of the settler monuments that perform whiteness throughout the park – most especially Matthews's statue of Lord Stanley's "dedication." Heeding this direction will not necessarily entail removing the existing monuments but could result in new works that layer and respond to them in such ways that their declarations and celebrations of white spaces will be contested. I argue that the direction to integrate these Indigenous elements into the public commemorations in the park is also intricately connected to the direction acknowledging that Aboriginal rights include Aboriginal languages, which are best strengthened by Aboriginal people and communities.

As has been demonstrated throughout this work, Indigenous ways of knowing are held within language, and when this sort of knowledge is shared, whole worlds can be opened up. Two of the eleven strategies engage directly with concepts of territory: first, the direction that Park Board staff should ensure respect for Indigenous territorial protocols at events and, if appropriate, the engagement of local Indigenous people; and, second, that the Park Board should continue its "precedent-setting intergovernmental approach to the future stewardship of Stanley Park and other relevant lands." Although this latter direction does not relinquish any settler claim to title of the park – which is claimed federally, meaning that such a change could not be accomplished at the municipal level – it does engage with collaborative stewardship of the lands on which city parks have been created. This idea in itself brings in the complicated discussion of property ownership and land title, an elemental Western concept on which coloniality and whiteness are built. To claim legal title to land is one strategy that many Indigenous peoples use in order to protect themselves and their lands from resource extraction and commodification. This is not, however, an expression of Indigenous reciprocal relation to land but an action necessitated by the context of colonial society. The collaborative stewardship of land that cannot be sold, as undertaken by the peoples who have lived here from time immemorial and by newcomers who respect their knowledge and authority, holds great hope for future good relations. Given the late-capitalist moment in which it is being implemented, those engaged in following the joint stewardship approach will need great strength to resist the risk that the eleven strategies will become subsumed within con-tinuing colonial logic.[5]

TO: Park Board Chair and Commissioners

FROM: General Manager – Vancouver Board of Parks and Recreation

SUBJECT: Truth and Reconciliation Commission Calls to Action

RECOMMENDATION

THAT, in response to the <u>Calls to Action</u> provided by the Truth and Reconciliation Commission of Canada (TRC), the Vancouver Park Board direct staff to:

A. Adopt the "<u>United Nations Declaration on the Rights of Indigenous Peoples</u>" as a reference framework for Park Board's Reconciliation initiatives;

B. Work with First Nations people's and other civic bodies to identify, create, and deliver appropriate and actionable staff training on indigenous issues and reconciliation;

C. Take a 360 degree approach to programming, including in the areas of culture, health, public dialogue, physical activity, and sport in order to increase public knowledge and awareness of reconciliation and to provide support to indigenous peoples including children, youth, Elders and families;

D. Continue Park Board's precedent-setting intergovernmental approach to the future stewardship of Stanley Park and other relevant lands;

E. Review the donation of monuments, memorials, and public art processes and policies to ensure integration of Indigenous history, heritage values, and memory practices;

F. Review archeological protocols to ensure that "Aboriginal protocols shall be respected before any potentially invasive technical inspection and investigation of a cemetery site" or soil disturbance of a midden site takes place on park lands;

G. Acknowledge that Aboriginal rights include Aboriginal language rights; that preservation, revitalization and strengthening of Aboriginal languages and cultures are best managed by Aboriginal people and communities;

H. Review partner and business contracts, relationships and procurement policies for alignment with <u>TRC Calls to Action</u>;

I. Establish and fund as a priority a program for Indigenous and non-Indigenous artists to undertake collaborative community-engaged projects and produce works that contribute to the reconciliation process;

J. Review event permitting and sports hosting opportunities to ensure that Indigenous peoples' territorial protocols are respected and that, if appropriate to the scale of the event, that local Indigenous communities are engaged;

K. Maintain current policy of no charge for changing a name on the OneCard, especially in relation to Indigenous people reclaiming names changed by the residential school system.

C.1   The strategic directions for reconciliation adopted by the Vancouver Park Board, 6 January 2016.

Lastly, the direction for the Park Board to establish and prioritize a fund for collaborative community-engaged art by Indigenous and non-Indigenous artists that contributes to the reconciliation process will continue work that has been produced throughout the twentieth century by Indigenous artists and activists along with their non-Indigenous allies, but it will do so with the promise of stability provided by institutional infrastructure as long as petty bureaucracies do not impede the articulation of decolonizing artistic visions. How this will affect the resulting works of art and performance on the site remains to be seen in the years to come.

Eighteen months after the adoption of the January 2016 policy document, I attended an event that I believe demonstrates the shift in the Park Board's engagement with Indigenous peoples and their lands, while also making more visible to non-Indigenous people the relations that have always existed. In Leanne Betasamosake Simpson's (2017a) phrasing, this event was a means of showing the public multiple Indigenous nations engaging with land and water, "as we have always done." The event, which combined a "Thunderbird Sharing Ceremony" and a "Pulling Together Canoe Journey," took place in a tourist-filled park on 15 July 2017. The event was connected to Vancouver's Canadian Confederation celebrations. Across the country, the 150th anniversary of Confederation was commemorated – at times with flag-waving and various proud expressions of nationalism but also with ambivalence and anger that a national narrative built on the cultural genocide of Indigenous people could be something to celebrate. In Vancouver, the city that has named itself a City of Reconciliation, the commemoration of Confederation could not happen without the engagement of local Indigenous people. Initially, representatives from the three local nations refused to take part, but after some negotiation, they agreed to participate in Confederation events that recognized their histories (Urban Aboriginal Peoples' Advisory Committee 2016b).

Included as a major listing in the event calendar was the previous day's landing in Vanier Park/sənaʔqʷ of the canoes that carried the participants in the "Pulling Together Canoe Journey." However, this journey was not organized solely to celebrate Confederation but was actually the sixteenth annual incarnation of this resurgence initiative by coastal Indigenous peoples, which included up to thirty canoes paddled by Indigenous youth and local public service employees on a ten-day journey (Silva 2017, 1; Pulling Together Canoe Society n.d.). On the next day, which was the final day of the journey, the group paddled across the inlet that separates the

C.2   Pulling Together Canoe Journey landing at χʷay̓χʷəy̓, 15 July 2017.

park from the North Shore, starting at Ambleside Beach near xʷməlċθən, crossing the First Narrows on an ebbing tide, landing at HMCS *Discovery* Royal Canadian Navy Reserve on x̌ces/Dead Man's Island, and then circumnavigating the complicated currents surrounding spapəy̓əq to land at χʷay̓χʷəy̓.

I arrived early for the landing of the canoes, with a backpack full of supplies I might need for a long hot day in the sun. I parked my bike near the back entrance of the former site of Klahowya Village, now a strangely empty place. The buildings still stood but the doors were closed, and there were very few people circulating. However, the Stanley Park Miniature Railway was still running. No longer called the Spirit Catcher Train, this year it was branded the Urban Forest Train and focused on the ecological history of the forest, including both the local and introduced flora and fauna.[6]

I walked down the slope to the beach, passing the stream of tourists flowing along the seawall on foot and on bicycles. I joined the growing group of people near the beach, who were looking out at the water. We all waited for a long time in the sun and clustered in the small patches of protective shade. Eventually, canoes began to appear offshore (see figure C.2). The paddlers carefully manoeuvred them to the beach one by one, remaining seated in the canoes while they were greeted by local Indigenous leaders who enacted landing protocols that required the representatives of each canoe to identify themselves and ask for permission to come ashore. The protocols included orature in multiple languages as well as song, which rang out in the clear summer air, heard by the participants of the "Thunderbird Sharing Ceremony" as well as by the people who just happened to be visiting Stanley Park that day. This landing process, with its attention to each group on shore and in the canoes, continued for almost an hour. When it was over, the large canoes were safely pulled up onto the beach, and people began to flow out of them. Because of all the time that I had spent thinking about the history of this park and the efforts of settlers to create it as an exclusively white space, this moment of reversal, marked by the striking visual of a large number of Indigenous people steadily streaming back into the park from the shores of χʷaẏχʷəẏ, struck me as a display of continuity, strength, and futurity.

The organizers had provided a lunch for the paddlers, which was set up on folding tables under the trees just beyond Lumberman's Arch. This was the tenth day of their journey, and the youth seemed tired. They also appeared to be a cohesive group as they sat together in small clusters, amiably chatting in the shade. After lunch, there was a welcome to χʷaẏχʷəẏ, which featured speakers from local Indigenous nations explaining the significance of the place and their ancestral connections to it as well as a performance by Butterflies in Spirit, a Vancouver dance group made up mostly of family members of missing and murdered Indigenous women and girls started by Lorelei Williams.[7] They explained the origins of their dance group and the significance of their costumes, which had the faces of their missing or murdered relatives silkscreened on the front. They danced and drummed in unity and with clear support for one another. All the while, park visitors passed on the sidewalk connecting the Vancouver Aquarium to Lumberman's Arch, which had the effect of separating the people participating in the canoe-landing ceremony from the speakers and performers. At times, this separation was distracting, but mainly it demonstrated the irrelevance of the passers-by to the important work that was going on.

After about forty-five minutes, the performers and speakers led everyone in a procession up to the Thunderbird Performance Grove and past the former Children's Farmyard, the Aquarium, Malkin Bowl, and the Stanley Park Pavilion to a place just between the Air Force Garden of Remembrance and the Rose Garden (see figure c.3). The trees in this specially selected

Aquarium Area *at Stanley Park*

c.3   Map of the Thunderbird Sharing Ceremony events.

grove stand near to each other, in pairs, but with enough space on the ground for people to gather. This performance was the third in a series of collaborations between the dance groups Aeriosa and Spakwus Slulem at this site.[8] These collaborations and the struggle to be permitted to dance in the park are extensively documented by Tsimshian-Tlingit art historian and dancer Mique'l Dangeli in her doctoral dissertation, "Dancing Sovereignty" (2015, 152–206). In this third iteration, Dangeli's dance group, Git Hayetsk, joined Spakwus Slulem on the ground (see figure c.4). As Dangeli details in her work, citing Erin Manning, the "*relationscapes*" of collaborative respectful performance are intricately connected to enactments of Indigenous law and reciprocal relationships to land (32–3, italics original). In the cool shade of the tall trees, this performance required the audience to gaze up into the sky and remain aware of the sounds and movements of dancers within the circle of the grove. It was also an example of generosity, welcome, and care toward the mainly non-Indigenous aerial performers who dangled precariously from ropes and harnesses and held onto the trees. The simultaneous occurrence on 15 July 2017 of the "Pulling Together Canoe Journey" and the collaborative performance by Git Hayetsk, Spakwus Slulem, and Aeriosa, which evoked this book's

C.4 Members of Aeriosa in the trees while members of Spakwus Slulem and Git Hayetsk on the ground sing and dance their welcome to the land and sky, 15 July 2017.

concerns with navigating water currents, the reciprocal relationship to land, and civic and national commemorations, made this performance event a salient illustration of grounded practices that also included a clear display of an eddy of influence at this densely layered site.

This book has focused on understanding how, when, and why Indigenous performance is employed to create and transfer historical knowledge, to affirm the connection to land, and to assert identity. Considered in the context of intercultural and related settler performances, this effort is intended to further our knowledge about the constructed nature of white settler identity in Vancouver and about the use of performance to construct and maintain colonial space. I have also attempted to locate histories that have been ignored by settlers in order to support the project of Indigenous resurgence, which seeks a transition away from existing settler colonial power structures. In light of extensive discussions of the importance of endangered language regeneration, I have tried to communicate my experience of the significant way that performance can act as a mode of language learning and as a method for settlers to learn from Indigenous people. Language informs the way that performance, either in employing Indigenous languages or in accessing Indigenous worldviews, can be part of a grounded practice.

It is vitally important that performance analysis be engaged with Indigenous historiographies. Although performance and visual arts are not necessarily separate practices, the imposed colonial policies, which deemed performance illegal but simultaneously encouraged visual arts, were intended to uncouple the power of combining these art forms. Visual arts or recorded expressive arts are static and controllable commodities and were therefore more permissible in colonial structures, whereas performance requires living bodies in space and thus entailed personal risk for the performers in their confrontation with colonial structures, which depend on Indigenous vanishing. The analysis of past performance practices by Indigenous peoples can play a part in locating Indigenous cultural continuity and histories.

This book has tried to reconsider the settler city of Vancouver; its potential applications are meant to inform scholarship and performance as well as civic life. My experiences studying the hən̓q̓əmin̓əm̓ language are shared to offer further understanding of the significance of Indigenous-language learning as a method of self-decolonizing for settlers/newcomers. Since I was given permission to share the language research, my experiences may also contribute to a wider understanding of the knowledge about this area held within hən̓q̓əmin̓əm̓ and to increased recognition for the people who are working to regenerate the language and the knowledge it contains. I nonetheless feel that a significant limitation of the process has been a too-fragile connection with people from the Tsleil-Waututh and Squamish Nations. As this book comes to an end, it is even clearer that the work is just begun.

Understanding the influence that James Skitt Matthews had on the City of Vancouver Archives as well as his interventions throughout the city to create a British imperial identity of whiteness may guide future researchers in a more critical engagement with the archives that he, in part, created. Matthews influenced the construction of an idealized Lord Stanley; this understanding helps us begin to deconstruct the settler vision of Stanley Park in order to fully acknowledge and eventually repatriate it as Indigenous land. The discussion of place names as well as the negative connotations of the settler name "Siwash Rock" for a rock formation in the park may aid in a reconsideration of the significance of place names used throughout the broader region. The use of performance to stage historical political interventions at a civic celebration and a contemporary tourist site reveals the possibility of obstructing continuing colonial actions in these spaces of commodification or spectacle. Instead of denigrating Indigenous people who choose to work in these venues, might we instead consider them to be frontline workers of decolonization?

Finally, it is my hope that the terms "grounded practices" and "eddies of influence," although initially rooted in a specific local investigation, may be of use to other scholars engaged in understanding the incredible work done by Indigenous performers whose work contributes to cultural continuation and to the maintenance of Indigenous spaces. Performers act as leaders in the way that the concept is understood by speakers of the hən̓q̓əmin̓əm̓ language: they are those who are strong enough to move against the current and into the light.

Self-Guided Walking Tour of spapəy̓əq/Brockton Point and χʷay̓χʷəy̓/Lumberman's Arch

There are many local Indigenous people who offer guided tours of various areas of the lands known as Stanley Park; some tours are operated by the Vancouver Park Board and the Stanley Park Ecology Society, and others are offered as part of business ventures. The Stanley Park History Group runs a variety of events focused on Stanley Park and Vancouver women's history throughout the year, and there are also other tours that either capitalize on or sensationalize local settler history. This self-guided walk has a different purpose, which is to make visible the construction of whiteness that happens through performance, commemoration, and monument in the park. Doing so may be more of a "disorientation" for non-Indigenous people who have spent time in the park over their lives, but this sort of new perspective, I hope, will have a positive result in creating new relations with both this land and local Indigenous peoples.

Directions: The walk is mostly flat, about one and a half hours long. Start around the 2 kilometre mark on the seawall – near the end of the point at the 9 O'Clock gun installation. If you are driving to the park, you can try to park near the rowing club or the miniature train. If you are biking, a good place to park your bike is near the rowing club.

(1) 9 O'Clock Gun

This walking tour begins standing on a concrete slab. You should be near to the 9 O'Clock Gun. It will be below you on your left. You should be looking at downtown Vancouver, where you can see a floating gas station, the white sails of Canada place, and lots of tall glassy buildings. On your right, you should see a big lilac bush. If you're here in the spring, it will probably have flowers on it. The rest of the year, it will be bushy and green. In front of you, there should be a small plaque.

This cannon was installed in 1894, when a community of families lived here, many of whose members were local Indigenous women married to newcomers who worked at the port. With the start of steamship service to Asia after the railway was completed in 1889, more colonial transport was being conducted on the coast than ever before, and there needed to be stable information in order to navigate into the inlet. For this reason, a lighthouse was built at the tip of the point, and the lighthouse keeper set off an explosion every night at 9:00 p.m. so that ships in harbour could synchronize their clocks in order to measure tides accurately. In 1894 this decommissioned British naval cannon was set up here and became the time signal. It was built in 1816 – and may have seen service in India as the British struggled to control their colonies there at the time. At some point, it was sent to the West Coast. It may have been part of the armaments used by the British while they worked to establish control over local Indigenous people who resisted coal mining in the Nanaimo area, and/or it may have spent time at the military installation in Esquimalt when there was tension with the United States over the establishment of a border. The gun, which is set off every night, is a symbol of the struggle for colonial control of this land – in terms of its ability to inflict violence on those opposing the British but also in terms of creating a method of keeping time that is synchronized worldwide and not necessarily in tune with local rhythms. This method of timekeeping enabled global transportation systems and commerce. It was essential to the establishment of a colonial space.

The British name for the surrounding body of water, the Burrard Inlet, was chosen by George Vancouver during his initial visit to the area in June 1792 to honour his friend Sir Harry Burrard (1765–1840), who was his shipmate on HMS *Europa* in the West Indies in 1785 (Akrigg and Akrigg 1997, 33). Although Captain George Vancouver is best known for his exploration of the Pacific, it is worth noting that his nine years in the West Indies were in service of maintaining the wealthiest centre of commodity exchange of the British Empire, which was based on the trade of enslaved African people. The brutality of the colony of Jamaica in particular created a "garrison society" in which white control of enslaved Africans was held only through the military's constant presence and intervention (see Dillon 2014, 169–71).

Before moving on around the point, look down at the concrete slab commemorated with a plaque explaining that it was set by the royal engineers in 1865 and used as a survey point in 1898. It is a relic of colonial efforts to exert control through mapping. The lilac bush to the right has no sign explaining its origin and seems to be just another part of the natural landscape; however, as Jean Barman details in the opening and closing chapters of *Stanley Park's Secret: The Forgotten Families of Whoi Whoi, Kanaka Ranch and Brockton Point* (2005), the bush was planted by Martha Smith (nee Thompson) by the front door of the family home shortly after her marriage in 1896 when she left the Coqualeetza Residential School (150–2). She married into the Smith family, who had lived on the point since Peter Smith arrived from Portugal and married a Squamish woman named Kenick in 1860. This family and their neighbours were dispossessed of their homes during a court case in the 1920s, and although the decision allowed them to stay on as tenants of the City of Vancouver until their deaths, the Vancouver Park Board decided in 1931 that the homes on the south shore of the point needed to be removed in order to allow the people of Vancouver to view the downtown harbour skyline. The families were offered moving expenses and two-year's free tenancy in other city-owned houses. They left and their homes were either burned or bulldozed (62, 200–31). There are no words embossed in brass commemorating the origins of this lilac bush to note this dispossession.

Directions: To get to the next stop on the tour, you have to go down the hill to the 9 O'Clock Gun. Once you get to the gun, turn left, walk along the walking path of the seawall, and continue around the point.

Keep walking along the seawall toward the mountains. The water should be on your right and a small hill with trees and bushes on your left. Continue until you see a round concrete lookout that juts out from the seawall. The next stop is in the middle of that lookout.

(2) Port of Vancouver Centennial Plaques at the Lighthouse

The second stop on the tour is inside a concrete semi-circle lookout that faces the water, North Vancouver, the mountains, and the port. The day that I'm here, there's a big kelp bed floating in front of me. The waves are crashing onto the shore, and there's a little bit of wind. All around me are different plaques.

Installed in 1988 during the celebrations to mark the park's centennial, these five bronze plaques emphasize the significance of the working port and resource-extraction industries. From left to right, they commemorate mineral, petroleum, forestry, and agricultural products as well as the method of shipping consumer goods by container and the cruise ship industry. Each plaque is embossed with a relief view of an area in the eastern inlet. This is a unique commemorative installation in this area of the park because it emphasizes industry and extraction, which are at the core of the colonial project. This point is named after Francis Brockton, an engineer on HMS *Plumper*, which surveyed the BC coast from 1857 to 1860 (Akrigg and Akrigg 1997, 30). In June 1859 a vein of coal was discovered in the harbour you see to the right, which is still called Coal Harbour. This find set off a flurry of mining activity and land speculation led by Robert Burnaby, who established a mining camp in August of that year. Sean Kheraj in *Inventing Stanley Park* (2013) speculates that this coal deposit was the reason why Colonel Richard Clement Moody in the colonial land office set aside the land as a "government reserve" in 1859, although it was mistakenly labelled a "military reserve" when surveyed in 1863 (35–8). Even though there was not much useable coal there, Kheraj suggests that this find changed Europeans' relations with this land because it necessitated the creation of detailed maps and prioritized extractive commodities.

After looking at the plaques and the distant port scenarios they portray, I encourage you to focus on the interactions of the water as it moves past this point of land, called "spapəy̓əq" in the hən̓q̓əmin̓əm̓ language, meaning "bent at the end." This lookout emphasizes the industrial interactions that occur at a port where land-based resources are prepared for transport over water. It is also, however, an excellent place to observe the swirling currents that occur when flowing water meets an obstacle. Such eddies are of material consequence for those who travel over water – as well as a way to think about the sort of dynamic intercultural interaction that has happened in this space. When water meets an obstacle, the flow of the current changes until, over time, the water eventually changes the shape of the obstacle, which in turn affects the current. The other sites on this self-guided walk trace installations, performances, and monuments that are instances of such dynamic "eddies of influence."

Directions: To get to the next spot, continue along the seawall, go around the point, and pass beneath the simulation lighthouse. With the water on your right, keep walking toward the little lighthouse. There should be a concrete wall on your left.

Continue along the walking path. You should now see the Lions Gate Bridge. Keep the water on your right and the concrete wall on your left. Eventually, you'll see a little set of stairs on your left next to a concrete platform. Go up the stairs and cross the street, watching for bikes and cars. You should be heading toward a café and gift shop.

Stop walking when you see a fire hydrant on your right. Look left into the treed area to see one of Musqueam artist Susan Point's house posts. It's a big wooden structure resembling a gate.

(3) Susan A. Point's *People amongst the People* (2008)

You should be standing near a small wooden fence on the gravel path. Behind you should be the road, and in front of you should be a café and gift shop. To your left is Susan Point's *People amongst the People*.

Installed as an intervention into the Northwest Coast totem pole display, the series of three works that make up Susan A. Point's *People amongst the People* (2008) are gateways into the area that assert local Indigenous histories and relationships to the land. As Musqueam curator Jordan Wilson (2016b) explains,

> Weaving motifs speak not only to the historic tradition of wool weaving amongst our communities in general, but also gesture toward nearby stiʔəwəq̓ʷ ("Second Beach"), where women gathered diatomaceous earth, used to prepare the wool of mountain goats and woolly dogs. An image of a mask dancer alludes to its relationship with χʷayχʷəy̓ (nearby "Lumberman's Arch"). Much like historic Coast Salish designs, depictions of human and non-human entities are given equal prominence, and portrayed together, conveying a reciprocal and spiritual relationship between each other. Herring and orcas are featured, two species once present in the "Burrard Inlet" ecosystem; the former critical in the sustenance of our ancestors, but frequently overlooked. Like her ancestors before her, Susan masterfully blends high-relief sculpture with low-relief engraving, as well as naturalistic representation with geometric design.

Wilson also comments on the significance of the house post as the enduring structure that remained in place during seasonal rounds and awaited a family's return, linking Point's gateway works to the return of Coast Salish peoples' authority over this land.

Directions: Continue walking toward the café, and turn left into the totem pole viewing area. This is the next stop on the tour.

(4) The Totem Pole Viewing Area

You should be in a gravel clearing in front of a number of totem poles. There're probably a lot of tourists taking pictures and milling about.

Originally installed at χʷay̓χʷəy̓ in 1924, the totem pole display was created by early settlers involved with the Art, Historical and Scientific Association of Vancouver who reified the Northwest Coast monumental poles – as opposed to local Indigenous peoples' work – as worthy of salvaging and intended to install an abandoned village from up the coast as an education and tourist site. The village installation began with a few totem poles, and then Squamish activist Andy Paull intervened, explaining to the organizers that it would be very insulting to have a village from the Northwest Coast on their land. The project was abandoned, but the totem poles remained, becoming more and more popular. They were moved to this spot in 1960 and have been added to over the years and updated. This is the most photographed site in the city of Vancouver, and depending on the season and the weather when you are visiting the park, there may be people who arrived there in full tour buses and are now milling around, using the washroom facilities, and buying refreshments at the gift store and café called Legends of the Moon. Although current signs indicate the origins of the poles themselves, this background regarding the involvement of the Art, Historical and Scientific Association of Vancouver and Andy Paull's intervention connects with the way that Susan A. Point's gateway works mark a contemporary intervention into a long history of local assertions of territorial control.

Directions: To get to the next stop, continue walking along the gravel path, leaving the totem poles on your left. Stay to the left and leave the viewing area, heading toward a sculpture in a separate clearing.

(5) Luke Marston's *Shore to Shore* (2015)

You should be in a gravel area between the totem pole viewing area and a road, looking at a large sculpture.

The sculpture *Shore to Shore* (2015) commemorates both Portuguese newcomer Joe Silvey, who arrived from the Azores Islands in the mid-1800s, and the women who married him: Khaltinaht (Musqueam-Squamish) and Kwatleemaat (Shíshálh). It was carved by Luke Marston (aka Ts'uts'umutl), who is the great-great-grandson of Silvey and Kwatleemaat. This work is placed near the family's home and was unveiled in April 2015. The process of the development of the project has been extensively documented in film and print and on a companion website that explains the symbolic details of the artwork. Of note for this tour is the complicated nature of the construction of whiteness. Silvey was from a southern European nation and did not have access to the same privileges as British colonial citizens. Whiteness could be achieved by non-British people only if they did not live in proximity to nonwhite people or work alongside them. According to the Indian Act, which decreed that Indigenous women who married non-Indigenous men lost their claims to status, the children of Silvey and his wives would also not have official Indian status. However, they lived in a way that asserted their relationship to their ancestral lands – which were not designated as an "Indian Reserve." Jean Barman's *Stanley Park's Secret* (2005) outlines the complicated nature of the status of the mixed Indigenous and non-Indigenous families that inhabited this point long after the land was designated a park, and her book *The Remarkable Adventures of Portuguese Joe Silvey* (2004) is a detailed biography of his life and family.

Directions: To get to the next stop, walk all the way back past the viewing area until you reach the gift shop and the café. Go around the back of the building.

Once you are at the back of the building, you should see a grove. Past the grove is a big field. Go and stand anywhere you want in the field. I like to sit on a bench underneath a big tree pretty close to the road. As this field is often used as a cricket pitch, be careful to stay out of the way of the possible flying balls.

(6) Cricket Pitch

If you *are* sitting on the bench and facing the water, on the other side of the road, next to the bicycle path, you can almost see a boulder.

The boulder has a brass plaque on it commemorating Edward Stamp's lumber mill project. The text reads, "Here/ Captain Edward Stamp/ pioneer industrialist and legislator/ started lumbering operations; then, finding / a better site, he moved elsewhere on / Burrard Inlet, and founded in the wilderness, / now the City of Vancouver, the famous / Hastings Sawmill / 1865." What is not spelled out by the plaque is that after having the land cleared, Stamp and his workers realized there were currents that

swirled around the point that made it too dangerous for his purposes. If
he had known the place name or its meaning ("bent at the end") or if he
had communicated with local people who navigated the waters, he would
never have made this mistake. Instead, after cutting down the trees, he
abandoned this space and set up farther down the inlet, close to where
Main Street meets the water and near CRAB Park. However, the land then
became a recreational resource, as you can see if there is a cricket game
underway. As one of the few cleared spaces in the early days of the city, it
was opened as an athletic grounds in 1891. The Vancouver Cricket Club
was formed in 1889 – the year after the inauguration of Stanley Park by
colonial authorities.

This was also the site of a performance of note, *The Jubilee Show*, which
celebrated the sixtieth anniversary of the incorporation of Vancouver and
was an ambitious dramatic pageant of Vancouver history. It ran from 1 to
17 July 1946 and included 4,200 performers on the purpose-built Timber
Bowl outdoor stage, which seated 15,000 spectators (see figures 3.1 to 3.4). It
began when the 9 O'Clock Gun was set off each night and opened with the
"Indian Sequence," which included a "Potlatch Ballet" where 125 Vancouver
settler citizens cast as Indigenous characters performed a dance that combined one of the most elite European forms with an outlawed West Coast
ceremony. It's also important to note that this assertion of whiteness and
settler society did not go without challenge, as the Native Brotherhood of
British Columbia strategically ran a performative installation and political
intervention called *The Indian Village and Show* at səṅaʔqʷ on the southern
shore of False Creek, near the present-day site of Vanier Park (see figures 3.5
to 3.12).

Directions: To get to the next stop, continue walking across the field. This is
one of the longer walks between stops, about 700 metres. When you reach
the hedges protecting the Brockton Oval playing field, walk between them
and the road, with the hedges on your left and the road on your right. You
should see a little cottage.

Keep the cottage on your right and the hedges on your left. Walk along
the concrete path and continue around the bend. When you see a fork in
the path, go right. You'll walk past a little garage structure, and the path will
turn to gravel. You'll see a road (Avison Way) that has a lot of parking on it.
Cross that road to a trail head. It's not marked, but there is a sign that says "No
stopping" and another that says "Pick up after your dog." This is Kinglet Trail, a

path that runs parallel to Stanley Park Drive through the woods. It should be a gravel path surrounded by a lot of foliage.

Head down the trail and follow it for quite some time until it opens up. Then cross the street and continue walking toward the big logs propped up on each other until you reach the signs commemorating both Lumberman's Arch and χʷaẏχʷəẏ on the north side of the path before the arch.

(7) Lumberman's Arch/χʷaẏχʷəẏ

You should be near to the base of Lumberman's Arch, a structure made up of very large logs propped up on each other. Make yourself comfortable. There should be benches to sit on or trees to stand under.

The sign on the right side of the path explains the history of the original Lumberman's Arch, first installed at this site shortly after its construction to celebrate the Duke of Connaught's visit to the city in 1912. It remained in place until 1947 when, due to rot, it was dismantled and replaced with the current arch in 1952. This sign also includes an image of workers digging in what archeologists call a "midden" mound next to the village of χʷaẏχʷəẏ in 1888. It included calcified shells, belongings, and possibly human remains. This mound was used as grading material for the first road put through the park. The material did not hold up to traffic and was replaced shortly afterward.

The building of this road was the topic of August Jack Khahtsahlano's speech at the "Rededication of Stanley Park" held here on 25 August 1943. Over 15,000 people attended this event, held near the end of the Second World War, when much of the perimeter of the park was off limits to the public due to Canadian military defence installations. For photos of the performance, which was conceived, cast, scripted, and directed by the city archivist James Skitt Matthews, see figures 2.1 to 2.4. Although this was in many ways a puzzling event orchestrated by Matthews to performatively enact his construction of Lord Stanley's visit to the park in 1889, the presence of Khahtsahlano, who told the story of his family's home being disturbed by road workers and asserted that they were still waiting to be paid, is an example of an Indigenous person's strategic use of a stage to reach a wide audience at a time when dancing, Indigenous languages, and land claims were prohibited.

Before moving on to the next site, look across the water to the mountains to see the twin peaks known as "The Sisters" to local Indigenous people or as "The Lions" since the 1890s when Judge John Hamilton Grey suggested the name because of his view of their similarity to the "lions couchant" of heraldry that adorn Trafalgar Square in London (Akrigg and Akrigg 1997, 154). If you would like, walk beneath the roadway and through the covered tunnel to the children's waterpark and small beach. From this vantage point, it is clear how easily the inlet could be crossed at the narrows to get to the North Shore by canoe, making it an ideal accessible landing place for large gatherings, such as the last recorded potlatch witnessed by white settlers in 1885.

Directions: After you finish exploring the area around χʷay̓χʷəy̓, head away from the water and go toward the concession to get to the next stop.

When you are facing the concession, turn left and walk with the water at your back along a concrete path. There should be a row of younger trees on your left and a wooded area on your right. Continue along the path. At the fork, go left on the main part of the path. Soon, a tall concrete pole will come into view among the trees. This is the Japanese War Memorial, the next stop on our tour.

(8) Japanese Canadian War Memorial

You should be in a circular concrete area surrounded by hedges, and there should be a concrete memorial pole surrounded by a small chain.

By August 1943, when the "Rededication of Stanley Park" was performed just north of here, the internment of Japanese people living on the West Coast was complete, and seized Japanese properties had been sold off – although this was not without controversy at the time. It is important to note the widespread fear of invasion that gripped the West Coast during the Second World War. The military infrastructure from Boundary Bay to Tofino included over 400 buildings and outposts. A civilian group called the BC Rangers, whose volunteers kept watch in isolated areas, included some Indigenous people who also wanted to protect their lands from further invasion.

The memorial structure in front of you, erected after the First World War to honour Japanese Canadian soldiers, was also affected by the fear of invasion. At the top of the structure is a lantern shape that was illuminated nightly when the memorial was first dedicated in 1920. On 16 December 1941 the lantern was extinguished, possibly due to blackout restrictions as well as Japan's status as an enemy of the Allies. It was not relit until 2 August 1985, just before the Canadian government issued an apology for its internment policy in 1988 and paid redress to survivors of the internment camps (Greenaway n.d.).

Directions: From the memorial, go around the hedges and walk up the hill on the concrete path. Keep the playground on your right, heading toward the Stanley Park Railway. Sometimes, it's closed, but in July, August, October, and December, it's open. If it's closed, stand at the gate and look in. If it's open, go inside the gate to explore the area and then stand near Stanley Park Junction, the small train station.

(9) Stanley Park Miniature Railway and Former Children's Farmyard

You should be standing near Stanley Park Junction, a small train station inside the former children's farmyard.

A small railway began operating in the park in the 1940s, but after Hurricane Freda blew through Vancouver in October 1962, the Park Board used some of the cleared area to build a more elaborate attraction. On 29 May 1964, city archivist James Skitt Matthews organized another "Rededication of Stanley Park" to celebrate the seventy-fifth anniversary of Lord Stanley's visit, which was followed by the opening of the Stanley Park Miniature Railway with a reenactment of the Last Spike ceremony, which had signalled the completion of the Canadian Pacific Railway in 1885 (see figure 2.7). Through this performative event, the miniature train – including its replica of Engine 374, which had pulled the first passenger train across the country – was explicitly connected to the completion of the Canadian Pacific Railway, forming a tidy circle that encompassed British Columbia's entrance into Confederation in 1871 based on the promise of a cross-country railway, the founding of the City of Vancouver and the rampant property speculation that occurred when it became clear that the terminus station would be in the city, and the colonial designation of this land as a park, which was the first act of City Council in 1886.

The original four-minute ride was embedded in celebrating resource extraction as it passed by "a prospector's cabin complete with water wheel, a fire ranger's lookout, [and] an Indian encampment" before continuing "over a rustic bridge, along the shoreline of a man-made lake and across the lake on a 140-foot-long trestle into a windowed 60-foot-long snow-shed, on through the blackness of a 60-foot-long tunnel, [and] around a view through the trees of Burrard Inlet" (Lindsay 1964, 30). During the Aboriginal Tourism Association of British Columbia's Klahowya Village events from 2010 to 2014, the ride was called the Spirit Catcher Train, and Indigenous iconography was laid over the many significations of the celebrated settler culture.

Directions: Go back through the gate where you entered and down the hill toward the Japanese War Memorial. The playground should be on your left. When you reach a fork, go right. You should pass a wooden structure on your right as you skirt along the top of a hill. Keep walking with the curve of the concrete path and then continue walking straight. You will pass the railway café on your right and go over a small creek. There should be a big tree in the middle of the path as you reach the bus loop.

As you face the bus loop, there will be a small concrete path to your left. Go down that path. You should be walking with a little waterfall on your left and the bus loop on your right. When you reach a fork, keep right, curving around the bus loop. You will see a green signpost. Go right and then continue walking straight until you reach a road. The bus loop should be on your right and the Stanley Park Pavilion on your left.

Once you reach the road, turn left. Walk along the road toward the pavilion parking lot, keeping the pavilion on your left and a small stone retaining wall on your right. Continue through the parking lot. You should see some gardens on your right and the entrance to Malkin Bowl on your left.

Once you reach the end of the parking lot, there're a number of paths you could take. Continue straight on the wider concrete path that goes alongside Malkin Bowl, which will be on your left. You'll pass a water fountain and some benches. The Rose Garden is just over the hill on your left. Keep walking straight.

You'll see a playground. Continue past the playground, keeping it on your right, until you see a statue across some grass on the right. It's a human figure with its arms in the air. You can cut across the grass to get there or take the path, which swoops around. Go and stand facing the statue.

(10) Lord Stanley Statue

You should be standing in front of a statue of Lord Stanley with a small garden right behind you.

This final stop on the tour sums up many of the ways that we have encountered the construction of whiteness in the previous nine spaces. This statue is also a result of the performative organizing efforts of city archivist James Skitt Matthews. In 1952 he became aware of Mayor David Oppenheimer's promise to Lord Stanley during his 1889 visit that Vancouver would commemorate his presence in the park with a cairn made up of all the mineral resources to be found in British Columbia. By mid-century, the cairn did not exist, and it is unclear whether such a cairn was ever built or whether the rocks were stolen or dispersed. Matthews took it upon himself to fulfil the promise of commemoration by designing this statue, commissioning the sculptor, crowd-sourcing the funding, and then hiding it away in a warehouse for years until the Vancouver Park Board agreed to place it prominently at the entrance to the park – rather than near Chaythoos on the high bluffs by current-day Prospect Point, which is where Lord Stanley actually stopped in the park. Matthews eventually had his way, and the statue was placed here during another ceremony attended by Governor General Georges Vanier in 1960 (see figure 2.6).

The shape of the statue is based on the ceremony Matthews first devised for the 1943 "Rededication of Stanley Park," as is the phrase etched on its base. Although there were some eyewitnesses to Lord Stanley raising his hands in this manner, there is no account recorded in the archives of him ever having made a speech. Indeed, since it was an overcast day, he may have been raising his hands to test for rain.

Since there is no verifiable account of a speech by Lord Stanley, the words on the stone may have another origin, one that is much more in keeping with a mid-century reaction to the rise of fascism in Europe than with the British colonial project of the late nineteenth century. Just before Matthews scripted the 1943 ceremony, he compiled a scrapbook of Dr J.L. Telford's mayoral activities in Vancouver from 1939 to 1940. One of Telford's tasks in 1939 was to write to the descendants of Lord Stanley as part of the city's fiftieth anniversary commemoration of his visit. In this letter, Telford described the park as "one thousand acres of primeval forest, interspersed with patches of smooth green sward; sea girt with sandy beaches where tens of thousands gambol on a summer's day," adding that he wished he could magically transport Lord and Lady Derby to "stand upon the same old Indian clearing above the rushing waters of our First Narrows on which your noble father, the Governor-General, stood, and, throwing his arms into the air as though embracing the whole expanse of towering forest before him, besought the Almighty to bless our great park to *the use and pleasure of future generations of all colors, creeds and customs*" ("His Worship" 1940, italics added).

This is the first reference in the city archives that attributes this utterance to Lord Stanley, and it is worth providing a little detail about Telford here. Before serving as Vancouver's mayor, he had been Vancouver East's Co-operative Commonwealth Federation (CCF) member in the provincial legislature from 1937 to 1939 (Elections British Columbia n.d.). He was a charismatic personality known throughout the province for his "spell-binding oratory" and as "the voice of the CCF." Some of Telford's own values seem to be imbued in the statement attributed to Stanley, as he demonstrated later during his term as mayor when he repeatedly made an effort to quell general anxiety about the Japanese at the time of their internment in 1942. This letter, by a socialist mayor in the context of the rise of fascism in Europe and anti-Japanese sentiment in British Columbia, is the first text recorded in the archives that reports Stanley making this generous dedication to people of all "colors, creeds and customs."

Although the sentiment expressed in the phrase is admirable, it is also dishonest and a method of creating a disaffiliation in order to attribute a retroactive benevolence to the original British society created here. This is a logic often used to allow white people to claim innocence. When Matthews attributed this statement to Lord Stanley, he cast the disaffiliation backward to the year 1889, powerfully asserting the absence of racializing discourses and practices that would limit the privileges available to some members of that society. In reframing the past, the statue also hails the contemporary white passer-by to recruit them into an admiration of the generosity of the British nobility. Not all observers, however, have been oblivious to the unlikeliness of Stanley's utterance. Stó:lo poet, scholar, and educator Lee Maracle picks up on it in her story "Mink Witnesses the Creation of Stanley Park" (2014), which ends with the words, "'Stanley Park, named after John Stanley. All races welcome in this park.' All races welcome, humph, good idea" (1).

As a conclusion to this tour, I ask you to consider the numerous spaces you have seen that emphasize the colonial commodification of these lands: the 9 O'Clock Gun, which emphasized British military power as well as the global industrial transportation system; the resource extraction celebrated by the plaques installed at the Port of Vancouver for the park's centennial; and the early years of the forestry industry as indicated by Edward Stamp's failed attempt to establish a mill in the park and by the celebration of that industry evident both in the name chosen for the Timber Bowl outdoor stage, constructed for *The Jubilee Show* of 1946, and in the presence of monumental Lumberman's Arch. A cairn made up of all the mineral resources of the province, although less spectacular than this statue, would have been a more honest expression of colonial interests.

And finally, I suggest that you turn your back to the statue and look in the direction that Lord Stanley is also looking. The edge of this beautiful parkland is spread out in front of you, along with the ocean's shore to the left as well as the tall buildings and traffic of the city in the distance. If it is summertime, you may be able to smell the roses from the garden nearby. If not, the wet green growth and ocean breeze may dominate. This a contested, complicated, and beautiful space, and I encourage you to consider, here and now, how you can use the knowledge you have gained during this tour to responsibly support the original caretakers of these lands in their continued stewardship and in their pursuit of restitution for the past wrongs on which all of this beauty has been built.

Notes

Introduction

1 This area extends from Musqueam, Katzie, Kwantlen, Langley, Marpole, Burrard, Jericho, and Coquitlam to Tsawwassen (Shaw and Campbell 2012, 1–3).

2 Throughout this book, I use various terms to refer to Indigenous peoples. When relevant, I refer to the specific person or group of people by name, such as Musqueam. "Coast Salish" is a term developed by linguists to describe the groups of people along the Pacific Northwest Coast in British Columbia, Washington, and Oregon who speak Salishan languages; I apply this term to describe spaces and activities that have engaged a wider number of coastal peoples. When referring to Canadian policies affecting Indigenous people, I use "Aboriginal" as an umbrella term for First Nations, Métis, and Inuit, and I use "Indian" only when referring specifically to concepts of status contained within Canada's Indian Act or when directly quoting from a source. I mainly use "Indigenous" because it is a transnational term that also connotes a connection to land while emphasizing the global project of decolonization.

3 Skwxwú7mesh is the language of the Squamish Nation, whose population lives among nine communities stretching from the Lower Mainland and especially North and West Vancouver to Squamish and the northern area of Howe Sound.

4 Dr Israel Wood Powell, the first BC superintendent of Indian Affairs, began pressuring the federal government to ban the "potlatch" because the ceremony was understood as a way that Elders could influence the younger generations by passing on their traditional values (Ray 2016, 224). Sir John A. Macdonald issued an Order in Council on 7 July 1883 requiring Indigenous people to abandon potlatching, and he followed it up with an amendment to the Indian Act on 19 April 1884 that made it a misdemeanor to participate in a potlatch or a "Tamanawas" dance, subject to imprisonment for a minimum of two months and a maximum of six (226). A 1927 Indian Act amendment expanded the ban to include all Indigenous people in the western provinces and territories

from dancing off their reserves or appearing in "aboriginal costume" at public
exhibitions (235). Both restrictions were lifted in 1951.

5 čəsnaʔəm was a village used by Musqueam people until approximately 1,500
years ago. In the city of Vancouver, this area became known as Marpole. In the
late 1800s the area became a site of research, and settlers began to remove buried
human remains and belongings. Considered one of the largest "pre-contact
middens" in western Canada, it was declared a National Historic Site in 1933. As
a result of the discovery of intact burials during the building of a condominium
development, Musqueam people and supporters held a vigil and protest from
January to May 2012. In October 2013 the Musqueam Nation purchased part
of the lot. In January 2015 a three-part exhibit, curated by Musqueam people,
opened at the Musqueam Cultural Centre, the University of British Columbia's
Museum of Anthropology, and the Museum of Vancouver ("Documentation"
2015). The City of Vancouver returned a portion of the čəsnaʔəm lands located
at 8902 Milton Street to the Musqueam Indian Band in October 2018 ("Portion
of čəsnaʔəm Village" 2018).

6 *Delgamuukw v. British Columbia* [1997] 3 SCR 1010. Anishinaabe-Ojibway legal
scholar John Borrows (1999) explains that the 1997 Supreme Court of Canada
decision regarding the Gitksan and Wet'suwet'en peoples' claim to legal title and
the right to self-government "extended the laws of evidence to accommodate
Aboriginal traditions and histories" so that they are placed on equal footing with
other types of historical evidence (555–6).

7 The Idle No More movement is a continuation of Indigenous peoples' efforts
to protect their lands for centuries – being similar to the "flashpoints" of the
Red Power movement of the 1960s and 1970s, mobilization against the 1969
White Paper, the Oka Crisis of 1990, the Gustafsen Lake Standoff of 1995,
and more (Kino-nda-niimi Collective 2014). The events of the winter of 2012
were sparked by Indigenous women's response to a federal omnibus bill that
left only 0.01 per cent of rivers and 0.03 per cent of lakes protected, notably
excluding from protection two rivers in British Columbia that lie along the route
of the contentious Enbridge Northern Gateway Pipelines project (Ecojustice
2012). The Standing Rock Sioux have been opposing the pipeline of Dallas-
based Energy Transfer Partners that crosses their territory; from April 2016
to February 2017, thousands of people representing over 300 Indigenous
nations joined the resistance camp (Crane-Murdoch 2016; Deerchild and
Fontaine 2016). Although within days of assuming power the new Republican
administration issued federal permits to complete the pipeline, there is ongoing
litigation by the Standing Rock Sioux ("Standing Rock Sioux" 2017).

8 The downriver hən̓q̓əmin̓əm̓ word is "xʷənitem" (Suttles 2004, 255–6).

Chapter One

1 Algonquin-Anishinabe theatre scholar and dramaturg Lindsay Lachance (2018)
   also discusses Coulthard's concept of *grounded normativity* in relation to the
   development of Indigenous political and theatrical performances.

2 The French word "propre," which Steven F. Rendall has translated as "proper,"
   has more nuance. It can mean "own" as in "my own" or "ma propre"; it can mean
   "clean" as in "the clean desk" or "la bureau propre"; or as in Rendall's translation,
   it can mean "correct" like the English word "proper." The translation of "propre"
   as "own," in consideration of the rest of de Certeau's definition of strategy, seems
   most accurate.

3 The curators and themes of each exhibit are listed as follows:

   > Musqueam Cultural Education Resource Centre and Gallery: Curated
   > by Leona Sparrow with co-curators Terry Point, Jason Woolman
   > and Larissa Grant, this minimum one-year exhibit focuses on the
   > sophistication of past and present knowledge and technologies of the
   > Musqueam people.
   >
   > Museum of Vancouver: The curatorial collective was comprised of Terry
   > Point, Susan Roy, Viviane Gosselin, Larissa Grant, Leona Sparrow, Jordan
   > Wilson, Jason Woolman and Susan Rowley. The minimum five-year
   > exhibit focuses on belongings, Indigenous ways of knowing, colonialism
   > and cultural resilience.
   >
   > Museum of Anthropology: Curated by Susan Rowley and Jordan
   > Wilson, this one-year exhibit focuses on language, oral history and recent
   > community actions taken to protect c̓əsnaʔəm. ("Unprecedented, Three-
   > Site Exhibition" 2014)

4 The word "ʔiməxneʔtən" (visitor) is composed of the word "walk" with lexical
   suffixes meaning "alongside"; thus a visitor is one who walks alongside (Shaw
   and Campbell 2013b, 333). This denotation echoes de Certeau's (1984) emphasis
   on the "pedestrian speech act" (97), but in this formulation the walkers are the
   newcomers to the unceded lands.

5 The voices belonged to Larry Grant, Howard E. Grant, Howard J. Grant, Dickie
   Louis, Mary Roberts, and Wendy Grant-John. My thanks to Larry Grant (2015)
   for this information.

6 I extend my thanks to Jill Campbell (2014) for this phrasing.

7 In *The Archive and the Repertoire* (2003), Diana Taylor also discusses the
   significance of performative immersive practices to language learning. She
   asserts that taking the teaching of languages seriously also includes "thinking

about reiterated, embodied social practice. Students learn ... by staging scenarios where the acquired language takes on meaning, by imitating, repeating, and rehearsing not just words but cultural attitudes. Theorizing these practices, not just as pedagogical strategies but as the transmission of embodied cultural behaviour, would enable scholars to branch out into new cultural thinking about the repertoire" (26).

8   For an audio recording of the December 2014 celebration, see Gaertner (2014a).

9   The language continuum is also responsive to the geography of the land and water. The boundary between hən̓q̓əmin̓əm̓ and Halq̓eméylem is close to the area where the ocean flood tide, at its highest in midwinter, produces slack water for 80 kilometres. It is said that it is possible to catch this up-bound tide from the mouth of the river and paddle to Katzie – the farthest upstream village with a community that speaks hən̓q̓əmin̓əm̓ (Suttles 2004, 514).

10 A lexical suffix is a grammatical unit added to the end of a stem. It is "often similar to what could be expressed as an independent 'lexical' root [but] there isn't always an independent root in the language which expresses quite the same range of meanings," nor is there "necessarily any similarity in sound or form between a lexical suffix and an independent root with a similar meaning" (Shaw and Campbell 2013a, 200). Patricia Shaw (2019) further explains, "Within hən̓q̓əmin̓əm̓, lexical suffixes can have semantic values characterizing shape (e.g., the -as ~ -əs suffix for 'round'), or quantificational meaning (e.g., -mat for 'part of a whole'), or relative location (e.g., -mən ~ -min), among others. The principal 'lexical' categories in grammar (at large) are noun, verb, adjective; so you could say that a lexical suffix is a grammatical unit that has semantic properties of a lexical category but functions morphosyntactically as a derivational suffix added to a lexical root/stem." Lexical suffixes have long been recognized as a distinct feature of languages of the Pacific Northwest. Laurence C. Thompson (1979) describes them as "legion" in Salishan languages, where they cover "a number of semantic classes such as parts of the body, other familiar elements of nature, various artifacts and some concepts; they are frequently extended to metaphorical and abstract uses" (700). Suttles (2004) identifies ninety-one lexical suffixes in his reference grammar and speculates on the existence of twenty-eight others (285–319).

11 An animated projection of this story, drawn by Suzanne Guerin and animated by Saki Murotani, looped continuously on the wall of the Museum of Vancouver c̓əsna?əm exhibit.

12 Historian Keith Thor Carlson and Stó:lō cultural adviser and historian Albert (Sonny) McHalsie (aka Naxaxalhts'i) of Shxw'ow'hamel First Nation also discuss

the significance of the skillful use of back eddies in upriver travel among the Stó:lō (speakers of Halq̓eméylem) and their use as natural defences against raiders (Carlson and McHalsie 1998, 78–80; Carlson 2010, 53). According to Stó:lō Tribal Council staff and Elders, "all the Indigenous people living along the lower 190 kilometres" of the Fraser River are "'Stó:lō'" (Carlson 2010, 13), which is the Halq̓eméylem word for "river." Although not all Lower Mainland First Nations have joined the Stó:lō Nation, Carlson asserts their cultural connection, while explaining how the multiple and creative affiliations are a part of Coast Salish identity formation (9–13).

13 Schneider's *Performing Remains* (2011) is an influential work on the implications of US Civil War reenactment, performance, and history that has usefully expanded the theoretical field of performance studies, but it must be read with an awareness of the absence of Indigenous peoples in terms of their participation in the war and with an understanding of Indigenous theorizing on the dynamics of temporality, memory, and what reenactment can do. Schneider acknowledges in an endnote that she "does not take up the matter of Native American approaches to history and reenactment" (201n73); however, given both the pervasive use of her theoretical terms in theatre studies and the topic of this research, it is necessary to acknowledge that I am applying her concepts while also connecting them to how local Indigenous peoples engage with performance, history, and time. My thanks to Ric Knowles (2015) for his comments on this subject.

14 To describe the movement, I employ the term "affective swirling" here to connect with theatre theory's concept of affect, which attends to the presence of the body and the full range of public feeling that can be triggered through performance activities (Hurley 2014).

15 As part of the "Park Board Reconciliation Strategies" (Soutar 2018), a process of renaming the rock, led by local Indigenous nations, was underway as of 2017. For more discussion of these strategies, see the book's conclusion.

16 According to Suttles's (2004) reference grammar, the diminutive form occurs only in the progressive (138, 172). In that case, if it is the diminutive "little," it is also a progressive. The full vowel in the first syllable could be explained by its being the plural progressive, as it follows the pattern given by Suttles (193, 196). Suttles also has three other examples of plural progressives that follow a similar pattern (167). I thank Patricia Shaw (2015) for her insight on these matters of hən̓q̓əmin̓əm̓ grammar.

17 As noted above, the nominalized version of this word, "sx̌ʷəy̓em̓," refers to events involving x̌e:l's and to the world before x̌e:l's came (Suttles 2004, 264). Keith Thor Carlson (2010) identifies the upriver word "sx̱wox̱wiyám" as "stories/

histories describing the activities of the Creator, the transformers, and sky-born heroes; often taking place in the distant past, but sometimes involving recent miraculous happenings" (283).

18 Suttles (2004) shows that the intransitive can change from "-əm" to "-em" in the durative form (174–7). Once again, I thank Patricia Shaw (2015) for the feedback on this idea.

19 Patricia Shaw (2015) advises, however, that for the word to become fully transitive, a suffix would have to be added. She also notes that the function of the subject of a "bare" root may well be different from the function of the subject of an overtly intransitivized verb; that is, each could take different kinds of nouns as its subject and thus perform different kinds of roles. She cautions that this is only one subclass or root onto which "-əm" can be added, although I can find no other mention of the suffix in Suttles (2004).

20 The "lions couchant" are meant to symbolize an attitude of restful vigilance and conscious power.

21 There is a continuing controversy over the use of the name Capilano, which is a hereditary name belonging to the Musqueam, to whom Chief Joe was connected by his mother. He was given use of the name while leading a West Coast Indigenous delegation to petition King Edward IV in 1906, but Musqueam people did not consider its continued use appropriate once he returned from London (Carlson 2005, 34). As he was a public figure known by this name, I will continue to use it along with his Squamish name, Su-á-pu-luck.

22 This organization worked with the Vancouver Organizing Committee for the 2010 Olympic and Paralympic Winter Games (VANOC) to officially represent the Lil'wat, Musqueam, Squamish, and Tsleil-Waututh people on whose territories the events were being held. Their involvement and representation were intended to ensure economic benefit to these First Nations groups while in return legitimating the Olympic movement's social impact (Silver, Meletis, and Vadi 2012, 294). Although they comprised a powerful organization, they did not represent all members of their nations – some of whom were very critical of the impact of the Winter Olympics. For more details, see Vancouver Media Co-op (n.d.).

23 For a discussion of iterations of this performance, see the intervention section after chapter 3.

24 Taylor (2003) uses the phrase "DNA of performance" (175) to critique Joseph Roach's concept of "surrogation," explaining that it is "urgent to note the cases in which surrogation as a model for cultural continuity is rejected precisely because, as Roach notes, it allows for the collapse of vital historical links and political moves" (46). Taylor then illustrates this point with the example of Catholic friars' attempts to impose new religious rituals on Indigenous

converts, asserting that the converts may have been "rejecting surrogation and continuing their cultural and religious practices in a less recognizable form. The performance shift and doubling, in this case, preserved rather than erased the antecedents ... [being] a form of multiplication and simultaneity rather than surrogation and absenting" (46). This is an important addition to Roach's genealogical method. When discussing the performative political protests of the grandmothers, mothers, and children of the disappeared in Argentina, Taylor adapts Roach's genealogy of performance to the DNA *of performance*, which she defines as transmissions "that refuse surrogation ... [where] nothing disappears; every link is there, visible, resistant to surrogation" (175). Taylor's use of the metaphor of DNA thus grounds genealogy more specifically in people and place.

25 Ogimaa Mikana: Reclaiming/Renaming is a project that aims "to restore Anishinaabemowin place-names to the streets, avenues, roads, paths, and trails of Gichi Kiiwenging (Toronto) – transforming a landscape that often obscures or makes invisible the presence of Indigenous peoples. Starting with a small section of Queen St., re-naming it Ogimaa Mikana (Leader's Trail) in tribute to all the strong women leaders of the Idle No More movement" (Ogimaa Mikana n.d.). Photos of the project's actions are available at http://ogimaamikana.tumblr.com.

Intervention

1 Co-produced by Raven Spirit Dance and Neworld Theatre, the play was first performed five times each afternoon from 14–16 July 2011, followed by a site-specific dance at the Dancing on the Edge festival. It was commissioned by Neworld Theatre and was developed and produced, in part, through the City of Vancouver's 125th Anniversary Grant Program (Neworld Theatre 2019). The podplay is also available through the theatre company and can be enacted independently at any time. Adrienne Wong acts as the host, opening and closing the audio recording. Quelemia Sparrow plays Song, narrates, and gives the walking directions, Elizabeth McLaughlin plays the mother, and Margo Kane plays the Indigenous woman.

2 A podplay, also known as an audiowalk, is a pre-recorded audio play that interacts with a specific location. Listeners/walkers experience it through the use of a personal media player on-site, listening to the play and simultaneously navigating the area by following directions interspersed throughout.

3 This increased use of podplays is especially evident in Vancouver due to the engagement with the form by Neworld Theatre's artistic associate Adrienne Wong, who in 2011 produced eleven works set in downtown Vancouver (Neworld Theatre 2019).

4   Also known as the CRAB Park boulder, this memorial was dedicated in July
    1997, ten years after the opening of the park. Local activist Don Larson and
    other CRAB park organizers conceived, designed, and placed it in response to
    violence in the neigbourhood and the refusal of authorities to take it seriously.
    The inscription on the granite boulder has the phrase "The Heart ... Has Its
    Own Memory" in larger text, with the following words in smaller text splitting
    the phrase where I have inserted the ellipsis: "In honour of the spirit of the
    people murdered in the Downtown Eastside. Many were women and many
    were Native Aboriginal women. Many of these cases remain unsolved. All my
    relations." The inscription closes with the date of its dedication: "July 29, 1997"
    (Burk 2010, 47–65).

5   Bob Baker (aka S7aplek) is the great-great-grandson of Su-á-pu-luck/Capilano,
    who led the 1906 delegation to London, discussed in chapter 1 (Dangeli 2015,
    171–2).

Chapter Two

1   See Sleigh (2008) on Matthews's education, his brother's death, and his family's
    departure from New Zealand (24–6); on his experience in the trenches during
    world war one (66–70); on his abduction of his first wife and his medical
    discharge (77); on his son's death (91); and on his postwar work difficulties
    (97–101).

2   The colonial place names of the area were formerly Kitsilano Park and the
    Squamish Indian Reserve. The village is known as sənaʔqʷ in hənḡəminəm̓ and
    Sen̓ákw in Sḵwx̱wú7mesh (Roy 2011, 87). Matthews refers to it as Snauq in his
    archival records. As multiple groups used this place, unless I am directly citing
    Matthews, I refer to it as sənaʔqʷ/Sen̓ákw.

3   The complete scanned text of Matthews's *Conversations with Khahtsahlano,*
    1932–1954 (1955) is also now available for download from the City of Vancouver
    Archives. This is the text I use here, and all the page numbers refer to the ones
    inserted at the bottom of the pages, not to the ones on the top right.

4   Although he never explains how he and August Jack Khahtsahlano developed
    a relationship, it may have had its genesis in 1911 when Matthews was one of
    the first settlers to build a home at Kitsilano Point, which had only recently
    been cleared for development (Sleigh 2008, 52). His new home was less than a
    ten-minute walk from where Khahtsahlano lived at what he called Snauq, also
    known as sənaʔqʷ/Sen̓ákw, until 1913 when families were illegally removed and
    their homes burnt to the ground (Roy 2011).

5   Matthews consistently uses "Supplejack" as the spelling of the name of
    Khahsahlano's father. Since Khahtsahlano was known as August Jack before this
    official name change, it seems that Jack was considered the family's surname in
    colonial terms. I will therefore use the spelling "Supple Jack" instead.

6   The process of the naming is described by Charles Hill-Tout in a letter to
    Matthews dated 8 May 1931. After the Canadian Pacific Railway released the
    land for settlement about 1910, the company requested that it no longer be
    named Greer's Beach after a man who had "erected a dwelling there." Railway
    personnel asked the postmaster for ideas, who then asked Hill-Tout, and he
    suggested "Kates-ee-lan-ogh," modifying it by taking off the final "gutteral"
    sound (Matthews 1931–56, vol. 1, 1932, 21).

7   "The Opening of the Park," *Vancouver Weekly News-Advertiser*, 26 September
    1888, 8; "Stanley Park," *Vancouver Weekly News-Advertiser*, 3 October 1888, 2,
    both in City of Vancouver Archives (CVA), Local Newspapers, Vancouver Weekly
    News-Advertiser, 19 September 1888 to December 1910, M-47.

8   "Stanley Park," *Vancouver Weekly News-Advertiser*, 3 October 1888, 2, CVA,
    Local Newspapers, Vancouver Weekly News-Advertiser, 19 September 1888 to
    December 1910, M-47.

9   "Lord Stanley's Arrival at the Terminal City," *Vancouver Weekly World*,
    31 October 1889, 6, CVA, Local Newspapers, Vancouver Weekly World, 5
    September 1889 to 27 September 1894, M-48.

10 Ibid.

11 Ibid.

12 Red hematite was used for the production of iron and steel ("Novel Piece of
    Mine Engineering" 1890), and as Oppenheimer explained in his book *The
    Mineral Resources of British Columbia: Practical Hints for Capitalists and
    Intending Settlers* (1889, 23), processed galena ore from the Kootenay District
    yielded silver and lead.

13 "Today's Events," *Vancouver Weekly World*, 31 October 1889, 1, CVA, Local
    Newspapers, Vancouver Weekly World, 5 September 1889 to 27 September
    1894, M-48. Contrary to this article's date of 31 October 1889, it is clear from the
    Vancouver Daily News-Advertiser that the events described occurred on Tuesday,
    29 October 1889 ("Today's Programme" 1889).

14 "Stanley Cairn," 1888, *Vancouver Weekly World*, 30 October 1888, 5, CVA, Local
    Newspapers, Vancouver Weekly World, 5 September 1889 to 27 September 1894,
    M-48.

15 Below, I discuss this placement of an Indigenous grave at the time and in the
    space of the ceremony.

16 On 17 August 1943, Matthews had a phone conversation with a former police officer, Dan Leatherman, who said that there was something wrong with Plante's story, noting that instead the carriage was drawn by four white horses. On 19 August, Hugh Campbell visited Matthews in his office and also contradicted Plante's story. He was a member of the fire brigade that had acted as the honour guard that day and also said that Stanley did not go out in a two-horse hack but in a carriage drawn by four white horses (Matthews, 1931–56, vol. 6, 1945, 124). Years later, in 1949, after the first reenactment in 1943 but before his work on the publications, Matthews heard from another man, James Martin, who described watching the procession going by with four horses pulling Stanley's carriage and claimed that there were somewhere between twelve and twenty buggies (Matthews, 1931–56, vol. 7, 1956, 298; "Stanley Park – Dedication, 1889," CVA, AM54-S23-2, box 505-C-5, folder 281).

17 The population of the city was approximately 275,000 at the time. The audience of 15,000 was 5.5 per cent of the citizenry; in terms of the 2016 census data, this figure would be the same as a contemporary audience of over 135,000 people (MacDonald 1992, 48; Statistics Canada 2017).

18 "Stanley Park – Rededication, 1943," CVA, AM54-S23-2, box 505-C-5, folder 283.

19 According to accounts of the day, although her name is included here, Armytage-Moore did not take part in the rededication. As she was one of the most politically active locals in support of Indigenous people – working to represent them in courts, as the original publisher of the *Native Voice*, and as a member of the Native Brotherhood of British Columbia – the fact that she did not participate may be an indication that she did not support the celebration of the taking of this land.

20 "Stanley Park – Rededication, 1943," CVA, AM54-S23-2, box 505-C-5, folder 283.

21 Ibid.

22 Ernest Vanderpoel Young (1878–1955) was an engineer and actor from London who had been living in Vancouver since 1911. He helped to form the Vancouver Little Theatre Association and worked in radio as well. He was the chair of Dramatic Entertainment during the city's Golden Jubilee festivities in 1936, staging William Shakespeare's *A Midsummer Night's Dream* and an operatic production of Samuel Coleridge-Taylor's *The Song of Hiawatha* (1898–1900), each performed with two casts – one for voice and the other for performance – outdoors at Brockton Oval. By 1940 he had founded Theatre Under the Stars, and he worked as a director and actor in many of the productions staged in the summers at Malkin Bowl (Sutherland 1993, 4–24).

23 See "1889 Pageant Plans" (1943, 13), "Throngs See 'Birth'" (1943, 13), "Foresight of Pioneers" (1943, 13), "Surveyors Came at Dawn" (1943, 13), "Wine Disappears" (1943, 13), "Vancouver Celebrates" (1943, 3), and "History Turns Back" (1943, 3).

24 "Album of 1943 Rededication of Stanley Park," CVA, AM54-S41, box 173-B-1, album A-10.

25 A revised version of this publication makes up chapter 4 of this book.

26 I also acknowledge the disturbing nature of settler and scholarly fixation on the graves and remains of Indigenous people (in general) and on those of August Jack Khahtsahlano's father in particular. I am not commenting on the actual grave but instead on the use of it by Matthews.

27 These are the conversations that Barman (2005) cites.

28 Matthews is clearly hailing white settlers when he uses the first-person plural possessive here to refer to this Indigenous gravesite. It was certainly not a first for the Indigenous people of the area.

29 For a book about the history of Vancouver, there is a marked absence of Matthews's archives as a source, and his *Conversations with Khahtsahlano* (1955) is used only once, when Roy (2011) cites Khahtsahlano's comment that the Musqueam had no claim to False Creek because the Squamish were the ones who built their houses there. She suggests that this perception "reveals how Aboriginal people have drawn on Western understandings of ownership in making their claims. Possibly August was responding in terms that would make sense to Matthews" (115).

30 See "Lord Stanley Statue – Dedication and Plans – Lord Stanley Statuette – 1956–1959," CVA, AM54-S11-4, box 577-C-3, folder 8; "Lord Stanley Statue File," CVA, AM54-S15-1, box 508-D-6, folder 19; and "Lord Stanley Statue – Oct. 29, 1889 – Lord Stanley Statuette," CVA, AM54-S11-4, box 577-B-1, folder 1.

31 "Unveiling of Lord Stanley Statue by Governor General," CVA, COV-S483, box 36-C-6, folder 105.

32 "Lord Stanley Statue – Oct. 29, 1889 – Lord Stanley Statuette," CVA, AM54-S11-4, box 577-B-1, folder 1.

33 This amount would be the equivalent of $67,500 in 2015 dollars (Bank of Canada n.d.).

34 "Lord Stanley Statue File," CVA, AM54-S15-1, box 508-D-6, folder 19.

35 "Lord Stanley Statue – Oct. 29, 1889 – Lord Stanley Statuette," AM54-S11-4, box 577-B-1, folder 1.

36 Yes, it is named after the same Stanley; he was an amateur hockey enthusiast and founded the competition in 1893.

37 Matthews (1964b) included them in his book about the event, as well as the images of Chaythoos, and he still mentioned Khay-tulk's "wooden mausoleum" but added that it was moved when the water pipes were put in (28).

38 "Stanley Park Railway," CVA, VPK-S652-MI-108, box 721-B-1, folder 12, movie.

39 Later known as Lord Strathcona, Smith was the same man who declined when asked by Vancouver city councillors to name the park in 1888, allowing Lord Stanley to do so instead.

Intervention

1 Julie Burelle's *Encounters on Contested Lands: Indigenous Performances of Sovereignty and Nationhood in Québec* (2019) is an important recent work that takes up this issue in depth.

2 A direct translation would be, "Once again, if you permit."

3 Kane was appointed a member of the Order of Canada on 30 June 2017. Loring has since been chosen as the first artistic director of the Indigenous Stage at the National Arts Centre.

Chapter Three

1 Dick Diespecker, Dorwin Baird, and Pierre Berton, "*Jubilee Show* Script 1, 2, 3," City of Vancouver Archives (CVA), Add. Mss. 226, 514-E-6, files 6, 7, 8, Correspondence, Programmes, and Other Materials, 1946. Details of event planning and newspaper reports can be found in "Diamond Jubilee Committee, Indian Village," CVA, City Clerk's Records, series 27, 80-C-6, file 5, Special Committee Supporting Documents, 1946; and in "Diamond Jubilee, Vancouver, 1946," CVA, Major J.S. Matthews Newspaper Clippings Collection, M2451.

2 While this show was being performed, Tim Cummings and his sister Agnes, descendants of James Cummings and Spukhpukanum (aka Lucy Cummings), still lived on the north side of Brockton Point. Since the Indian Act relied on paternal descent to establish status, this family was not legally considered Indigenous, but it was treated as such in that all of the children were taken to residential schools. When the last family member died in 1958, all evidence of their lives there was erased (Barman 2005, 276; 2007, 23–6).

3 Not only was the ceremony considered uncivilized, but it was also illegal since the potlatch ban remained in force until 1951.

4 "Jubilee Show Cut; More Pep in It Now," CVA, Add. Mss. 226, 564-F-5, file 1, Vancouver Diamond Jubilee Publicity and Advertising Scrapbook, vol. 2. The play ended at 2:00 a.m. on opening night, so three hours had to be cut.

5   This amount would be the equivalent of $3,546,195.65 in 2017 dollars (Bank of
    Canada n.d.).

6   "Vancouver Citizens' Diamond Jubilee Committee to William Scow:
    Assignment," CVA, Mayor's Office Fonds, 34-C-4, file 19.

7   "Correspondence, Programmes, and Other Materials, 1946," CVA, Vancouver
    Citizens' Diamond Jubilee Committee Fonds, Add. Mss. 226, 514-E-6, file 5.

8   Maisie Armytage-Moore was the daughter of R.C. Campbell, who was involved
    with the efforts to install the Kwakwaka'wakw village in Stanley Park in the
    early 1900s (Fortney 2010). After her second marriage, she was known as
    Maisie Hurley.

9   "Vancouver Diamond Jubilee *Indian Village and Show* Program," 3–4, CVA,
    AM1519, PAM 1946–5.

10 "Correspondence, Programmes, and Other Materials, 1946," CVA, Vancouver
    Citizens' Diamond Jubilee Committee Fonds, Add. Mss. 226, 514-E-6, file 5. The
    "Canadian Warriors Pageant" may be a reference to the ceremony involving the
    governor general and the Indigenous war veterans, discussed below.

11 "Vancouver Diamond Jubilee *Indian Village and Show* Program," 17, CVA,
    AM1519, PAM 1946–5.

12 Fortney (2010) also quotes a personal communication with former BC Supreme
    Court justice Thomas Berger, who explains Hurley's and Armytage-Moore's
    influence on his understanding of the significance of the Royal Proclamation of
    1763 and the concept that Aboriginal title had never been extinguished (83).

13 Eric Jamieson's *The Native Voice: The Story of How Maisie Hurley and Canada's
    First Aboriginal Newspaper Changed a Nation* (2016) details Hurley's life and
    long-time collaborative relationships with Indigenous activists from her arrival
    in Vancouver in 1891 to her meeting with Haida Elder Alfred Adams in 1944 on
    a Vancouver street just before his death from cancer, stating that he advised her
    to "give your life to my people by telling the white people about them" (15).

14 "Vancouver Diamond Jubilee *Indian Village and Show* Program," 2, CVA,
    AM1519, PAM 1946–5.

15 Ibid., 5.

16 Ibid., 7.

17 Ibid., 9–11.

18 Ibid., 12–13.

19 Initial discussions with representatives from the Musqueam Language and
    Culture Program indicate that the names listed are not Musqueam or Tsleil-
    Waututh people (Grant 2015). A representative of the Tsleil-Waututh Nation
    Treaty, Lands and Resources Department agreed with this assessment but also
    hypothesized that the performers of the "Twin Wolf Dance" might possibly have

been members of the Tsleil-Waututh Nation dance group Children of Takaya, which was formed shortly after this time (Morin 2015).

20 Matthews saved multiple copies of *The Indian Village and Show*'s program, on some of which he wrote commentary disputing the information included. The one with this comment on the inside cover is in "Correspondence, Programmes, and Other Materials, 1946," CVA, Vancouver Citizens' Diamond Jubilee Committee Fonds, Add. Mss. 226, 514-E-6, file 5. There are three other copies in "Vancouver Diamond Jubilee *Indian Village and Show* Program," CVA, AM1519, PAM 1946-5. In this file, on a copy with "Siwash Rock" written on the cover in the top right-hand corner, Matthews disparaged the stories of Deadman's Island and Siwash Rock. It is clear that this is his writing, as he initialled all of his comments.

21 "36 Indians to Reveal Secret Dances," *Vancouver News-Herald*, 29 June 1946, "Diamond Jubilee, Vancouver, 1946," CVA, Major J.S. Matthews Newspaper Clippings Collection, M2451.

22 "Correspondence, Programmes, and Other Materials, 1946," CVA, Vancouver Citizens' Diamond Jubilee Committee Fonds, Add. Mss. 226, 514-E-6, file 5.

23 "Disgruntled Indians May Quit Show," *Vancouver News-Herald*, 9 July 1946, "Diamond Jubilee, Vancouver, 1946," CVA, Major J.S. Matthews Newspaper Clippings Collection, M2451.

24 "Indians, Jubilee Smoke Peace Pipe," *Vancouver News-Herald*, 10 July 1946, "Diamond Jubilee, Vancouver, 1946," CVA, Major J.S. Matthews Newspaper Clippings Collection, M2451.

25 "Correspondence, Programmes, and Other Materials, 1946," CVA, Vancouver Citizens' Diamond Jubilee Committee Fonds, Add. Mss. 226, 514-E-6, file 5.

26 The letter was a pitch to the organizing committee and may or may not accurately describe all the details of the eventual "giant tom-tom" stage as it was built, although it does correspond with the drawing in the program.

27 "Vancouver Diamond Jubilee *Indian Village and Show* Program," 8, CVA, AM1519, PAM 1946-5.

28 The word "braves" is comparable to "tom-tom" in terms of its usage.

29 "Vancouver Diamond Jubilee *Indian Village and Show* Program," 16, CVA, AM1519, PAM 1946-5.

30 Scow likely spoke in his own language, Kwak'wala.

31 After Alexander received the pole in 1946, it was installed in the garden at Rideau Hall, the official residence of the governor general in Ottawa, and in 1997 it was repainted by Richard Hunt, Martin's grandson.

32 "Mungo Martin," *Vancouver News-Herald*, 1946, "Diamond Jubilee, Vancouver, 1946," CVA, Major J.S. Matthews Newspaper Clippings Collection, M2451.

33 "Vancouver Citizens' Diamond Jubilee Committee to William Scow:
    Assignment," CVA, Mayor's Office Fonds, 34-C-4, file 19. I do not include the
    photos here, as I am still unclear of their status as restricted cultural knowledge.

34 The Royal BC Museum (item 16499) holds a portrait of Cranmer painted during
    this event by Mildred V. Thornton. The inscription on the back reads, "No. 23
    Chief Dan Cranmer, Nimpkjh Tribe of the Kwakiutl at Alert Bay, BC Announcer
    of Cedar Bark Dance Ceremonies at Vancouver, 1946. Painted in a tent at
    Kitsilano grounds at that time. Held on to old practices until about 1949.
    Mildred V. Thornton."

35 Hawker's chapter "The Cranmer Potlatch and Indian Agent Halliday's Display"
    in *Tales of Ghosts: First Nations Art in British Columbia, 1922–61* (2003) is
    an analysis of the significance of this event in the history of Indigenous art in
    British Columbia. Much of the regalia seized from participants has since been
    repatriated and is on display at the U'Mista Cultural Centre in Alert Bay.

36 "Totem-Land Society Correspondence, 1954," CVA, Add. Mss. 336, 547-C-7,
    file 6.

37 The letter is not explicit but is likely talking about what was known as the
    Marpole Midden, or čəsnaʔəm.

38 "Totem-Land Society Correspondence," CVA, Add. Mss. 336-S2, 547-C-7, file 6.
    For an image of the letter, see "Archive / Totem-Land" (1954).

Intervention

1 I am using here modes described by Bert States in "The Actor's Presence:
   Three Phenomenal Modes" (2002). His modes are the "self-expressive,"
   during which we have an awareness of the virtuosic artistry of the actor (26);
   the "collaborative," which breaks down the distance between performer and
   audience, making a more dynamic relationship possible, one that says "we are in
   this together" (29, 33); and the "representational," which is in the "key of *he, she,
   it* and *they*" when an actor becomes a character (33, italics original).

2 red diva projects is committed to "the development, creation, and production
   of innovative works of live performance and new media ... that are ready to
   shape and shift, encircling artists of all disciplines who are willing to answer the
   call for social change through artistic expression ... [by] specializ[ing] in the
   development of original works that reflect an integrated Aboriginal perspective
   and a highly actualized creative process towards production" (PuSh 2013, 3).

3 The PuSh International Performing Arts Festival happens every year for
   three weeks in January and presents "work that is visionary, genre-bending,

multi-disciplined, startling and original. The Festival showcases acclaimed international, Canadian and local artists and mixes them together with an alchemy that inspires audiences, rejuvenates artists, stimulates the industry and forges productive relationships around the globe" (PuSh n.d.).

4 The film was made available for free community screenings throughout 2017 as part of an National Film Board program celebrating the 150th anniversary of Confederation (National Film Board 2019).

5 Clements's *The Road Forward* explicitly credits the Native Brotherhood *and* Sisterhood of British Columbia, and it seems that doing so is her effort to credit the women's work retroactively. Following her lead, I also refer to the brotherhood and sisterhood as working together.

6 The program states, "[P]hotographs from the Constitution Express, besides the obvious difference in clothing and hairstyles, look fairly similar to the photos and videos you've no doubt seen of the Idle No More protests" (PuSh 2013, 2).

7 I use the term "traditional" here to describe songs based on Indigenous cultural knowledge that has been passed down through generations, employing forms, lyrics, and musicality that are connected to past practices but also responsive to contemporary experience.

8 The 1969 White Paper was a policy paper put forward by Prime Minister Pierre Elliott Trudeau and Minister of Indian Affairs Jean Chrétien that aimed to put an end to the legal relationship between Canada and Aboriginal peoples through the dismantling of the Indian Act. It was met with great opposition by Indigenous leaders, as it was considered another attempt at assimilation (First Nations and Indigenous Studies 2009). Further information on the political organizing in response to the White Paper can be found in Arthur Manuel's *Unsettling Canada: A National Wake-Up Call* (2015, ch. 3), written by George Manuel's son. The response to Bill C-45, which triggered the Idle No More movement, can be compared to this earlier instance of Indigenous organizing.

9 Begun by the Working Group on Indigenous Populations in 1985, the United Nations Declaration on the Rights of Indigenous Peoples (UNDRIP) was adopted by the United Nations General Assembly on 13 September 2007, with 144 in favour, 11 abstentions, and 4 against, namely Australia, Canada, New Zealand, and the United States (Blackstock 2013, 20). Canada's main problem was stated to be about Article 19, which requires governments to seek consent from Indigenous peoples regarding policy, as well as Articles 26 and 28, which involve land rights and restitution. The UNDRIP is mentioned twenty-three times in the Truth and Reconciliation Commission of Canada's *Calls to Action* (2015), which repeatedly calls for all levels of Canadian governing bodies and

educational institutions to adopt and implement the declaration as well as to educate students regarding its content. For more details, see Manuel (2015, ch. 13). In May 2016, Canada officially removed its objector status regarding the UNDRIP. An excellent resource for the UNDRIP is *Know Your Rights! United Nations Declaration on the Rights of Indigenous Peoples for Indigenous Adolescents* (2013), prepared by Gitksan scholar Cindy Blackstock, who is the executive director of the First Nations Child and Family Caring Society of Canada.

Chapter Four

1 From 2002 to 2010, I was a co-organizer of a youth exchange program at the Purple Thistle Centre, an arts and activism collective run by youth in East Vancouver. The program involved exchanges between East Vancouver youth and Sahtu Dene youth of Fort Good Hope, Northwest Territories, and was intended to build ongoing relationships between the two communities.

2 The same could be said for much of this book.

3 Raheja (2010) is careful to explain that in using the word "sovereignty" she engages with the discourse concerning those Indigenous concepts of sovereignty that predate European nation-to-nation conceptualizations, asserting that the "English word 'sovereignty', then, becomes the placeholder for a multitude of Indigenous designations employed to describe the concept that also takes into account the European origins of the idea" (198).

4 One of these shows was the closing performance of the first iteration of Marie Clements's *The Road Forward*, discussed in the previous intervention section.

5 ATBC has since changed its name to Indigenous Tourism BC.

6 This is the same miniature railway that was opened in 1964 with a reenactment of the dedication of the park and the hammering of the Last Spike, discussed in chapter 2.

7 Campbell-Johnston was the father of Maisie Armytage-Moore, whose influence with the Native Brotherhood of British Columbia and *The Indian Village and Show* is discussed in chapter 3.

Intervention

1 The live music interacted with a film score created in 2012 by Derek Charke in collaboration with Tagaq for the first commissioned performance at the Toronto International Film Festival (Altman 2012; Martineau 2014).

2   "Monopolylogues," a term originated by Matthews, are performances wherein one actor plays many characters.

3   The Polaris Music Awards began in 2005 to honour, celebrate, and reward "creativity and diversity in Canadian recorded music by recognizing, then marketing the albums of the highest artistic integrity, without regard to musical genre, professional affiliation, or sales history, as judged by a panel of selected music critics" (Polaris Music Prize 2019).

4   The on-screen "Preface by Robert Flaherty" that opens *Nanook of the North* explains that he gained the actors' approval for the project by showing them the developed film as he went along. The only credit given for the film is Robert Flaherty's name as producer. Information regarding the Inuit experiences of working on the film is from Claude Massot's documentary *Nanook Revisited* (1988), in which he returned with a film crew to the community where Flaherty was based to discuss its making.

5   Moderated by Michelle Raheja, the panel discussion featured Tagaq as well as Yellowknives Dene filmmaker Amos Scott and biologist Joel Heath examining the question "How do we best tell Indigenous stories?"

Conclusion

1   The Tsilhqot'in's court case and their blockades in an effort to stop logging operations in their territory south and west of Williams Lake had been going on for over twenty years. Then, on 26 June 2014, the Supreme Court of Canada unanimously affirmed the Aboriginal title of the Tsilhqot'in to 1,700 square kilometres. This was the first confirmation of Aboriginal title outside of an Indian reserve in Canada. It includes not only old village sites but also sites that have been used for resource gathering and hunting. The court decision also clarified how to prove Aboriginal title and when Aboriginal consent is needed for resource development projects (McCue 2014).

2   All information regarding this committee's activities is from the minutes of their meetings posted on the City of Vancouver's website (Urban Aboriginal Peoples' Advisory Committee n.d.).

3   One such example is detailed by Tsimshian-Tlingit art historian and dancer Mique'l Dangeli (2015), who describes how a Park Board staff member, while attempting to enforce the board's conception of local protocols, delayed a collaborative performance by a Squamish dance group and a non-Indigenous aerial dance company for over a year (152–206). The learning that resulted from this fraught process has influenced subsequent Park Board policy and decisions.

4   weaving spells her name without capital letters.

5   An update on achievements related to the strategies adopted in 2016 was
    released in April 2018, including an articulation of statements to guide the
    ongoing process:

> Mission: Decolonize the Vancouver Park Board. The Park Board
> recognizes the institution's colonial history and upholds the Board's
> commitment to the eleven Reconciliation Strategies.
>
> Vision: For the Park Board to be an evolvable organization in which
> every employee and Commissioner recognizes the humanity in themselves
> by recognizing and respecting the humanity of First Peoples; an
> organization that sets a worldwide example in treating Reconciliation as a
> decolonization process.

It also identifies the values that guide the work:

> Patience: Colonialism didn't happen overnight. Untangling it takes time.
> We will pace ourselves for the marathon, not the sprint. We will adjust
> deadlines to ensure things are done well and respectfully.
>
> Clarity: We will focus on how colonialism functions to exclude, not on
> how to include.
>
> Pragmatism: All staff are inheriting a system not of our making.
> The Park Board Reconciliation Team is here to assist colleagues with
> examining the ways colonialism continues to damage others. Blame is
> unproductive.
>
> Leadership: We will nurture and sustain each other, demonstrating
> Indigenous principles in the way we function as a team.
>
> Learning: We consent to learn in public. We will make mistakes. We
> will sit with those mistakes, be transparent about them, and use them both
> to learn and to teach. Our mistakes will be diagnostic tools. (Soutar 2018,
> 7–8)

6   The audio on the train in 2017 described the 2006 blowdown of trees during a
    windstorm, pond algae and frogs, the squirrels' highway through the trees, the
    meadow, and eagles. In the tunnel, where murals of nocturnal animals glowed
    in the dark, it included sounds of their noises. It also discussed the history of
    wolves, deer, bears, and cougars in the park – noting that the last cougar was
    killed in 1911 and that there was logging in the park from 1860 to 1880. It ended
    with a statement about the forest as First Nations lands, the importance of the
    western red cedar as a tree of life, and commentary on the changing forest
    community and the balance necessary for survival.

7 For more on Williams and her collaboration with Kathara Dance, see
   CBC Arts (2017).
8 The two previous ones were "Trees Are Portals," 30 August to 4 September
   2015, and "Psuedotsuga-Earth to Sky," 13–14 July 2016. The performances
   that have occurred in the park are in part a result of Mique'l Dangeli's (2015)
   documentation of the Park Board process in her doctoral dissertation, as
   was explained by jil weaving during the public question session at Dangeli's
   oral defence of her dissertation on 14 April 2015 at the University of
   British Columbia.

References

Archives, Special Collections, and Municipal Records

British Columbia Provincial Archives, City of Vancouver Records
City Council Minutes, https://covapp.vancouver.ca/councilMeetingPublic/
    CouncilMeetings.aspx.
Urban Indigenous Peoples' Advisory Committee Minutes, https://vancouver.ca/
    your-government/urban-aboriginal-peoples-advisory-committee.aspx.
Vancouver Park Board Minutes, https://parkboardmeetings.vancouver.ca/2019/
    index.htm.
City of Vancouver Archives (CVA)
    City Clerk's Records.
    Local Newspapers.
    Major J.S. Matthews Newspaper Clippings Collection.
    Mayor's Office Fonds.
    Vancouver Citizens' Diamond Jubilee Committee Fonds.
University of British Columbia
British Columbia Historical Newspapers.
Special Collections.

Secondary Sources

Aboriginal Affairs and Northern Development Canada. 2009. "Canada Boosting
    Aboriginal Tourism in British Columbia." News release, 20 March.
    https://www.canada.ca/en/news/archive/2009/03/canada-boosting-
    aboriginal-tourism-british-columbia.html.
"About the Early Vancouver Project." n.d. City of Vancouver Archives.
    http://former.vancouver.ca/ctyclerk/archives/digitized/EarlyVan/
    aboutearlyvancouver.htm.

Abraham, Chris. 2010. "Mother, Mentor and Muse." In *Stratford Festival: For the Pleasure of Seeing Her Again*. Playbill. Stratford, ON: Stratford Festival.

Abraham, Johnny, Gary Flegehen, Zach George, Deborah Jacobs, Aaron Nelson-Moody, and Debbie Sparrow. 2009. *People of the Land: Legends of the Four Host First Nations*. Syilx territory on the Penticton Indian Reserve, BC: Theytus Books.

Ahmed, Sara. 2004. "Declarations of Whiteness: The Non-Performativity of Anti-Racism." *Borderlands e-journal* 3, no. 2. http://www.borderlands.net.au/vol3no2_2004/ahmed_declarations.htm.

– 2006. *Queer Phenomenology: Orientations, Objects, Others*. Durham, NC: Duke University Press.

– 2007. "A Phenomenology of Whiteness." *Feminist Theory* 8, no. 2: 149–68.

Akrigg, G.P.V., and Helen Akrigg. 1997. *British Columbia Place Names*. Vancouver: UBC Press.

Alfred, Taiaiake. 2014. "Idle No More and Indigenous Nationhood." In *The Winter We Danced: Voices from the Past, the Future and the Idle No More Movement*, ed. Kino-nda-niimi Collective, 347–9. Winnipeg: ARP Books.

Altman, W.L. 2012. "Derek Charke." *Musicworks Magazine*, no. 113. https://www.musicworks.ca/featured-article/featured-article/derek-charke.

"Archive / Totem-Land Stationery and Mission Statement." 1954. *Ruins in Process: Vancouver Art in the Sixties*. http://vancouverartinthesixties.com/archive/188.

"Around the Park." 1889. *Vancouver Daily News-Advertiser*, 30 October, 8.

AtBC. 2010. *Klahowya Village Final Report 2010*. West Vancouver: Aboriginal Tourism Association of British Columbia. https://www.indigenousbc.com/assets/corporate/AtBC%20-%20Klahowya%20Village%20in%20Stanley%20Park%20-%20Final%20Report%202010.pdf.

– 2012a. *Klahowya Village in Stanley Park: Final Report 2012*. West Vancouver: Aboriginal Tourism Association of British Columbia. https://www.indigenousbc.com/assets/Klahowya%20Village%20Final%20Report%202012.pdf.

– 2012b. *2011–12 Annual Report*. West Vancouver: Aboriginal Tourism Association of British Columbia. https://www.indigenousbc.com/assets/corporate/AtBC%20Annual%20Report%202011-12.pdf.

Auslander, Philip. 2012. "The Performativity of Performance Documentation." In *Perform, Repeat, Record: Live Art in History*, ed. Amelia Jones and Adrian Heathfield, 47–58. Bristol, UK: Intellect.

Baldwin, Andrew, Laura Cameron, and Audrey Kobayashi. 2011. "Introduction: Where Is the Great White North? Spatializing History, Historicizing

Whiteness." In *Rethinking the Great White North: Race, Nature and the Historical Geographies of Whiteness in Canada*, ed. Andrew Baldwin, Laura Cameron, and Audrey Kobayashi, 1–15. Vancouver: UBC Press.

Balme, Christopher. 2006. "Audio Theatre: The Mediatization of Theatrical Space." In *Intermediality in Theatre and Performance*, vol. 2, ed. Freda Chapple and Chiel Kattenbelt, 117–24. Amsterdam: Rodopi.

– 2007. *Pacific Performances: Theatricality and Cross-Cultural Encounter in the South Seas*. Basingstoke, UK: Palgrave Macmillan.

Bank of Canada. n.d. "Inflation Calculator." https://www.bankofcanada.ca/rates/related/inflation-calculator.

Barman, Jean. 2004. *The Remarkable Adventures of Portuguese Joe Silvey*. Maderia Park, BC: Harbour.

– 2005. *Stanley Park's Secret: The Forgotten Families of Whoi Whoi, Kanaka Ranch and Brockton Point*. Madeira Park, BC: Harbour.

– 2007. "Erasing Indigenous Indigeneity in Vancouver." *BC Studies*, no. 155: 3–30.

– 2008. "Foreword." In Daphne Sleigh, *The Man Who Saved Vancouver: Major James Skitt Matthews*, x–xiii. Vancouver: Heritage House.

Basso, Keith H. 1996. *Wisdom Sits in Places: Landscape and Language among the Western Apache*. Albuquerque: University of New Mexico Press.

Berner, Geoff. 2014. "Introduction Speech for Tanya Tagaq." *CBC Music*, 23 September. https://polarismusicprize.ca/blog/geoff-berners-introduction-speech-for-tanya-tagaq.

Bierwert, Crisca. 1999. *Brushed by Cedar, Living by the River: Coast Salish Figures of Power*. Tucson: University of Arizona Press.

Black, Martha. 2012. "Re: Dance Photos." Personal communication, 25 May.

Blackstock, Cindy. 2013. *Know Your Rights! United Nations Declaration on the Rights of Indigenous Peoples for Indigenous Adolescents*. New York: UNICEF, Secretariat of the United Nations Permanent Forum on Indigenous Issues, and Global Indigenous Youth Caucus.

Blomley, Nicholas. 2004. *Unsettling the City: Urban Land and the Politics of Property*. New York: Routledge.

Borgstrum, C. Henrik. 1999. "Performance Review: For the Pleasure of Seeing Her Again." *Theatre Journal* 51, no. 3: 323–5.

Borrows, John. 1999. "Sovereignty's Alchemy: An Analysis of Delgamuukw v. British Columbia." *Osgoode Hall Law Journal* 37, no. 3: 537–96.

Bratton, Jacky. 2003. *New Readings in Theatre History*. Cambridge, UK: Cambridge University Press.

Brewer, Mary F. 2005. *Staging Whiteness*. Middleton, CT: Wesleyan University Press.

Brown, Lorna. 2011. "Mixing Messages." In *Digital Natives: Other Sights for Artists' Projects*, ed. Lorna Brown and Clint Burnham, 52–7. Vancouver: City of Vancouver Public Art Program.

Burk, Adrienne L. 2010. *Speaking for a Long Time: Public Space and Social Memory in Vancouver*. Vancouver: UBC Press.

Burelle, Julie. 2019. *Encounters on Contested Lands: Indigenous Performances of Sovereignty and Nationhood in Québec*. Evanston, IL: Northwestern University Press.

Butler, Judith. 1988. "Performative Acts and Gender Constitution: An Essay in Phenomenology and Feminist Theory." *Theatre Journal* 40, no. 4: 519–31.

Campbell, Jill. 2014. Personal communication, 3 February.

Carlson, Keith Thor. 2005. "Rethinking Dialogue and History: The King's Promise and the 1906 Aboriginal Delegation to London." *Native Studies Review* 16, no. 2: 1–38.

– 2010. *The Power of Place, the Problem of Time: Aboriginal Identity and Historical Consciousness in the Cauldron of Colonialism*. Toronto: University of Toronto Press.

Carlson, Keith Thor, and Albert (Sonny) McHalsie. 1998. *I am Stó:lō: Katherine Explores Her Heritage*. Chilliwack, BC: Stó:lō Heritage Trust.

Carter, Jill. 2010. "Repairing the Web: Spiderwoman's Children Staging the New Human Being." PhD diss., University of Toronto.

– 2015. "Discarding Sympathy, Disrupting Catharsis: The Mortification of Indigenous Flesh as Survivance-Intervention." *Theatre Journal* 67, no. 3: 413–32.

CBC Arts. 2017. "Bridging Cultures to Inspire Healing through Dance." *YouTube*, 1 February 2017. https://www.youtube.com/watch?v=bB-ipVt2LYU.

Chambers, Iain. 1994. *Migrancy, Culture, Identity*. New York: Routledge.

Chapman, Malaya Qaunirq. 2014. "People Hating on Tanay Tagaq's 'Fuck PETA' Polaris Speech Are Missing the Point." *Vice*, 27 September. https://www.vice.com/en_ca/article/4w5bb3/people-hating-on-tanya-tagaqs-fuck-peta-polaris-speech-are-missing-the-point-943.

Charlebois, Gaeten. 2013. "Encore une fois, si vous le permettez." *Canadian Theatre Encyclopedia*, 14 June. http://www.canadiantheatre.com/dict.pl?term=Encore%20une%20fois%2C%20si%20vous%20le%20permettez.

Chow, Rey. 2002. *The Protestant Ethnic and the Spirit of Capitalism*. New York: Columbia University Press.

City of Vancouver. 2013. "Ride the Stanley Park Miniature Train." 5 April. http://archive.li/fntxI.

– 2014. "Motion on Notice: Protocol to Acknowledge First Nations Unceded Traditional Territory." 24 June. https://council.vancouver.ca/20140624/documents/motionb3.pdf.

– 2016. "Park Board Approves 11 Recommendations in Response to Truth and Reconciliation Commission." 12 January. https://vancouver.ca/news-calendar/park-board-approves-11-recommendations-response-to-truth-reconciliation-commission.aspx.

– 2019. "First Nations Art and Totem Poles." https://vancouver.ca/parks-recreation-culture/totems-and-first-nations-art.aspx.

Comaroff, John L., and Jean Comaroff. 2009. *Ethnicity, Inc.* Chicago: University of Chicago Press.

Coulthard, Glen Sean. 2014. *Red Skin, White Masks: Rejecting the Colonial Politics of Recognition.* Minneapolis: University of Minnesota Press.

Couture, Selena. 2010. "Frames of Mind: *Beyond Eden* and *The Edward Curtis Project*." *alt.theatre: cultural diversity and the stage* 8, no. 2: 10–17.

– 2011. "Margo Kane's Creative and Community Work: Moving Towards Social Change." MA thesis, University of British Columbia.

– 2014. "Indigenous Interventions at Klahowya Village, χʷayχʷəy Vancouver/Unceded Coast Salish Territory." In *Recasting Commodity and Spectacle in the Indigenous Americas*, ed. Helen Gilbert and Charlotte Gleghorn, 235–53. London: Institute of Latin American Studies, School of Advanced Study, University of London.

Crane-Murdoch, Sierra. 2016. "Standing Rock: A New Moment for Native-American Rights." *New Yorker*, 12 October. https://www.newyorker.com/news/news-desk/standing-rock-a-new-moment-for-native-american-rights.

Crey, Karmen, and Erin Hanson. 2009. "Indian Status." First Nations and Indigenous Studies, University of British Columbia. https://indigenous foundations.arts.ubc.ca/indian_status.

Crosby, Marcia. 2004. "Haida, Human Being and Other Myths." In *Bill Reid and Beyond: Expanding on Modern Native Art*, ed. Karen Duffek and Charlotte Townsend-Gault, 108–32. Vancouver: Douglas and McIntyre.

Dangeli, Mique'l. 2015. "Dancing Sovereignty: Protocol and Politics in Northwest Coast First Nations Dance." PhD diss., University of British Columbia.

Dawn, Leslie. 2008. "Cross-Border Trading: Mungo Martin Carves for the World of Tomorrow." BC *Studies*, no. 159: 7–44.

de Certeau, Michel. 1984. *The Practice of Everyday Life*. Trans. Steven F. Rendall. Berkeley: University of California Press.

Deerchild, Rosanna, and Tim Fontaine. 2016. "CBC's Tim Fontaine Shares Stories from Standing Rock and the Fight against the Dakota Access Pipeline." Podcast. *Unreserved*, 15 September 2016. https://www.cbc.ca/listen/shows/unreserved/segment/10216288.

Deloria, Philip J. 1998. *Playing Indian*. New Haven, CT: Yale University Press.

– 2004. *Indians in Unexpected Places*. Lawrence, KS: University Press of Kansas.

Derrida, Jacques. 1996. *Archive Fever: A Freudian Impression*. Chicago: University of Chicago Press.

Diamond, Beverley. 2008. *Native American Music in Eastern North America: Experiencing Music, Expressing Culture*. New York and Oxford: Oxford University Press.

Dickinson, Peter. 2013. "PuSh 2013: The Road Forward." *Performance, Place, and Politics*, 2 February. http://performanceplacepolitics.blogspot.com/2013/02/push-2013-road-forward.html.

– 2014. "PuSh 2014: Nanook of the North/Tanya Tagak [*sic*: Tagaq]." *Performance, Place, and Politics*, 2 February. https://performanceplacepolitics.blogspot.com/search?q=nanook.

Digital Natives. 2011. "Video Burrard St Bridge." 24 April. http://digitalnatives.othersights.ca/press-room/video-of-burrard-st-bridge.

Dillon, Elizabeth Maddock. 2014. *New World Drama: The Performative Commons in the Atlantic World, 1649–1849*. Durham, NC: Duke University Press.

"Documentation: Unceded Self-Guided Tour." 2015. *UBC Wiki*. 19 February. https://wiki.ubc.ca/Documentation:Unceded_self_guided_tour.

Duffek, Karen. 2012. "Re: Scow Copyright Document." Personal communication, 24 May.

Dumont, Marilyn. 1996. "Letter to Sir John A. McDonald." In *A Really Good Brown Girl*, 52. London, ON: Brick Books.

Dyer, Richard. 1997. *White*. New York: Routledge.

Ecojustice. 2012. "Environmental Groups, First Nations Join in Opposition to Omnibus Bill C-45." 28 November. https://www.ecojustice.ca/pressrelease/environmental-groups-first-nations-join-in-opposition-to-omnibus-bill-c-45.

Ehren, Christine, and Robert Simonson. 2002. "San Fran's ACT Has the Pleasure of Seeing Dukakis May 4–June 9." *Playbill*, 4 May. http://www.playbill.com/article/san-frans-act-has-the-pleasure-of-seeing-dukakis-may-4-june-9-com-105525.

Elections British Columbia. n.d. "Electoral History of British Columbia, 1871–
1986." https://elections.bc.ca/docs/rpt/1871-1986_ElectoralHistoryofBC.pdf.

"Electronic Billboards Coming to Vancouver: Squamish Nation." 2009.
CBC News, 23 September 2009. https://www.cbc.ca/news/canada/
british-columbia/electronic-billboards-coming-to-vancouver-squamish-
nation-1.834162.

Emberley, Julia. 2007. Defamiliarizing the Aboriginal: Cultural Practices and
Decolonization in Canada. Toronto: University of Toronto Press.

Favel, Floyd. 2005. "Waskawewin." Topoi 24, no. 1: 113–15.

– 2013. "Theatre: Younger Brother of Tradition." In Indigenous North American
Drama: A Multivocal History, ed. Birgit Däwes, 115–22. Albany, NY:
SUNY Press.

Fee, Margery, and Lynette Russell. 2007. "'Whiteness' and 'Aboriginality' in
Canada and Australia: Conversations and Identities." Feminist Theory 8,
no. 2: 187–208.

First Nations and Indigenous Studies, University of British Columbia. 2009.
"The White Paper 1969." https://indigenousfoundations.web.arts.ubc.ca/
the_white_paper_1969.

"Foresight of Pioneers Wins Public Thanks." 1943. Vancouver Sun, 26 August, 13.

Fortney, Sharon. 2010. "Entwined Histories: The Creation of the Maisie Hurley
Collection of Native Art." BC Studies, no. 167: 71–95.

Francis, Daniel. 2011. The Imaginary Indian: The Image of the Indian in
Canadian Culture. 2nd ed. Vancouver: Arsenal Pulp.

Francis, Margot. 2011. Creative Subversions: Whiteness, Indigeneity and the
National Imaginary. Vancouver: UBC Press.

Gaertner, Dave. 2014a. "End of Term Celebration Language Celebration."
Podcast. Aloud: Literature for Your Ears, 2 December. https://www.citr.ca/
radio/aloud/episode/20141202.

– 2014b. "How Do We Articulate Cyberspace (a Landless Territory) within the
Discourse of Indigenous Studies." Lecture, Centre for Teaching Learning and
Technology, University of British Columbia, 29 October.

Garner, Ray. 1960. "How Lord Stanley Finally Got into His Own Park."
Maclean's, 8 October. 52. City of Vancouver Archives, "Lord Stanley Statue –
Oct. 29, 1889 – Lord Stanley Statuette," AM54-S11-4, box 577-B-1, folder 1.

Gerson, Carole, and Veronica Strong-Boag. 2002. "Introduction: The Firm
Handiwork of Will." In E. Pauline Johnson, Tekahionwake: Collected Poems
and Selected Prose, ed. Carole Gerson and Veronica Strong-Boag, xiii–xliv.
Toronto: University of Toronto Press.

Gilbert, Helen, and Joanne Tompkins. 1996. *Post-Colonial Drama: Theory, Practice, Politics*. New York: Routledge.

Glass, Aaron. 2010. "Objects of Exchange: Material Culture, Colonial Encounter, Indigenous Modernity." In *Objects of Exchange: Social and Material Transformation on the Late Nineteenth-Century Northwest Coast*, ed. Aaron Glass, 3–35. West Haven, CT: Yale University Press.

Government of Canada. 1996. "The Veterans' Land Act." In *Report of the Royal Commission on Aboriginal Peoples*, vol. 1, *Looking Forward Looking Back*, 550–6. Ottawa, ON: Canada Communication Group. http://data2.archives. ca/e/e448/e011188230-01.pdf.

"Governor General Made Honorary Chieftain." 1946. *The Native Voice: Official Organ of the Native Brotherhood of British Columbia, Inc.* 1, no. 1: 2.

Grant, Larry. 2015. Personal interview, 9 April.

Greenaway, John Endo. n.d. "Japanese Canadian Timeline." *Canadian Nikkei.* http://www.canadiannikkei.ca/blog/japanese-canadan-timeline.

Hanson, Erin. 2009a. "Aboriginal Rights." First Nations and Indigenous Studies, University of British Columbia. https://indigenousfoundations.arts.ubc.ca/ aboriginal_rights.

– 2009b. "Aboriginal Title." First Nations and Indigenous Studies, University of British Columbia. https://indigenousfoundations.arts.ubc.ca/aboriginal_title.

– 2009c. "Constitution Act, 1982 Section 35." First Nations and Indigenous Studies, University of British Columbia. https://indigenousfoundations.arts. ubc.ca/constitution_act_1982_section_35.

Harris, Cole. 1997. *The Resettlement of British Columbia: Essays on Colonialism and Geographical Change*. Vancouver: UBC Press.

Harry, Katrin. 2012. "Fire at Klahowya Village in Stanley Park Causes Thousands of Dollars in Damage to Artwork and Artist Tools." *Nation Talk*, June 24. http://nationtalk.ca/story/fire-at-klahowya-village-in-stanley-park-causes-thousands-of-dollars-in-damage-to-artwork-and-artist-tools.

Hawker, Ronald W. 2003. *Tales of Ghosts: First Nations Art in British Columbia, 1922–61*. Vancouver: UBC Press.

"Here's Key to Pictures." 1943. *Vancouver Sun*, 26 August, 13.

Highway, Tomson. 2005. "On Native Mythology." In *Aboriginal Drama and Theatre: Critical Perspectives on Canadian Theatre in English*, vol. 1, ed. Rob Appleford, 1–3. Toronto: Playwrights Canada.

Hillson, Norman. 1952. *Alexander of Tunis: Biographical Portrait of a Distinguished Soldier Statesman*. London: Allen and Co.

"His Worship the Mayor Dr. James Lyle Telford, M.D., M.L.A." 1940. City of Vancouver Archives, AM54-S14-503-D-4.

"History Turns Back 54 Years." 1943. *Vancouver Daily Province*, 25 August, 3.

Hosokawa, Shuhei. 1984. "The Walkman Effect." *Popular Music* 4: 165–80.

Hurley, Erin. 2014. "Introduction: Theatre Matters." In *Theatre of Affect: New Essays on Canadian Theatre*, vol. 4, ed. Erin Hurley, 1–11. Toronto: Playwrights Canada.

Irlbacher-Fox, Stephanie. 2014. "Traditional Knowledge, Co-Existence and Co-Resistance." *Decolonization: Indigeneity, Education and Society* 3, no. 3: 145–58. https://jps.library.utoronto.ca/index.php/des/article/view/22236.

Jamieson, Eric. 2016. *The Native Voice: The Story of How Maisie Hurley and Canada's First Aboriginal Newspaper Changed a Nation*. Halfmoon Bay, BC: Caitlin.

Jane, John. 2014. "For the Pleasure of Seeing Her Again." *Review Vancouver*. http://www.reviewvancouver.org/th_pleasure_of_seeing2014.htm.

Johnson, Pauline. 1911. *Legends of Vancouver*. Vancouver and Victoria: David Spencer Limited.

Jones, David C. 2014. "Tremblay Transformed: A Play Is Adapted for the Talking Stick Festival Exploring Aboriginal Culture through the Arts." *Charlebois Post: Canada's Online Opera and Dance Magazine*, 27 February. http://charpo-canada.blogspot.com/2014/02/review-vancouver-theatre-for-pleasure.html.

Joseph, Robert. 1998. "Behind the Mask." In *Down from the Shimmering Sky: Masks of the Northwest Coast*, ed. Peter L. Macnair Robert Joseph, and Bruce Grenville, 18–35. Vancouver: Douglas and McIntyre.

The Jubilee Show. 1946. Souvenir program. Vancouver: Sun Publishing Company.

Keirstead, Robin G. 1986–87. "J.S. Matthews and an Archives for Vancouver, 1951–1972." *Archivaria* 23: 86–106. https://archivaria.ca/index.php/archivaria/article/view/11368/12309.

Kheraj, Sean. 2013. *Inventing Stanley Park: An Environmental History*. Vancouver: UBC Press.

King, Thomas. 2012. *The Inconvenient Indian: A Curious Account of Native People in North America*. Toronto: Anchor Canada.

Kino-nda-niimi Collective. 2014. "Idle No More: The Winter We Danced." In *The Winter We Danced: Voices from the Past, the Future and the Idle No More Movement*, ed. Kino-nda-niimi Collective, 21–6. Winnipeg: ARP Books.

Knowles, Ric. 2015. Personal communication, 10 July.

– 2016. "Indigenous Declarations: ARTICLE 11 at the National Arts Centre." *Canadian Theatre Review* 166: 101–5.

Kramer, Jennifer. 2006. *Switchbacks: Art, Ownership, and Nuxalk National Identity*. Vancouver: UBC Press.

Lachance, Lindsay. 2018. "The Embodied Politics of Relational Indigenous Dramaturgies." PhD diss., University of British Columbia.

Langston, Patrick. 2013. "For the Pleasure of Seeing Her Again: Margo Kane Shines Brightly." *Capital Critics Circle*, 7 June. http://capitalcriticscircle.com/for-the-pleasure-of-seeing-her-again-margo-kane-shines-brightly.

Lawrence, Bonita. 2004. *"Real" Indians and Others: Mixed Blood Urban Native Peoples and Indigenous Nationhood*. Lincoln: University of Nebraska Press.

LeBlanc, Roméo. 1997. "The Unveiling of an Inuksuk at Rideau Hall." Office of the Governor General of Canada, 21 June. http://archive.li/itr4t.

Leyshon, Glynis. 2014. "Re: Questions about WCT 2012 Production of 'For the Pleasure of Seeing Her Again.'" Personal communication, 25 November.

Lindsay, Eric. 1964. "Park Board News 2.11, 5 June 1964." City of Vancouver Archives, "Stanley Park Rededication 1889–1964," AM54-S23-2, box 505-C-5, folder 293.

"A Loving Tribute, Warts and All." 2013. *Ottawa Citizen*, 4 June. https://ottawacitizen.com/life/style/our-ottawa/a-loving-tribute-warts-and-all.

MacDonald, Bruce. 1992. *Vancouver: A Visual History*. Vancouver: Talonbooks.

Manuel, Arthur. 2015. *Unsettling Canada: A National Wake-Up Call*. Toronto: Between the Lines.

Maracle, Lee. 2014. "Mink Witnesses the Creation of Stanley Park." *Voicings Literary Magazine* 2: 1.

Martineau, Jarrett. 2014. "Tanya Tagaq Remixes 'Nanook of the North.'" *RPM – Revolutions Per Minute: Indigenous Music Culture*, 28 January. http://rpm.fm/interview/tanya-tagaq-remixes-nanook-of-the-north.

Matthews, James Skitt. 1931–56. *Early Vancouver*. 7 vols. Vancouver: City of Vancouver Archives. http://former.vancouver.ca/ctyclerk/archives/digitized/EarlyVan/index.htm.

– 1955. *Conversations with Khahtsahlano, 1932–1954: Conversations with August Jack Khahtsahlano, Born at Snauq, False Creek Indian Reserve, circa 1877, Son of Khaytulk and Grandson of Chief Khahtsahlanogh*. Vancouver: City of Vancouver Archives. https://archive.org/details/ConversationsWithKhahtsahlano1932-1954_346/page/n7.

– 1959. *Naming, Opening and Dedication of Stanley Park, Vancouver, Canada 1888–1889*. Vancouver: City of Vancouver Archives.

– 1964a. *Naming, Opening and Dedication of Stanley Park, Vancouver, Canada 1888–1889*. 2nd ed. Vancouver: City of Vancouver Archives.

– 1964b. *Stanley Park, Vancouver: The Rededication 19th May 1964*. Vancouver: City of Vancouver Archives.

Mawani, Renisa. 2003. "Imperial Legacies (Post)Colonial Identities: Law, Space and the Making of Stanley Park, 1859–2001." *Law Text Culture* 7: 98–141.

– 2004. "From Colonialism to Multiculturalism? Totem Poles, Tourism and National Identity in Vancouver's Stanley Park." *Ariel* 35, nos 1–2: 31–57.

– 2005. "Genealogies of the Land: Aboriginality, Law, and Territory in Vancouver's Stanley Park." *Social and Legal Studies* 14, no. 3: 315–39.

McCue, Duncan. 2014. "Tshilqot'in Land Ruling Was a Game Changer for B.C." *CBC News*, 23 December. https://www.cbc.ca/news/indigenous/tsilhqot-in-land-ruling-was-a-game-changer-for-b-c-1.2875262.

McDonald, Robert A.J. 2013. "'Telford Time' and the Populist Origins of the CCF in British Columbia." *Labour/Le Travail* 71: 87–100.

McHalsie, Albert (Sonny). 2001. "Halq'eméylem Place Names in Stó:lō Territory." In *A Stó:lō–Coast Salish Historical Atlas*, ed. Keith Thor Carlson, 134–53. Vancouver: Douglas and McIntyre; Seattle: University of Washington Press; Chilliwack: Stó:lō Heritage Trust.

McLeod, Kimberley. 2014. "Finding the New Radical: Digital Media, Oppositionality, and Political Intervention in Contemporary Canadian Theatre." *Theatre Research in Canada* 35, no. 2: 203–20.

McNally, B.M. 2013. "Magnetic North Review: For the Pleasure of Seeing Her Again." *Ottawa Tonight*, 8 June. https://www.ottawatonite.com/2013/06/magnetic-north-review-for-the-pleasure-of-seeing-her-again.

Mojica, Monique. 2012. "In Plain Sight: Inscripted Earth and Invisible Realities." In *New Canadian Realisms*, ed. Roberta Barker and Kim Solga, 218–42. Toronto: Playwrights Canada.

– 2013. "Chocolate Woman Dreams the Milky Way." In *Indigenous North American Drama: A Multivocal History*, ed. Birgit Däwes, 123–40. Albany, NY: SUNY Press.

Morin, Jesse. 2015. "Re: Meeting." Personal communication, 29 April.

Moreton-Robinson, Aileen. 2015. *The White Possessive: Property, Power, and Indigenous Sovereignty*. Minneapolis: University of Minnesota Press.

musicisayer. 2009. "Tanya Tagaq – The Sounds of Throat Singing." *YouTube*, 7 July. https://www.youtube.com/watch?v=Nb2ZDjeiU4.

Myers, Fred. 2001. "Introduction: The Empire of Things." In *The Empire of Things: Regimes of Value and Material Culture*, ed. Fred Myers, 3–61. Santa Fe, NM: School of American Research Press.

National Film Board. 2019. "Aabiziingwashi [Wide Awake]: NFB Indigenous Cinema on Tour." https://www.nfb.ca/wideawake.

Native Languages of the Americas. 2015. "American Indian Drums." http://www.
    native-languages.org/drums.htm.

Nelles, Drew. 2015. "Howl: Why Tanya Tagaq Sings." *The Walrus*, 15 January.
    https://thewalrus.ca/howl.

Neworld Theatre. 2019. "Podplays." https://neworldtheatre.com/portfolio-item/
    podplays.

"A Novel Piece of Mine Engineering." 1890. *The Miner* (Nelson, BC),
    27 December, 2. https://open.library.ubc.ca/collections/bcnewspapers/
    xminer/items/1.0182491#p1z-1r0f.

O'Bonsawin, Christine M. 2010. "'No Olympics on Stolen Native Land':
    Contesting Olympic Narratives and Asserting Indigenous Rights within the
    Discourse of the 2010 Vancouver Games." *Sport in Society* 13, no. 1: 143–56.

O'Donnell, Jacqueline P. 1985. "The Native Brotherhood of British Columbia
    1931–1950: A New Phase in Native Political Organization." MA thesis,
    University of British Columbia.

Ogimaa Mikana: Reclaiming/Renaming. n.d. http://ogimaamikana.tumblr.com.

Oliver, Kathleen. 2014. "For the Pleasure of Seeing Her Again Gets Everything
    Right." *Georgia Straight*, 24 February. https://www.straight.com/arts/593031/
    pleasure-seeing-her-again-gets-everything-right.

Olson, Michelle. 2019. Personal communication, 22 January.

olympicvancouver2010. 2010. "Complete Vancouver 2010 Opening Ceremony –
    Vancouver 2010 Winter Olympics." *YouTube*, 11 April. https://www.youtube.
    com/watch?v=MxZpUueDAvc.

Oppenheimer, David. 1889. *The Mineral Resources of British Columbia: Practical
    Hints for Capitalists and Intending Settlers: With Appendix Containing the
    Mineral Laws of the Province and the Dominion of Canada*. Vancouver:
    News-Advertiser Manufacturing Stationers, Printers and Bookbinders.
    https://open.library.ubc.ca/collections/chung/chungpub/items/1.0056409.

Pederson, Wendy, and Jean Swanson. 2009. *Our Place & Our Words: Mapping
    Downtown Eastside Community Assets and Challenges*. Vancouver: Carnegie
    Community Action Project and Vancity. http://www.carnegieaction.org/wp-
    content/uploads/2016/08/Our-Place-and-Our-Words.pdf.

Perry, Adele. 2001. *On the Edge of Empire: Gender, Race, and the Making of
    British Columbia, 1849–1871*. Toronto: University of Toronto Press.

Peters, Mwalim Daphunkeeprofessor. 2013. "Mwalim DaPhunkeeProfessor &
    The Road Forward Players – 'Come & Get Your Love' (Tribute to REDBONE)."
    YouTube, 7 March. https://www.youtube.com/watch?v=Bi6e-PhbOIc.

Phelan, Peggy. 1993. *Unmarked: The Politics of Performance*. New York: Routledge.

Phillips, Kimberly J. 2000. "Making Meaning in Totemland: Investigating a Vancouver Commission." MA thesis, University of British Columbia.

Polaris Music Prize. 2019 "About Polaris." https://polarismusicprize.ca/about.

Polley, Alex. 2015. "The Aboriginal Turn: Analysing Tagaq's Animism and the Changing Relationships between Canada and Its Aboriginal Populations." *Idle No More*, 9 February. http://www.idlenomore.ca/alex_polley_ma_ student_in_music_and_culture_carleton_university.

"Portion of c̓əsnaʔəm Village and Burial Site Returned to Musqueam." 2018. *Musqueam: A Living Culture*, 16 October. https://www.musqueam.bc.ca/ portion-of-c%CC%93%C9%99sna%CA%94%C9%99m-village-and-burial-site-returned-to-musqueam-indian-band.

Pratt, E.J. *Towards the Last Spike*. Toronto: Macmillan of Canada, 1952.

Pulling Together Canoe Society. n.d. "History of Pulling Together Journeys." https://pullingtogether.ca/previous-pulling-together-journeys.

PuSh. n.d. "About & History." PuSh International Performing Arts Festival. https://pushfestival.ca/about-the-festival/about-the-festival.

– 2013. "The Road Forward Program." PuSh International Performing Arts Festival, Club PuSh, Vancouver.

– 2014. "PuSh Panel Discussion: *Nanook of the North*." PuSh International Performing Arts Festival, York Theatre, Vancouver, 1 February.

Raheja, Michelle. 2010. *Reservation Reelism: Redfacing, Visual Sovereignty, and Representations of Native Americans in Film*. Lincoln: University of Nebraska Press.

Raibmon, Paige. 2000. "Theatres of Contact: The Kwakwaka'wakw Meet Colonialism in British Columbia and at the Chicago World's Fair." *Canadian Historical Review* 81: 157–90.

Ray, Arthur. 2016. *An Illustrated History of Canada's Native Peoples*. 4th ed. Montreal and Kingston: McGill-Queen's University Press.

Roach, Joseph. 1996. *Cities of the Dead: Circum-Atlantic Performance*. New York: Columbia University Press.

Robinson, Dylan. 2016. "Welcoming Sovereignty." In *Performing Indigeneity: New Essays on Canadian Theatre*, vol. 6, ed. Yvette Nolan and Ric Knowles, 5–32. Toronto: Playwrights Canada.

Roy, Patricia E. 2003. *The Oriental Question: Consolidating a White Man's Province, 1914–41*. Vancouver: UBC Press.

Roy, Susan. 2002. "Performing Musqueam Culture and History at British Columbia's 1966 Centennial Celebrations." *BC Studies*, no. 135: 55–90.

– 2010. *These Mysterious People: Shaping History and Archaeology in a Northwest Coast Community*. Montreal and Kingston: McGill-Queen's University Press, 2010.

– 2011. "A History of the Site: The Kitsilano Indian Reserve." In *Digital Natives: Other Sights for Artists' Projects*, ed. Lorna Brown and Clint Burnham, 87–93. Vancouver: City of Vancouver Public Art Program.

Ruprecht, Alvina. 2013. "For the Pleasure of Seeing Her Again: The Production Pulls through on the Strength of the Play." *Capital Critics Circle*, 10 June. http://capitalcriticscircle.com/for-the-pleasure-of-seeing-her-again-the-production-pulls-through-on-the-strength-of-the-play.

Schneider, Rebecca. 2011. *Performing Remains: Art and War in Times of Theatrical Reenactment*. New York: Routledge.

Scott, F.R. 1966. *Selected Poems*. Toronto: Oxford University Press, 1966.

Seabrook, John. 2015. "Free." *New Yorker*, 2 February. https://www.newyorker.com/magazine/2015/02/02/free-6.

"Shaping the Future of Aboriginal Tourism." 2019. *Indigenous Tourism BC*. https://www.indigenousbc.com/corporate/news/archive.

Shaw, Patricia. 2015. Personal interview, 22 April.

– 2019. Personal communication, 13 January.

Shaw, Patricia, and Jill Campbell. 2012. *hənq̓əmin̓əm̓qən ct ceʔ: We're Going to Speak hənq̓əmin̓əm̓! Book One*. Vancouver: Musqueam Indian Band and University of British Columbia First Nations Languages Program.

– 2013a. *hənq̓əmin̓əm̓qən ct ceʔ: We're Going to Speak hənq̓əmin̓əm̓! Book Two*. Vancouver: Musqueam Indian Band and University of British Columbia First Nations Languages Program.

– 2013b. *hənq̓əmin̓əm̓qən ct ceʔ: We're Going to Speak hənq̓əmin̓əm̓! Book Three*. Vancouver: Musqueam Indian Band and University of British Columbia First Nations Languages Program.

Shaw, Patricia, Jill Campbell, Larry Grant, and Victor Guerin, eds. 2010. šxʷqʷəltən: The Sounds of Musqueam. Vancouver: Musqueam Indian Band and First Nations Languages Program, University of British Columbia.

Silva, Octavio. 2017. "Gathering of Canoes – Pulling Together Canoe Journey – Canada 150+ Event." Vancouver Park Board, 12 June. https://parkboard meetings.vancouver.ca/2017/20170619/REPORT-GatheringOfTheCanoes-Canada150Event-20170619.pdf.

Silver, Jennifer, Zoë Meletis, and Priya Vadi. 2012. "Complex Context: Aboriginal Participation in Hosting the Vancouver 2010 Winter Olympic and Paralympic Games." *Leisure Studies* 31, no. 3: 291–308.

Simpson, Leanne Betasamosake. 2011. *Dancing on Our Turtle's Back.* Winnipeg: Arbeiter Ring.

– 2014. "The PKOLS Reclamation: Saturating Our Land with Stories." In *The Winter We Danced: Voices from the Past, the Future and the Idle No More Movement,* ed. Kino-nda-niimi Collective, 359–63. Winnipeg: ARP Books.

– 2017a. *As We Have Always Done: Indigenous Freedom through Radical Resistance.* Minneapolis: University of Minnesota Press.

– 2017b. "Decolonizing Solidarity." Conversation and film screening. No More Silence Collective, Native Canadian Centre of Toronto, 27 May.

Sleigh, Daphne. 2008. *The Man Who Saved Vancouver: Major James Skitt Matthews.* Vancouver: Heritage House.

Smith, Linda Tuhiwai. 2012. *Decolonizing Methodologies: Research and Indigenous People.* 2nd ed. New York: Zed Books.

Snelgrove, Corey, Rita Kaur Dhamoon, and Jeff Corntassel. 2014. "Unsettling Settler Colonialism: The Discourse and Politics of Settlers, and Solidarity with Indigenous Nations." *Decolonization: Indigeneity, Education and Society* 3, no. 2: 1–32. https://jps.library.utoronto.ca/index.php/des/article/view/21166.

Soutar, Rena. 2018. "Park Board Reconciliation Strategies – TRC Update." Vancouver Park Board, 10 April. https://parkboardmeetings. vancouver.ca/2018/20180416/REPORT-PBReconciliationStrategies-TRCUpdate-20180416.pdf.

"The Standing Rock Sioux Tribe's Litigation on the Dakota Access Pipeline." 2017. *EarthJustice,* 4 December. https://earthjustice.org/features/faq-standing-rock-litigation.

States, Bert O. 2002. "The Actor's Presence: Three Phenomenal Modes." In *Acting (Re)considered: A Theoretical and Practical Guide,* ed. Phillip B. Zarrilli, 23–39. New York: Routledge.

– 2007. "The Phenomenological Attitude." In *Critical Theory and Performance,* ed. Janelle G. Reinelt and Joseph Roach, 26–36. Ann Arbor: University of Michigan Press.

Statistics Canada. 2017. "Vancouver, (CMA) – British Columbia." In *Focus on Geography Series, 2016 Census.* https://www12.statcan.gc.ca/census-recensement/2016/as-sa/fogs-spg/Facts-cma-eng.cfm?GC=933&GK=CMA&LANG=Eng.

Stoller, Ann Laura. 2002. "Colonial Archives and the Arts of Governance." *Archival Science* 2, nos 1–2: 87–109.

– 2009. *Along the Archival Grain: Epistemic Anxieties and Colonial Common Sense.* Princeton, NJ: Princeton University Press.

Stueck, Wendy. 2010. "No Name Change for Stanley Park: Stockwell Day." *Globe and Mail*, 5 July. https://www.theglobeandmail.com/news/british-columbia/no-name-change-for-stanley-park-stockwell-day/article1386877.

"Surveyors Came at Dawn: Corner Cut off House for Stanley Park Road." 1943. *Vancouver Sun*, 26 August, 13.

Sutherland, Richard. 1993. "Theatre Under the Stars: The Hilker Years." MA thesis, University of British Columbia.

Suttles, Wayne. 1996. "Linguistic Evidence for Burrard Inlet as Former Halkomelem Territory." Paper presented at the 31st International Conference on Salish and Neighbouring Languages, Vancouver. https://lingpapers.sites.olt.ubc.ca/files/2018/03/1996_Suttles.pdf.

– 2004. *Musqueam Reference Grammar.* Vancouver: UBC Press.

"Talking Stick: Sharing Perspectives Panel." 2013. Talking Stick Festival, Vancouver East Cultural Centre, Vancouver, 25 February.

Taylor, Diana. 2003. *The Archive and the Repertoire: Performing Cultural Memory in the Americas.* Durham, NC: Duke University Press.

– 2006. "Performance and/as History." *Drama Review* 50, no. 1: 68–86.

Thomas, Richard. 1993. *The Imperial Archive: Knowledge and the Fantasy of Empire.* New York: Verso.

Thompson, Laurence C. 1979. "Salishan and the Northwest." In *The Languages of Native America: Historical and Comparative Assessment*, ed. Lyle Campbell and Marianne Mithun, 692–765. Austin: University of Texas Press.

"Throngs See 'Birth' of Stanley Park." 1943. *Vancouver Sun*, 26 August, 13.

"Today's Programme." 1889. *Vancouver Daily News-Advertiser*, 29 October 1889, 8.

Tremblay, Michel. 1998. *For the Pleasure of Seeing Her Again.* Trans. Linda Gaboriau. Vancouver: Talonbooks.

– 2002. *Twelve Opening Acts.* Trans. Sheila Fischman. Vancouver: Talonbooks.

– 2003. *Birth of a Bookworm.* Trans. Sheila Fischman. Vancouver: Talonbooks.

– 2011. *Crossing the Continent.* Trans. Sheila Fischman. Vancouver: Talonbooks.

Tremblay, Michel, and Eleanor Wachtel. 2000. "Three Decades of Success for Michel Tremblay." Radio broadcast. *The Arts Today*, 27 March. https://www.cbc.ca/archives/entry/three-decades-of-success-for-michel-tremblay.

– 2003. "Novelist Michel Tremblay Interview." Encore radio broadcast. *Writers and Company*, 23 March 2013. https://www.cbc.ca/player/play/2353490281.

Truth and Reconciliation Commission of Canada. 2015. *Calls to Action*. http://trc.ca/assets/pdf/Calls_to_Action_English2.pdf.

Tsleil-Waututh Nation. n.d. "Community Services: Culture & Language." https://twnation.ca/for-our-community/for-our-members/community-services.

Tuck, Eve, and K. Wayne Yang. 2012. "Decolonization Is Not a Metaphor." *Decolonization: Indigeneity, Education and Society* 1, no. 1: 1–40. https://jps.library.utoronto.ca/index.php/des/article/view/18630.

Union of British Columbia Indian Chiefs. "Education Workshop." 1979. *Union of British Columbia Indian Chiefs Education Bulletin*, 5 October. http://gsdl.ubcic.bc.ca/cgi-bin/library.cgi?a=d&c=ubcicbu1&d=HASH 017e3d56e2ca96b8994e7faa.

"Unprecedented, Three-Site Exhibition Reveals Archeological & Cultural Origins of Vancouver." 2014. *Museum of Vancouver*, 3 December.

Urban Aboriginal Peoples' Advisory Committee. n.d. "Meetings." https://vancouver.ca/your-government/urban-aboriginal-peoples-advisory-committee.aspx.

– 2016a. "Minutes, January 18, 2016." https://vancouver.ca/docs/council/uapc20160118min.pdf.

– 2016b. "Minutes, March 3, 2016." https://vancouver.ca/docs/council/uapc20160303min.pdf.

Usmiani, Renate. 2013. "Margo Gwendolyn Kane." *The Canadian Encyclopedia*. https://www.thecanadianencyclopedia.ca/en/article/margo-gwendolyn-kane.

"Vancouver Celebrates Stanley Park Dedication in Colorful Ceremony." 1943. *Vancouver Daily Province*, 25 August, 3.

Vancouver Park Board. 2010. "Minutes of the Meeting of the Board of Parks and Recreation Held at the Park Board Office on Monday, May 17, 2010." 17 May. https://parkboardmeetings.vancouver.ca/2010/100607/Minutes17May2010.pdf.

Vancouver Media Co-op. n.d. "Anti-Olympics Archive: Indigenous Peoples + Olympics." http://vancouver.mediacoop.ca/olympics/indigenous-peoplesolympics.

Vancouver Organizing Committee for the 2010 Olympic and Paralympic Winter Games (VANOC). 2010. *Vancouver 2010 Sustainability Report*. https://stillmed.olympic.org/Documents/Games_Vancouver_2010/VANOC_Sustainability_Report-EN.pdf.

Wasserman, Jerry. 2012. "Michel Tremblay." In *Modern Canadian Plays*, vol. 1, 5th ed., ed. Jerry Wasserman, 59–64. Vancouver: Talonbooks.

Werb, Jessica. 2014. "PuSh Festival: Tanya Tagaq Wrestles with Feelings about

Nanook of the North." *Georgia Straight*, 15 January. https://www.straight.com/arts/566076/push-festival-tanya-tagaq-wrestles-feelings-about-nanook-north.

White, Bob. 2010. "Michel Tremblay: A Revolutionary and His Roots." In *Stratford Festival: For the Pleasure of Seeing Her Again*. Playbill. Stratford, ON: Stratford Festival.

Wildcat, Matthew, Mandee McDonald, Stephanie Irlbacher-Fox, and Glen Sean Coulthard. 2014. "Learning from the Land: Indigenous Land Based Pedagogy and Decolonization." *Decolonization: Indigeneity, Education and Society* 3, no. 3: i–xv. https://jps.library.utoronto.ca/index.php/des/article/view/22248.

W!ld Rice Theatre. 2004. "For the Pleasure of Seeing Her Again: About the Show." https://www.wildrice.com.sg/productions/123-for-the-pleasure-of-seeing-her-again2004.

Wilson, Jordan. 2016a. "Gathered Together: Listening to Musqueam Lived Experiences." *Biography* 39, no. 3: 469–94.

– 2016b. "25in25: A Public Art Retrospective – People amongst the People by Susan A. Point." *Our City. Our Art. Our Vancouver*, 11 September. https://ourcityourart.wordpress.com/2016/09/11/25in25-a-public-art-retrospective-people-amongst-the-people-by-susan-a-point.

"Wine Disappears, So Christening Is Dry." 1943. *Vancouver Sun*, 26 August, 13.

Wong, Adrienne, and Martin Kinch. 2012. "Performing Neighbourhoods: An Interview with the Creators of PodPlays." *West Coast Line: A Journal of Contemporary Writing and Criticism* 46, no. 1: 38–43.

Ybarra, Patricia. 2009. *Performing Conquest: Five Centuries of Theater, History, and Identity in Tlaxcala, Mexico*. Ann Arbor: University of Michigan Press.

Youds, Mike. 2012a. "Beyond 'Leathers and Feathers': WCT Play Represents Gradually Shifting Perceptions." *Kamloops Daily News*, 1 February.

– 2012b. "For the Pleasure of Seeing Them Again: Lorne Cardinal and Margo Kane Perform in Michel Tremblay's Heartrending Homage to His Mother." *Kamloops Daily News*, 19 January.

– 2012c. "Review: Kane and Cardinal in Loving Portrait." *Kamloops Daily News*, 27 January.

Zittlau, Andrea. 2014. "Nora Naranjo-Morse's 'Always Becoming': Enacting Indigenous Identity on a Museum Stage." In *Recasting Commodity and Spectacle in the Indigenous Americas*, ed. Helen Gilbert and Charlotte Gleghorn, 97–111. London: Institute of Latin American Studies, School of Advanced Study, University of London.

Index

həṅq̓əmiṅəm̓

The alphabetical order of
həṅq̓əmiṅəm̓ is as follows: c, c̓, č, h,
k, kʷ, k̓ʷ, l, l̓, λ, ƚ, m, m̓, n, n̓, p, p̓, q, q̓,
qʷ, q̓ʷ, s, š, t, t̓θ, t., θ, w, w̓, x, xʷ, χ, χʷ,
y, y̓, ʔ, a, a:, e, e:, i, i:, u, u:, ə.

c̓əsnaʔəm, the city before the city
   (Museum of Anthropology, UBC),
   22–4, 32, 197n3
c̓əsnaʔəm village, 7, 82, 167, 196n5

hiw̓aʔqʷ (head person, chief), 15, 29
həṅq̓əmiṅəm̓-Hul̓q̓um̓inum-
   Halq̓eméylem language
   continuum, 26
həṅq̓əmiṅəm̓ language: boundary
   with Halq̓eméylem, 198n9;
   as downriver dialect, 26; on
   electronic billboard, 132;
   grammar, 3, 29–30, 34–6, 198n10,
   199n16, 200n18, 200n19; Larry
   Grant speaking, 22; orthographic
   system, 149; study of, 24–9; words
   for place names, 202n2; words of
   welcome, 137

λ̓ces/Dead Man's Island, 173

məθkʷəy̓ grass, 30

niʔ (be there), 3, 29
"nə maʔəqʷ, nə ƚək̓ʷəm̓ maʔəqʷ"
   ("Alouette"), 27

qam̓əθət (to get into the back eddy),
   30–1
qem̓ (to get in the eddy), 30
qeqəm̓ (in the back eddy), 30
qiyəplenəxʷ, 28

q̓əmq̓əmələłp (big leaf maple trees,
   CRAB Park), 49

sƚχil̓əx (Siwash Rock), 34–5, 116, 178,
   208n20
snəw̓eyəł (teachings received since
   childhood), 23
spapəy̓əq (bent at the end, Brockton
   Point), 6, 14, 58, 79, 103, 173, 182.
   See also *The Jubilee Show*; walking
   tour
sq̓əq̓ip (gathered together), 23
stit̓əwəq̓ʷ (Second Beach), 183
sχʷayχʷəy dance, 35–6, 145
sχʷəy̓em̓, 34–5, 36, 199n17
sʔiłqəy̓ monster, 30
səlil̓w̓ətaʔł Nation (People of the
   Inlet), 148–9
səṅaʔqʷ/Senʼákw (Vanier Park/
   Kitsilano/Squamish Indian

Reserve), 7, 14, 101, 104, 186, 202n2, 202n4. *See also* Snauq (sənaʔqʷ/Senákw); Vanier Park, Vancouver

təməxʷ (land, earth), 30

t̓ᶿaɫᶿəɫəm̓ (shivering from cold), 34

xʷməlċθən (in North Vancouver), 173
xʷməθkʷəy̓əm (area, named by people of the land), 30
xʷiwəl (move upstream/move toward the centre of the house/move toward the fire), 29
xʷəlməxʷ təṅa təməxʷ (people of this land), 30
xʷənəθət (first ancestors), 39

χe:l̓s, 34, 199n17

χʷay̓χʷəy̓ village (near Lumberman's Arch): about, 3, 6, 35, 148, 158; disturbance of, 169; Pulling Together Canoe Journey, 173, 174. *See also* walking tour
χʷəy, 35
χʷəyem (tell a story), 35–6

ʔi (be here), 3, 29
"ʔi ct ceʔ xʷcəməstəl̓ qələt" ("We Will Meet Again"), 27
ʔiməxneʔtən (visitor), 42, 197n4

Non-həṅq̓əmiṅəm̓

Page numbers in *italics* denote photographs or illustrations.

Aboriginal Tourism Association of British Columbia (ATBC), 142, 146–7, 149, 150, 158–9, 190, 211n5
Abraham, Johnny, 38
"The Actor's Presence: Three Phenomenal Modes" (States), 209n1
Adams, Alfred, *114*, 207n13
Aeriosa (dance group), 175–6, *176*
Ahmed, Sara, 13, 54–6, 59, 63, 73, 78, 81, 87, 91
Alexander, Harold, 119–25, *123*, *126*
Alfred, Taiaiake, 40
Allen, Chadwick, 21
"All the Spikes but the Last" (F.R. Scott), 89
American Conservatory Theatre, 93
Anderson, Chris, 59
Animism (Tagaq), 161–3
Anishinaabemowin place names, 40, 201n25
The Archive and the Repertoire (Taylor), 19, 197n7
Archive Fever: A Freudian Impression (Derrida), 91
archives: City of Vancouver, 5, 7, 53–6, 60–3, 83, 178; Klahowya Village, 147–50; of NBBC, 14; role of, 91, 143–4, 152; Vancouver's 1946 Diamond Jubilee, 13–14, 101–4, 110–11, 129–32. *See also* Matthews, James Skitt; Taylor, Diana

Armytage-Moore, Maisie (Maisie
    Hurley), 70, 110–12, 124, 131,
    204n19, 211n7
arson, 157–8
Art, Historical and Scientific
    Association of Vancouver, 149, 184
Ashes on the Water (Q. Sparrow), 13,
    42–51
As We Have Always Done: Indigenous
    Freedom through Radical
    Resistance (L.B. Simpson), 11
ATBC (Aboriginal Tourism Association
    of British Columbia), 142, 146–7,
    149, 150, 158–9, 190, 211n5
August, William, 77
Auslander, Philip, 75–6

Baker, Bob (S7aplek), 50, 202n5
Baker, Frank, 87–8
Baldwin, Andrew, 86
Balme, Christopher, 147, 152–3, 156
Bard on the Beach Shakespeare
    Festival, 132
Barman, Jean, 5, 60, 63, 69, 78–9, 181,
    185
Barricelli, Marco, 93
Bass, Fred, 70–1
Basso, Keith, 33, 41
BC Métis Federation, 147, 149
BC Rangers, 188
Belmore, Rebecca, 11–12
Benjamin, Walter, 138
Berger, Thomas, 207n12
Berner, Geoff, 161
Beynon, William, 114
Beyond Eden (Ruddell), 146
Bierwert, Crisca, 33
billboards, electronic, 132

Bill C-31, 97
Birth of a Bookworm (M. Tremblay),
    94
Black, Martha, 129
Blackstock, Cindy, 210n9
Blaney, Charles, 88
Blomley, Nicholas, 76, 102
Borrows, John, 196n6
Bourdieu, Pierre, 55
Brassard, Andre, 93
Bratton, Jacky, 161, 163
Brewer, Mary, 57
Brockton, Francis, 182
Brockton Oval, 150
Brockton Point (spapəy̓əq, bent at the
    end), 6, 14, 58, 79, 103, 173, 182.
    See also The Jubilee Show; walking
    tour
Brushed by Cedar, Living by the River:
    Coast Salish Figures of Power
    (Bierwert), 33
Burnaby, Robert, 182
Burrard, Harry, 180
Burrard Inlet, BC, 180
Butler, Judith, 37
Butterflies in Spirit (dance group), 174

cairn, 65–8, 78, 83, 191, 193. See also
    gravesite
Calls to Action (TRC), 15, 159,
    167–9, 210. See also Truth and
    Reconciliation Commission of
    Canada (TRC)
Cameron, Laura, 86
Campbell, Hugh, 204n16
Campbell, Ian (Xàlek or Sekyú
    Siýam), 137, 158
Campbell, Jill, 25

Campbell, R.C., 207n8

Campbell, Vanessa, 22

Campbell-Johnston, R.C., 149, 211n7

Canadian Pacific Railway (CPR), 57, 64, 88, 89, 147, 180, 189, 203n6

Canadian Theatre Encyclopedia, 94

"Can I Kick It?" (A Tribe Called Quest), 27

Capilano, Joe (Su-á-pu-luck), 38–9, 200n21

capitalism, 17, 57

Cardinal, Lorne, 95–6

Carlson, Keith Thor, 198n12, 199n17

Carter, Jill, 11, 156

Catholicism, 200n24

Cavendish, Nicola, 93

Centaur Theatre, Montreal, 93

Challenge (newspaper), 67

Chapman, Malaya Qaunirq, 162

Charke, Derek, 211n1

Charlebois, Gaeten, 94

Charles, Christine, 26

Chaythoos, 62, 79–80, 169, 191, 206

Chi Engikiiwang/Tkaranto/Toronto, 40, 201n25

Children's Farmyard, Stanley Park, 147, 152, 174, 189–90

Chinese railway workers, 89–90

Chinook language, 35, 148

Choinière, Olivier, 42–3

Chow, Rey, 54–5

Chrétien, Jean, 210n8

Cities of the Dead: Circum-Atlantic Performance (Roach), 31, 53

Civil War (US) reenactment, 199n13

CKWX radio station, 70–1

Clements, Marie, 15, 39, 98, 134–41, 146

Clifton, Heber, *114*

Coal Harbour, BC, 182

Coast Salish peoples: communities, 117, 195n2, 198n12; a genealogy of cultural performance, 144–6; lands/territory of, 101, 132, 137, 148, 158; visual representations of, 142, 150, 183. *See also* səlil̓wətaʔɬ Nation; x̌ʷayx̌ʷəy̓ village (near Lumberman's Arch); Musqueam Nation; Sḵwx̱wú7mesh Nation (Squamish Nation)

coercive mimeticism, 55

Colclough, Alice, 118, 120

Comaroff, Jean and John, 127

"Come and Get Your Love" (Redbone), 136

commodification of Indigeneity, 142

Common Experience Payments, 168

Constitution Express, 135, 139, 210n6

Conversations with Khahtsahlano, 1932–1954 (J.S. Matthews), 61–2, 78–9, *81*

Cook, Herbert, 113, *114*

Co-operative Commonwealth Federation (CCF), 67, 192

Coqualeetza Residential School, 181. *See also* Indian residential schools

Corntassel, Jeff, 10

Coulthard, Glen Sean, 16–22, 32, 90–1, 197n1

CPR (Canadian Pacific Railway), 57, 64, 88, 89, 147, 180, 189, 203n6

CRAB Park (Create a Real Available Beach), 43–4, 48–9, 202n4

Cranmer, Dan, 130, 209n34

Creative Subversions: Whiteness, Indigeneity and the National Imaginary (M. Francis), 57, 89

Cree people, 13, 92, 94–6, 99–100

cricket pitch, Stanley Park, 185–7

Crosby, Marcia, 107, 110

cultural genocide, 97

Cummings, James and Lucy
(Spukhpukanum), 206n2

Cummings, Tim and Agnes, 206n2

Curtis, Edward, 146

Dakota Access Pipeline, 196n7

dances, secret, 121, 127–8, 130

Dancing on the Edge festival, 201n1

Dancing on Our Turtle's Back (L.B.
Simpson), 24

"Dancing Sovereignty" (Dangeli), 175

Dangeli, Mique'l, 175, 212n3, 214n8

Dawn, Leslie, 145

de Certeau, Michel, 16–17, 18–21, 24,
28, 86, 197n4

"Declarations of Whiteness: The Non-
Performativity of Anti-Racism"
(Ahmed), 54–5

decolonization: process of, 28, 36, 51,
130–3, 156; self-decolonization, 8,
12, 24, 26, 177; term usage/concept
of, 8–9, 20; Vancouver Park Board,
213n5

"Decolonization Is Not a Metaphor"
(Tuck and Yang), 9

Decolonizing Methodologies
(L.T. Smith), 9

"Decolonizing Solidarity"
(L.B. Simpson), 10

Delgamuukw v. British Columbia, 7,
196n6

Deloria, Philip J., 5, 154, 163

Deloria, Vine, Jr, 20

Derby, Earl of/Lord and Lady, 66–9,
74, 77, 192

Derrida, Jacques, 56, 91

Desrosiers, Maria, 94

Dhamoon, Rita Kaur, 10

Dickinson, Peter, 136–7, 161, 164

Digital Natives, 132

displaced transmission, 54, 66, 69,
87, 91

displacement, 14, 53, 76, 78, 102, 131

DNA of performance, 40, 200n24

*Down from the Shimmering Sky:
Masks of the Northwest Coast*
(Joseph), 129

Downtown Eastside, Vancouver, 43,
49, 202n4

Duffek, Karen, 129

Dukakis, Olympia, 93

Duker, Harry, 131

Dumont, Marilyn, 90

Dyer, Richard, 57

Early Vancouver (J.S. Matthews), 62

earthworks, 21

eddies (physical, water), 30–2, 168,
198n12

eddies of influence, 17, 22–32, 39–40,
50, 143, 159, 177–8, 182

Edward IV, King, 38

Elders, 23, 27–8, 33–4, 38, 40, 195n4,
198n12, 207n13

Enbridge Northern Gateway Pipelines
project, 167, 196n7

Encore une fois, si vous le permettez
(M. Tremblay), 93

"Entwined Histories: The Creation
of the Maisie Hurley Collection of
Native Art" (Fortney), 112

Ethnicity, Inc. (Comaroff), 127

Expo 86, 48–9

False Creek, Vancouver, 205n29

False Creek Indian Reserve, 62

Fanon, Frantz, 56

Favel, Floyd, 36

Fee, Margery, 78

Filewod, Alan, 42

"Finding the New Radical: Digital Media, Oppositionality, and Political Intervention in Contemporary Canadian Theatre" (McLeod), 42

First Nations and Endangered Languages Program (FNEL, UBC), 25–9

First Nations Languages Program (FNLG), 9

Flaherty, Robert, 14, 160

Fort Good Hope, Northwest Territories, 211n1

For the Pleasure of Seeing Her Again (M. Tremblay), 13, 92–100, 160–1

Fortney, Sharon, 112, 207n12

Four Host First Nations (FHFN), 7, 39, 145–6, 148–50, 200n22

"Fracking" (Tagaq), 163

Francis, Daniel, 154

Francis, Margot, 57, 89, 99

Fraser River/Delta, BC, 3, 26, 195n1

Full Circle First Nations Performance (FCFNP), 9, 97, 98

Gaertner, David, 42–3

galena ore, 65, 203n12

"Gathered Together: Listening to Musqueam Lived Experience" (Wilson), 23

gender issues, 37, 57, 92, 96

"Genealogies of the Land: Aboriginality, Law, and Territory in Vancouver's Stanley Park" (Mawani), 58

George, Dan, 149

gestures, 36–7

Gichi Kiiwenging/Toronto, 201n25

Gilbert, Helen, 139

Gilford Village, 129

Git Hayetsk (dance group), 175–6

Gitksan peoples, 196n6

Glass, Aaron, 112

God Is Red (V. Deloria Jr), 20

Gold Rush, 10

Goldsbie, Jonathan, 42–3

Gosselin, Viviane, 197n3

Gradual Enfranchisement Act of 1869, 96–7

Grafton, William, 80

Grant, Edna, 25

Grant, Gina, 28

Grant, Howard E., 23, 197n5

Grant, Howard J., 23, 197n5

Grant, Larissa, 197n3

Grant, Larry, 22, 23, 25, 27–28, 197n5

Grant-John, Wendy, 23, 197n5

gravesite, 62, 64, 69, 78–83, *81*, 203n15, 205nn26–7. *See also* Jack, Supple; statue of Lord Stanley

Great Fire of 1886, 13

Greer's Beach, BC, 203n6

Grey, John Hamilton, 37, 188

Greyeyes, Michael, 134

grounded normativity, 17, 20, 32, 197n1

grounded practices, 7, 17–22, 120–8, 178

Guerin, Arnold, Sr, 25–6

Guerin, Suzanne, 198n11

Gustafsen Lake Standoff, 196n7

"Haida, Human Being and Other
    Myths" (Crosby), 107, 110
Haida Nation, 107, 146, 207n13
Halq̓eméylem, 26, 198n9
Harris, Cheryl, 58
Harris, Cole, 57, 89
Harris, Frank, 66, 80–1
Harris, Ronnie Dean (Ostwelve),
    138–9
Hastings Mill, 49, 65
Hawaii's Polynesian Cultural Centre,
    147, 152
Hawker, Ronald, 119, 125, 209n35
Heath, Joel, 212n5
Heng, Ivan, 93
Highway, Tomson, 50
Hill-Tout, Charles, 203n6
Hiltz, Ralph E., 111, 112–13, 118, 120
HMS Europa, 180
HMS Plumper, 182
hockey, 86, 205n36
Hoey, R.A., 144
Holland, R. Rowe, 71–2
Houle, Robert, 11
Howard, Blanche Muirhead, 115–16
Howe, Leanne, 21
Humchitt band, 119
Hunt, Richard, 208n31
Hurley, Maisie, 207n8, 207n13.
    See also Armytage-Moore, Maisie
    (Maisie Hurley)
Hurley, Tom, 111

Idle No More, 8, 40, 135–40, 167–8,
    196n7, 201n25, 210n6, 210n8
imperialism, 89
"Imperial Legacies (Post) Colonial
    Identities: Law, Space and the

Making of Stanley Park, 1859–
    2001" (Mawani), 82–3
The Inconvenient Indian (T. King), 16
Indian Act, 83, 96–7, 102, 115, 124,
    185, 195n4
Indian Affairs, 106, 144, 195n4
"Indian Ceremonial Dances" (Scow),
    110, 129–30
Indian Reserve Commission, Joint,
    101
Indian residential schools, 28, 143,
    168, 181, 206n2
Indians in Unexpected Places (P.J.
    Deloria), 154
The Indian Village and Show, 103–20,
    108, 109, 117, 132, 186, 208n20
Indigeneity, commodification of, 142
"Indigenous artistic research
    methodology" (Mojica), 50
Indigenous Nationhood restoration
    movement, 40
Indigenous peoples: cultural
    genocide, 97; Elders, 23, 27–8, 33–
    4, 38, 40, 195n4, 198n12, 207n13;
    land title, 82, 102, 167, 170; status,
    96, 153, 185; war veterans, 124,
    127–8. See also individual bands/
    nations/peoples
"In Plain Sight: Inscripted Earth and
    Invisible Realities" (Mojica), 21
"Introduction to the Musqueam
    People, Their Territory, and Their
    Language" (FNEL), 28
Inuit, 12, 15, 160–6, 195n2, 212n4.
    See also Nanook of the North
    (Flaherty)
Inuktitut, 166
Inventing Stanley Park (Kheraj), 182

Irlbacher-Fox, Stephanie, 26–7

Jack, Supple, 68–9, 79–82, *81*, 203n5, 205n26. *See also* gravesite
Jamieson, Eric, 207n13
Japanese, internment of, 67, 71–2, 188–9, 192
Japanese Canadian War Memorial, Stanley Park, 71–2, 188–9
Jericho, BC, 26
Joe, Matthias, 71, 76, 77–8
Joe, Rita, 98
Johnson, Pam, 95
Johnson, Pauline (Tekahionwake), 37–9, 116
Joseph, Robert, 129
The Jubilee Show, 103–10, *105*, *106*, *107*, 118, 129, 131, 150, 186, 193, 206n4

Kane, Margo, 13, 92, 95–9, 201n1, 206n3
Katzie (village), 26, 198n9
Kenick (Squamish woman), 181
Khahtsahlano, August Jack: on False Creek, 205n29; former family home, 101; *The Indian Village and Show*, 113; name change, 62–3, 169; photos of, *75*, *115*; rededication of Stanley Park in 1964, 87; reenactment of the dedication, 1943, 70–82, 187. *See also* Chaythoos
Khaltinaht (Musqueam-Squamish woman), 184–5
Kheraj, Sean, 63, 69, 182
kinesthetic imagination, 54
King, Gerald, 95

King, Thomas, 16
Kitsilano Park, Vancouver, *126*, 202n2, 203n6
Klahowya Village, 142–59; archive, 147–50; Coast Salish performances, 144–6; continuing plans, 158–9; headdress, 154–7, *155*, 163; knowledge transmission, 151–8; Miniature Train Station, *157*; teepee in farmyard, *148*
knowledge transmission, 15, 124, 151–9, 160–1, 177. *See also* traditional knowledge
Kobayashi, Audrey, 86
Kramer, Jennifer, 127
Kreisberg, Jennifer, 134, 136–7
Kwakwaka'wakw village, Stanley Park, 129–31, 149–50, 207n8
Kwak'wala language, 132, 208n30
Kwantlen, 26
Kwatleemaat (Shíshálh woman), 184–5

Lachance, Lindsay, 197n1
"Lady Marmalade" (Labelle), 136
Lafontaine, Rita, 93
Lamb, William K., 62
land, 16–41; as breast milk, 30; commodification of, 16; eddies of influence, 22–32; grounded practices, 17–22; Indigenous title, 82, 102, 167, 170; naming of places, 32–41; and performance-based strategies and tactics, 21–2, 32–3; sale of, 106, 207n5
Langston, Patrick, 95
Larson, Don, 202n4
Last Spike, 89

Lavallee, Wayne, 136

Lawrence, Bonita, 13, 93, 96

Leatherman, Dan, 204n16

L'École des femmes (Molière), 43

Legends of Vancouver (Johnson),
    37–8, 116

Lek'leki (grove of beautiful trees,
    CRAB Park), 49

Les belles-soeurs (Tremblay), 92–3

"Letter to Sir John A. McDonald"
    (Dumont), 90

Leyshon, Glynis, 13, 92, 95, 99

lilac bush, 179–81

Lil'wat people, 39, 145–6, 200n22

Lin, Neo Swee, 93

The Lions (mountains), 37–8, 200n20

Little Big Man (Penn), 149

Loring, Kevin, 95, 98, 206n3

Louis, Dickie, 23, 197n5

Lower Mainland, BC, 26

Lower Mainland First Nations,
    198n12

Lumberman's Arch, Stanley Park, 6,
    35, 70–1, 150, 174, 187–8, 193.
    See also χʷay̓χʷəy̓ village (near
    Lumberman's Arch)

Macdonald, John A., 195n4

Magnetic North Theatre Festival, 92,
    95

Maitland, Skye, 166

Malkin Bowl, Stanley Park, 6, 87, 150,
    174

Manning, Erin, 175

Manuel, George, 138–9

*The Man Who Saved Vancouver:
    Major James Skitt Matthews*
    (Sleigh), 53

Maracle, Cheri, 136–7

Maracle, Lee, 90, 192

March, Sydney, 83

Maritime Museum, 132

Marpole/Marpole Midden, BC, 26,
    131, 195n1, 196n5, 209n37. *See
    also* c̓əsnaʔəm village; midden

Marston, Luke (Ts'uts'umutl), 184–5

Martin, James, 204n16

Martin, Jean, 160

Martin, Mungo, 125, 127, 128, 132,
    208n31

masks, 121, *122*

Massot, Claude, 212n4

Matthews, Charles, 161, 163, 212n2

Matthews, James Skitt, 52–100; and
    August Jack Khahtsahlano, 169,
    202n4, 203n5; imitating Lord
    Stanley statue, *84*; influence
    as archivist, 13, 178; program
    comments, 116–17, *117*, 208n20.
    See also archives; Stanley Park,
    Vancouver, dedication and
    rededications; statue of Lord
    Stanley

Mawani, Renisa, 58, 69, 82–3, 90–1

McDonald, Robert J., 67

McHalsie, Albert "Sonny"
    (Naxaxalhts'i), 35, 198n12

McLaughlin, Elizabeth, 201n1

McLeod, Kimberley, 42, 43

McNally, B.M., 95

Merleau-Ponty, Maurice, 55

Métis–First Nations uprising, North-
    West Resistance of 1885, 89

midden, 6, 169, 187. *See also* c̓əsnaʔəm
    village; Marpole/Marpole
    Midden, BC

The Mineral Resources of British Columbia: Practical Hints for Capitalists and Intending Settlers (D. Oppenheimer, Mayor), 203n12

Miniature Train Station, Klahowya Village, *157*

"Mink Witnesses the Creation of Stanley Park" (L. Maracle), 90, 192

missing and murdered Indigenous women, 49, 137, 174, 202n4

Mojica, Monique, 21, 36, 50

Molière, 43

monopolylogues, 161, 212n2

Moody, Richard Clement, 182

Moonlodge (Kane), 98

Moreton-Robinson, Aileen, 58–9, 69–70

multiculturalism, 86

Murotani, Saki, 198n11

Museum of Anthropology, c̓əsnaʔəm exhibit, 32, 197n3

Museum of Vancouver, c̓əsnaʔəm exhibit, 132, 197n3, 198n11

Musqueam Cultural Education Resource Centre and Gallery, 22, 26, 196n5, 197n3

Musqueam Language and Culture Program, 8, 9

Musqueam Nation (People of the River Grass): *c̓əsnaʔəm, the city before the city* (Museum of Anthropology, UBC), 22–3, 32, 197n3; c̓əsnaʔəm village, 7, 82, 167, 196n5; courses with, 27–9; early times, 4–6, 30; involvement in the Jubilee celebrations, 145–6; land title dispute, 101–2, 169–70. *See also* hən̓q̓əmin̓əm̓ language; Four Host First Nations (FHFN)

Musqueam Reference Grammar (Suttles), 26, 29

Myers, Fred, 128

Nagaeselaq band, 119

Nakapunkim (Governor General Harold Alexander), *126*, 127. *See also* Alexander, Harold

Naming, Opening and Dedication of Stanley Park Vancouver, Canada 1888–1889 (J.S. Matthews), 69, *81*

naming of places, 32–41, 117

Nanook of the North (Flaherty), 15, 160, 163, 211n1, 212n4

Nanook Revisited (Massot), 212n4

National Arts Centre, 206n3

National Native Role Model program, 98

Native Brotherhood of British Columbia (NBBC): about, *114*, 117–18; and grounded practices, 103; involvement in *The Indian Village and Show*, 14, 127–8, 130–3, 145; legitimization of, 121–4. See also *The Indian Village and Show*; *Native Voice*

Native Sisterhood of British Columbia (NSBC), 113, 134–5, 137, 210n5

Native Voice, 112, 119, 121, 124–7, 128, 139, 204n19

The Native Voice: The Story of How Maisie Hurley and Canada's First Aboriginal Newspaper Changed a Nation (Jamieson), 207n13

NBBC (Native Brotherhood of

British Columbia). *See* Native
Brotherhood of British Columbia
(NBBC)
Neworld Theatre, 43, 201n1, 201n3
New Readings in Theatre History
(Bratton), 161
Nicolson, Marianne, 132
9 O'Clock Gun, 6, 150, 179–81, 186
Nolan, Yvette, 98
Norris, Leonard, 83
North American Phonetic Alphabet,
25
North-West Resistance of 1885, 89
NSBC (Native Sisterhood of British
Columbia), 113, 134–5, 137, 210n5

*Objects of Exchange: Material Culture,
Colonial Encounter, Indigenous
Modernity* (Glass), 112
O'Bonsawin, Christine, 146
O'Connor, Dennis, 93
Ogimaa Mikana: Reclaiming/
Renaming, 40, 201n25
Oka Crisis, 196n7
Olympics, 2010 Winter, 7, 14, 39, 132,
134, 145–150, 200n22
*On the Edge of Empire: Gender, Race,
and the Making of British Columbia,
1849–1871* (A. Perry), 61
Oppenheimer, David (grand-nephew
of Mayor David Oppenheimer),
71–2, 72, 73, 74
Oppenheimer, David (Mayor), 64–8,
77–8, 80, 83, 191, 203n12
oral histories, 23, 95
"The Origin of the Name
'Musqueam'" (J. Point), 30

Owad band, 119
Owakalagalis band, 119

paddle song, 50
Park Board. *See* Vancouver Park
Board
"Park Board Reconciliation Strategies"
(Soutar), 199n15
Patira, 94
Paull, Andrew/Andy, 111, 150, 184
Peacock, Lucy, 93–4
Peircean semiotics, 24–5
Penn, Arthur, 149
People amongst the People (S.A.
Point), 150, 183
*People of the Land: Legends of
the Four Host First Nations*
(Abraham), 38–9
People of the River Grass (Musqueam
Nation). *See* Musqueam Nation
(People of the River Grass)
Performance, Place, and Politics
(Dickinson), 136–7
performance studies/theories/
practices, 21, 27, 33, 36, 53, 163,
197n7
"The Performativity of Performance
Documentation" (Auslander),
75–6
*Performing Conquest: Five Centuries
of Theater, History, and Identity in
Tlaxcala, Mexico* (Ybarra), 19
*Performing Remains: Art and War in
Times of Theatrical Reenactment*
(Schneider), 31, 199n13
Perry, Adele, 61
Perry, C.C., 150

Peters, Mwalim (Morgan) James, 136
"A Phenomenology of Whiteness"
    (Ahmed), 55
Pilnaquwilwakwas band, 119
Pine, Aidan, 27
Pitt Meadows, BC, 26
PKOLS (Mount Douglas), 40
"Place of Birth Chaythoos, not Snauq"
    (J.S. Matthews), 62
Planetarium, Vancouver, 132
Plante, Frank, 67–8, *73*, 73–4, 77,
    204n16
podplay (audiowalk), 42–3, 201nn2–3
poiēsis, 18
Point, Adeline, 25
Point, Dominic, 25
Point, James, 30, 34
Point, Marny, 25
Point, Susan A., 150, 183
Point, Terry, 23, 197n3
Polaris Music Prize for best Canadian
    album, 161, 212n3
Port of Vancouver centennial plaques
    at the lighthouse, 181–3
Post-Colonial Drama: Theory,
    Practice, Politics (Gilbert and
    Tompkins), 139
potlatch: in 1885, 188; ballet of, 5,
    103–4, *105*, 186; ban on, 6, 46,
    119, 129–30, 144–5, 195n4, 206n3;
    stories of, 70
Powell, Israel Wood, 195n4
The Practice of Everyday Life
    (de Certeau), 17, 18, 24, 86
Prairie Theatre Exchange, 98
Pratt, E.J., 89
"Preface by Robert Flaherty"
    (Flaherty), 212n4
Projet blanc (Choinière), 42

proper (propre), 18, 197n2
Prospect Point, Stanley Park, *81*
The Protestant Ethnic and the Spirit of
    Capitalism (Chow), 54–5
"Pulling Together Canoe Journey,"
    Vancouver, 172, *173*, 175–6
Purple Thistle Centre, 211n1
PuSh International Performing Arts
    Festival, 134, 209n3

Queer Phenomenology: Orientations,
    Objects, Others (Ahmed), 55–6
Quiet Revolution, 99
qujannamiik (thank you), 166

Raheja, Michelle, 7–8, 14, 143,
    156–60, 163, 165–6, 211n3, 212n5
Raibmon, Paige, 23, 128
Rathie, William, 88
Rathier, Rhéauna, 94
Ravensbergen, Lisa, 98
Raven Spirit Dance, 201n1
"Real" Indians and Others: Mixed
    Blood Urban Native Peoples
    and Indigenous Nationhood
    (Lawrence), 96
Reconciliation Canada, 168
Redbone, 136
red diva projects, 134, 209n2
red hematite, 65, 203n12
Red Power movement, 196n7
Red Skin, White Masks: Rejecting the
    Colonial Politics of Recognition
    (Coulthard), 16, 17–18
Reid, Ambrose, *114*
Reid, Bill, 107, 146
The Remarkable Adventures of
    Portuguese Joe Silvey (Barman), 60
Rendall, Steven F., 197n2

"Repairing the Web: Spiderwoman's Children Staging the New Human Being" (Carter), 156

Reservation Reelism: Redfacing, Visual Sovereignty, and Representations of Native Americans in Film (Raheja), 160

The Resettlement of British Columbia: Essays on Colonialism and Geographical Change (Cole Harris), 57

residential schools, 28, 143, 168, 181, 206n2

Rethinking the Great White North: Race, Nature and the Historical Geographies of Whiteness in Canada (Baldwin, Cameron, and Kobayashi), 86

Roach, Joseph, 31, 53–4, 82, 200n24

The Road Forward (Clements), 39, 134–41, 146, 210nn4–5, 211n4

Roberts, Mary, 23, 197n5

Robertson, Gregor, 168

Robinson, Dylan, 10

Rooney, Tom, 93–4

Rose Garden, Stanley Park, 6

Route #501 Revisited (Goldsbie), 42

Rowley, Susan, 197n3

Roy, Patricia, 67, 72

Roy, Susan, 82, 102, 128, 145, 197n3, 205n29

Ruddell, Bruce, 146

Ruprecht, Alvina, 95

Russell, Lynette, 78

Ryga, George, 98

Sasq'ets (Sts'ailes creature), 151

Sasquatch. *See* Sasq'ets (Sts'ailes creature)

Schneider, Rebecca, 31, 36–7, 53–4, 86, 91, 135–6, 138, 199n13

Scott, Amos, 212n5

Scott, F.R., 89

Scow, William, 110–13, *114*, 118, *123*, 123–5, *126*, 129–30, 208n30

Searle, John, 24

secret dances, 121, 127–8, 130

Shakespeare Garden, Stanley Park, 6, 150

Shaw, Patricia, 9, 25, 30, 198n10, 200n19

Shore to Shore (sculpture, Marston), 184

Shxw'ow'hamel First Nation, 198n12

Sideshow Freaks and Circus Injuns (Howe and Mojica), 21

Silvey, Joe, 184–5

Simpson, Audra, 12

Simpson, Leanne Betasamosake, 10, 11–12, 24, 40, 172

The Sisters (mountains), 37–8, 116, 187–8

Siwash Rock, Stanley Park. *See* słx̱iÌəx (Siwash Rock)

Sḵwx̱wú7mesh Nation (Squamish Nation), 37, 49, 78, 132, 148–9, 195n3, 202n2

Sleigh, Daphne, 53, 60

Smith, Donald (Lord Strathcona), 64, 89, 206n39

Smith, Linda Tuhiwai, 9

Smith, Peter, 181

Smith (nee Thompson), Martha, 181

Snauq (sənaʔqʷ/Sen'ákw), 79, 202n2, 202n4

Snelgrove, Corey, 10

sovereignty, visual, 14, 143–4, 149, 156, 164, 211n3

Spakwus Slulem (Eagle Song
     Dancers), 50, 175–6
Spanish Banks, Vancouver, 34
Sparrow, Debra, 149
Sparrow, Ed, 25
Sparrow, Leona, 197n3
Sparrow, Quelemia, 13, 42–51
Spence, Teresa, 137
Spirit Catcher Train, 147, 151, 157,
     190, 211n6
Spukhpukanum (Lucy Cummings),
     206n2
Squamish Nation, 101–2, 106, 114,
     145–6, 167–9, 200n22, 202n2,
     205n29. *See also* Skwxwú7mesh
     Nation (Squamish Nation)
Staging Whiteness (Brewer), 57
Stamp, Edward, 185, 193
Standing Rock Sioux, 8, 196n7
Stanley, Lord: about, 61, 64–7, 69, 70,
     77; dedication of park to people
     of all "colors, creeds and customs,"
     67–8, 71, 192; statue of, 69, 78,
     83–8, 84, 91, 170, 190–3
Stanley Cup, 86, 205n36
Stanley Park, Vancouver, about, 6, 158
Stanley Park, Vancouver, dedication
     and rededications, 52–92; 1888–89,
     naming, opening, and "dedication,"
     63–70; 1943 reenactment of the
     dedication, 70–8; 1964 reenactment
     of the dedication, 87–90; about, 13,
     187, 189; archives, 60–3; gravesite
     of Supple Jack, 78–83; The Last
     Spike, reenactment of, 87–90;
     whiteness, 54–9. *See also* statue of
     Lord Stanley

*Stanley Park, Vancouver: The
     Rededication 19th May 1964*
     (J.S. Matthews), *81*
Stanley Park Miniature Railway, 87,
     88, 89, 147, 189–90
Stanley Park Pavilion, 6, 174
*Stanley Park's Secret: The Forgotten
     Families of Whoi Whoi, Kanaka
     Ranch and Brockton Point*
     (Barman), 60, 69, 78, 181, 185
States, Bert, 98, 135, 209n1
statue of Lord Stanley, 69, 78, 83–8,
     84, 91, 170, 190–3
Stek'in people, 38
St John, Michelle, 134, 136–7
A Stó:lo–Coast Salish Historical Atlas
     (McHalsie), 35
Stó:lō Tribal Council, 198n12
storytelling, 153–4
strategies (de Certeau), 18–20
Stratford Festival, 93–4
Strathcona, Lord (Donald Smith), 64,
     89, 206n39
Sts'ailes Nation, 149, 151–2
Surrey, BC, 26
surrogation, 40, 54, 91, 200n24. *See
     also* Taylor, Diana
"Surveyors Came at Dawn: Corner
     Cut off House for Stanley Park
     Road" (*Vancouver Sun*), 76
Suttles, Wayne, 26, 29, 34, 35, 198n10,
     199n16, 200n18
Swanamia, 87, 116
*Switchbacks: Art, Ownership,
     and Nuxalk National Identity*
     (Kramer), 127
sxwoxwiyám (stories/histories

describing the activities of the Creator), 199n17

tactics (de Certeau), 18–20
Tagaq, Tanya, 15, 160–6, 211n1, 212n5
Tales of Ghosts: First Nations Art in British Columbia, 1922–61 (Hawker), 119, 209n35
Talking Stick Festival, 13, 92, 96, 97
Taylor, Diana: archive and repertoire, 19, 103, 124, 143–4, 147, 197n7; multiplication and simultaneity, 40, 53–4, 77, 200n24; on place, 19–21
teepee, 147, *148*
Telford, J.L., 66–8, 69, 73, 191–2
temporal drag, 77, 135–6
Théâtre du Nouveau Monde, 43
Théâtre du Rideau Vert, 93
"Theatres of Contact: The Kwakwaka'wakw Meet Colonialism in British Columbia and at the Chicago World's Fair" (Raibmon), 128
Theatre under the Stars, 150
These Mysterious People: Shaping History and Archaeology in a Northwest Coast Community (S. Roy), 82, 205n29
Thompson, Charlie, 131
Thompson, Laurence C., 198n10
Thornton, Mildred V., 209n34
"Thunderbird Sharing Ceremony," 172, 174, *175*
tillicum (friend), 38
Timber Bowl, 103, 150, 186, 193

Tlaxcaltecans, 20
Tompkins, Joanne, 139
tom-tom, 120–1, *122*, 208n26
"To My Indian Brother" (Howard), 115–16
Totem-Land Society, 131
totem poles, 5, 125, 132, 145, 150, 183, 184, 208n31
Towards the Last Spike (Pratt), 89
traditional knowledge, 36, 110, 127, 138, 143, 210n7. *See also* knowledge transmission
trains. *See* Miniature Train Station, Klahowya Village; Spirit Catcher Train; Stanley Park Miniature Railway; Urban Forest Train, Stanley Park
Trans Mountain Pipeline, 167
Tremblay, Armand, 94
Tremblay, Michel, 13, 92–100, 160–1
Trudeau, Pierre Elliott, 210n8
Truth and Reconciliation Commission of Canada (TRC), 15, 167–8, 210n9. See also *Calls to Action* (TRC)
Tsawwassen, BC, 26, 145
Tsilhqot'in decision on Aboriginal title, 167, 212n1
Tsleil-Waututh Nation, 9, 26, 101, 102, 145–6, 167–9, 200n22, 207n19
Tuck (Unangax̂), Eve, 9
Twelve Opening Acts (M. Tremblay), 94

U'Mista Cultural Centre, Alert Bay, 209n35
United Nations Declaration on the Rights of Indigenous Peoples (UNDRIP), 139, 168, 169, 210n9

Unsettling the City: Urban Land and the Politics of Property (Blomley), 76, 102

"Unsettling Settler Colonialism" (Snelgrove, Dhamoon, and Corntassel), 10

Urban Aboriginal Peoples' Advisory Committee, 168

Urban Forest Train, Stanley Park, 159, 173, 213n6

Usmiani, Renate, 98

Vancouver, BC, 26; 125th anniversary, 48, 201n1; as City of Reconciliation, 169; Great Fire of 1886, 13; map with həṅ̓q̓əmiṅ̓əṁ place names, 4; newspapers, 64, 66, 69, 83, 118; population in 1943, 204n17; Port of Vancouver, 44, 46, 181–3, 193. *See also* archives

Vancouver, George, 180

Vancouver Aquarium, 6, 150, 174

Vancouver Citizens' Diamond Jubilee Committee (VCDJC), 103, 111–12, 116, 118, 120, 128, 131. *See also* Vancouver's 1946 Diamond Jubilee

Vancouver Cricket Club, 186

Vancouver Organizing Committee for the 2010 Olympic and Paralympic Winter Games (VANOC), 39, 145–6, 200n22. *See also* Winter Olympics, 2010

Vancouver Park Board: and Chinese railway workers, 90; decolonization, 15, 169–72, *171*, 172, 212n3, 213n5, 214n8; dispossession of houses, 181; "Park Board Reconciliation Strategies"

(Soutar), 199n15. *See also* Stanley Park, Vancouver, dedication and rededications; statue of Lord Stanley

Vancouver's 1946 Diamond Jubilee, 101–33; decolonization, 130–3; grounded practices at səṅaʔq̓ʷ/Senákw, 120–8; *The Indian Village and Show*, 103–20; *The Jubilee Show*, 103–10; William Scow's copyright assignment, 129–30

Vanier, Georges, 83, 191

Vanier Park, Vancouver, 60, 172. *See also* səṅaʔq̓ʷ/Senákw (Vanier Park/Kitsilano/Squamish Indian Reserve)

VANOC (Vancouver Organizing Committee for the 2010 Olympic and Paralympic Winter Games), 39, 145–6, 200n22. *See also* Winter Olympics, 2010

VCDJC (Vancouver Citizens' Diamond Jubilee Committee), 103, 111–12, 116, 118, 120, 128, 131. *See also* Vancouver's 1946 Diamond Jubilee

visual sovereignty, 14, 143–4, 149, 156, 164, 211n3

"vortices of behavior" (Roach), 31

walking tour of spapəy̓əq/Brockton Point and χʷay̓χʷəy̓/Lumberman's Arch (self-guided), 179–93; cricket pitch, 185–7; Japanese Canadian War Memorial, 188–9; Lord Stanley statue, 191–3; Luke Marston's *Shore to Shore*, 184–5; Lumberman's Arch/χʷay̓χʷəy̓, 187–8; 9 O'Clock Gun, 179–81;

Port of Vancouver centennial plaques at the lighthouse, 181–3; Stanley Park Miniature Railway and Former Children's Farmyard, 189–90; Susan A. Point's *People amongst the People*, 183; totem pole viewing area, 184

walrus, 165–6

wayfinding, 36–7

We Are Here (film), 39, 146

weaving, jil, 169, 213n4, 214n8

"Welcoming Sovereignty" (Robinson), 10

Weledeh dialect of Dogrib, 17

Western Apache, 33

Western Canada Theatre (WCT), 13, 92, 94, 97, 99

Wet'suwet'en peoples, 196n6

"What Do Indians Want?" (T. King), 16

White (Dyer), 57

whiteness/whiteness studies, 10, 13, 54–9, 73–4, 78, 90–1, 170, 178–9, 185

White Paper (Canada, 1969), 97, 139, 196n7, 210n8

The White Possessive: Property, Power, and Indigenous Sovereignty (Moreton-Robinson), 58–9

Wildcat, Matthew, 26

W!ld Rice Theatre, 93

Williams, Guy, 113, *114*

Williams, Lorelei, 174

Wilson, Jordan, 23, 183, 197n3

Winter Olympics, 2010, 7, 14, 39, 132, 134, 145–50, 200n22

Wisdom Sits in Places: Landscape and Language among the Western Apache (Basso), 33

Women's Memorial Rock, 48–9, 202n4

Wong, Adrienne, 43, 48, 201n1, 201n3

Woolman, Jason, 197n3

WSÁNEĆ nations, 40

xwelítem (starving ones), 10

Yang, K. Wayne, 9

Ybarra, Patricia, 19–20, 21

York Theatre, 160, 161, 163

Youds, Mike, 95

Young, Ernest Vanderpoel, 72, *73*, 77, 204n22

youth exchange program, 142, 211n1

Zittlau, Andreas, 154

Zubot, Jesse, 160